BLACK AMERICANS:
A Statistical Sourcebook

1990 Edition

Alfred N. Garwood
Editor

Numbers & Concepts
Boulder, Colorado

ISBN 0-929960-02-5 trade paper
ISBN 0-929960-03-3 library edition

Numbers & Concepts
Suite E4-221
2525 Arapahoe Avenue
Boulder, CO 80302

TABLE OF CONTENTS

Chapter 3 - Education

Chapter 4 - Government, Elections, and Public Opinion

Chapter 5 - Crime, Law Enforcement, and Corrections

Chapter 7 - Earnings, Income, Poverty, and Wealth

INTRODUCTION

Black Americans: A Statistical Sourcebook is the second in a series of statistical sourcebooks covering significant topics in American life. It is the first in this series designed to be an annual publication. Black Americans resulted from the view that, despite the fact that there is coverage of Black Americans in a assortment of reference sources, there is indeed a need for a single volume statistical reference devoted entirely to this important segment of the population.

Black Americans provides an extensive collection of tables which display information on a wide variety of topics. With a few exceptions, each table presents information about the Black population, the White population, and a total for Americans of all races. The purpose in doing so is not to advance a specific perspective about Black Americans but to provide a context within which the tabular data can be more fully understood and evaluated.

Presenting data by race always puts one at risk of being labeled racist. Although undoubtedly there will be persons on both sides - those who see Black Americans as a propagandistic derogation of the Black community; and those who feel that the book eloquently proves the inherent racism and repression of the majority culture - the intent here is to serve neither cause. In fact, Black Americans, is not intended to serve any cause or advance any point of view, but to serve as a reportorial resource, providing access to federal government information. By researching and presenting this sometimes difficult to find, hard to understand information, Black Americans can serve students, business persons, social scientists, researchers, and others who need basic data about Black Americans.

The use of the term 'Black' itself can also be a cause for controversy. A number of terms have been used by Black Americans to name themselves, and in fact, as this is written there seems to be some evidence that 'Afro-American' is coming to replace the term Black. Black is used here solely because it is the word currently used by the federal government in gathering data. Federal usage has changed over the years, and as it continues to change, those changes will be reflected here.

The next sensitive question is, just who is Black? For federal data collection purposes, Black persons are those who say they are Black (or, in some surveys, Negro, or Afro-American). For statistical reporting purposes, being Black is based solely on self-identification.

The federal government considers Black to be a racial group (like White, Asian, etc.). However, being of Spanish origin, or identifying as Hispanic is not counted as a racial group. For almost all federal data collection programs, persons may be of any race and also of Hispanic origin (the major exception concerns some U.S. Department of Education data which counts Hispanics separately from non-Hispanic Blacks, and non-Hispanic Whites). As a general guideline, it is believed that the overwhelming majority of persons identifying themselves as Hispanic for federal data collection purposes also are counted as White, although there persons who are both Black and Hispanic.

Organization

The main portion of this book has been divided into eight chapters of tables:

Chapter 1 Demographics and Characteristics of the Population

Chapter 2 Vital Statistics and Health

Chapter 3 Education

Basically, the tables in each chapter represent results of a comprehensive review of all of the available federal government statistical information on the Black population. This material was edited and organized into chapters, and arranged in a sequence roughly following the pattern found in publications of the U.S. Bureau of the Census.

Each table presents pertinent information from the source (or sources) in a clear, comprehensible fashion. As users of this book will likely be a diverse group, ranging from librarians to business planners, from social scientists to marketers, all with different uses for the same data, the information selected for presentation was chosen for its broad scope and general appeal.

The Sources

All of the information here comes from U.S. Government sources, (if not originally, by way of republication by the federal government). In turn, most of the federal information is from the U.S. Bureau of the Census. Without question, the Bureau is the largest data gathering organization in the nation. It collects information on an exceptionally broad range of topics, not only for its own use and for the use of Congress and the Executive, but also as a data collection purveyor under contract with other federal agencies and departments. The reach of the Bureau is wider than most people realize, encompassing not only the decennial Census of Population, the Current Population Survey, and the Annual Housing Survey, but extending, in cooperation with other agencies, to the Consumer Expenditure Survey, the National Crime Survey, and the National Family Growth Survey, to name just a few. In addition to the scope and depth of its own activities (and those on behalf of other agencies), the fact that the Bureau is responsible for so much of the federal government's data collection adds uniformity to the statistical information published by different agencies. (Of course, much of this uniformity results from federal agencies that coordinate statistical policy, including the Office of Management and Budget. However, the fact that the Bureau of the Census is actually the main data collector has substantial impact.) As a result, many terms have become standardized (for example "household" has the same meaning whether it is used by the departments of Commerce, Health, Labor, or Education), and although the uniformity is not complete (especially regarding the underlying methodologies of data collection), there is enough to make the work of data users a lot easier.

The influence of the Bureau of the Census extends beyond federal government data collection. Because of the shear volume of data it collects, many private data collectors have adopted some of its procedures and terminology. This has the added value for researchers of making private and public data more compatible.

Observant readers will note that, with some frequency, the source of many tables is a Census publication, Statistical Abstract of the United States. There are a number of reasons for this, however none have anything to do with short cuts in our research. First, due perhaps to federal budget cuts, a growing quantity of information used in Statistical Abstract has never been published elsewhere before or it has never been published in such a detailed way (and may never be, even by the agency responsible for the data). Second, as the preeminent federal data publisher, the Bureau has access to a wealth of raw data in machine readable form. It is able to aggregate data geographically on regional lines (and break out other detail such as age, sex, race, etc.), using its own parameters for publication. Thus, even when information is published elsewhere, the manner of presentation in Statistical Abstract is likely to be unique, in that data is presented in a more general way so as to be useful to many different types of data users.

On all tables where Statistical Abstract is cited as the source, the original source also has been checked for additional information. To make more detailed research easier for readers who would do likewise, Statistical Abstract's own source (if it is not the Bureau itself), is listed as well.

Types of Information

Regardless of its source, there are basically two types of data presented in the tables of this book.

The first is complete count data. For example, the five questions asked of all Americans by the Bureau of the Census in the 1980 Census of Population was an attempt at a complete count of a given universe.

The second type of data is survey information. Here a fairly large, specifically chosen segment of a population or universe is studied. This sample is intended to be so scientifically drawn as to be representative of the entire population or universe. Information about consumer expenditures, money income, and the like are some of the items in this book based on this type of survey information. Of course, survey information is only as good as the survey itself, therefore the reader should always be the judge of the significance and accuracy of the material presented as it applies to his or her own research. Although specific survey methodology is not discussed here, a full reference to each source is made on every table. Interested readers are thus able to consult the original source materials, which in most cases contain a detailed explanations of survey methodology.

The Tables

In order to understand the material itself, (and to use the book efficiently), it is necessary to know how the tables have been prepared and presented.

First, let's look at table titles:

Table 4.01 Black Elected Public Officials, by Type of Office Held, 1970 - 1988

The table number contains the chapter number (to the left of the decimal) and the location of the table within the chapter (to the right of the decimal). This is the first table of Chapter 4. With a few exceptions, tables have been arranged within a chapter to present the oldest, most general information first, followed by newer, more specific information. This pattern is mirrored in the tables themselves, which present the oldest, most general information at the beginning.

In a table title, the word or words before the first comma identify the general topic of the table. After the first comma descriptive wording which identifies the detail presented about the general topic (i.e., the data is presented by age, sex, marital status, etc., or in this case, by type of office held) appears. After the description of the presentation of the data, the years for which data is presented are shown. If one, two or three years of data are provided, these specific years are listed. If more than three years of data are provided, a hyphenated range is shown beginning with the first year of data and ending with the last (as is the case in the example above).

This may all be somewhat arcane (or perhaps a garrulous statement of the obvious) but some table titles may look rather odd at first. However if the users understand how the tables are numbered and titled, it makes using the Table of Contents and the Index easier and more informative.

It should also be noted that the table titles (and the tables themselves) retain the original terms of the source material. This too may make for some fairly abstruse table titles (and some unusual line descriptors), but it has the advantage of making the book compatible with the original sources. Additionally, government terminology is not as arbitrary and irrelevant as it appears on first reading. Of course to newcomers some terms can be either confusing or deceptive (sometimes both), but all specialized terms are defined in the glossary. Needless to say, it is absolutely vital to understand the meaning of all terms used in a table before drawing any conclusions from the data.

Being clear about the terminology is especially important because not only does the government have overtly specialized terms which clearly require a definition or explanation, but many government agencies use ordinary words in specialized ways. There are real differences between: a household and a family (and, for that matter, a family and a married couple); the resident population and the civilian non-institutional population; a service industry and a service occupation; an urban area and a metropolitan area; to name just a few. When in doubt, consult the glossary.

To further facilitate use, every table in the book presents data in two, three, five, or six columns. The first column (or two columns if the data is presented by sex) are for the Black population; the second column (or third and fourth columns), are for the White population; and the final column or columns present data for all races.

Along the left margin of each table appears a column of line descriptors. Here, after a general heading, subgroups of the heading (usually indented) are shown. Two principles cover arranging and presenting the line descriptors: the oldest, most general information appears first, progressing to the newer, more specific; and quantities appear first, followed by percentages, medians, means, and per capita amounts. In this way parallels can be drawn between tables in a chapter and chapters in the book.

In selecting the data itself, wherever available (and wherever appropriate), a time span of data is presented, usually going back to 1975 or 1980. This provides readers with a historical context for the information and may show trends over a period of time. However readers should be cautioned that the years selected have been chosen from no special knowledge of the subject, nor to make any specific point. Thus the fact that there has been a decrease or increase in a given indicator for the period displayed does not mean that the same trend will continue, or that it represents the continuation of a historical trend, or even that which appears to be a trend within this period actually is one (showing a beginning, middle, and end year does not necessarily describe what happened in intervening years). The time span and specific dates have been chosen largely to create a congruity of data, and a basis of comparison between different categories of information.

Readers are also urged to pay special attention to the units shown (identified at the bottom of the table), noting the quantity, and whether a median, mean, percent, rate, or a per capita amount is provided.

At the bottom of each table three key paragraphs appear: Source, Notes, and Units. The source paragraph lists the source of the data presented in the table. When more than one source was used, the sources are listed in the same order in which the data itself appears in the table. As all sources are government publications, the issuing agency is listed as the author. All citations provide both the page and table number in the source from which the material was taken. This bibliographic detail on each table makes a separate bibliography at the end of the book unnecessary. A Superintendent of Documents Classification Number is also provided. This number is used as a locator number in most government depository libraries, and documents are shelved or filed according to it, just the way books in smaller public libraries are usually organized by the Dewey Decimal System.

The paragraph of notes includes pertinent facts about the data, the time of year covered by the survey, and the scope of the survey universe. One general note can be made here at the outset about all tabular data: detail (subgroups) may not add to the total shown, due to either rounding or the fact that only selected subgroups are displayed.

The final paragraph of a table, Units, identifies the units used, specifically stating that the quantity is millions of persons, thousands of workers, dollars per capita, etc.

The Glossary

For many tables, it is not possible to fully define a term or concept in the table notes, so the glossary serves as an important tool in using the tables. All terms that appear in either the title or text of a table which may be unclear or are used in a special way are defined in the glossary. Wherever possible, the definition is adapted (and in many cases taken verbatim) from the definition provided in the source publication. Not all source materials provide definitions, so sometimes a definition has been constructed by reviewing and summarizing the explanatory and supplementary material from the source.

In compiling the glossary, finding or drawing appropriate definitions was not as difficult as knowing when to stop. There is a clear temptation to move from a definition of a term to an explanation of the underlying methodology. The line was drawn at providing short clear definitions, including only as much background material as necessary to make a term understandable. In practice this results in compromises. For example, it is important for a reader looking at Consumer Expenditure Survey data to understand that it is based on a consumer unit, and that a consumer unit is very much like a household. But although it may be advantageous for some readers to have a further understanding of how consumer units are selected and interviewed, this goes beyond the scope of the glossary. On the other hand, some methodological background is essential to understand certain terms (such as crime data). Where such background is vital it has been included. Readers requiring more methodological definition are referred to the sources for detailed explanations.

The Index

Every key term from the tables has been indexed, and, in combination with the table of contents, readers should be able to find what they want without thumbing through the entire book or chapter. Readers should also note that the index provides table numbers as opposed to page numbers.

A Suggestion on How to Use This Book

One way to use this book is by locating the subject of general interest in the Table of Contents, and turning to that chapter. While the Table of Contents is detailed enough to narrow a search (and the index can certainly speed access to specific items), sometimes paging through the dozen or so tables in a given field uncovers unanticipated information of genuine importance. It is just this type of serendipity that has lead to the inclusion of information in this book, and sometimes such an unexpected find can greatly enhance a research project.

A Final Word

As this book will be updated on an annual basis, questions, comments, and criticisms from users are vital to making informed editorial choices about succeeding editions. If you have a suggestion or comment, be assured that it will be both appreciated and carefully considered. If you should find an error here, please let us know so that it may be corrected. Our goal is to provide accurate, easy to use, statistical compendiums which serve our readers needs. Your help enables us to do our job better.

Table 1.01 Resident Population and Median Age, 1790 - 1988

	Black		White		All Races	
	total	median age	total	median age	total	median age
1790 (August 2)	757	na	3,172	na	3,930	na
1800 (August 4)	1,002	na	4,306	16.0	5,308	na
1820 (August 7)	1,772	17.2	7,867	16.5	9,638	16.7
1840 (June 1)	2,874	17.3	14,196	17.9	17,069	17.8
1860 (June 1)	4,442	17.7	26,923	19.7	31,443	19.4
1880 (June 1)	6,581	18.0	43,403	21.4	50,156	20.9
1900 (June 1)	8,834	19.4	66,809	23.4	75,995	22.9
1920 (January 1)	10,463	22.3	94,821	25.6	105,711	25.3
1940 (April 1)	12,866	25.3	118,215	29.5	131,669	29.0
1960 (April 1)	18,872	23.5	158,832	30.3	179,323	29.5
1970 (April 1)	22,581	22.4	178,098	28.9	203,302	28.0
1980 (April 1)	26,683	24.9	194,713	30.9	226,546	30.0
1985 (July 1)	28,878	26.6	202,765	32.4	235,736	31.5
1986 (July 1)	29,306	26.9	204,301	32.7	241,096	31.8
1987 (July 1)	29,736	27.2	205,820	33.0	243,400	32.1
1988 (July 1)	29,300	27.3	na	33.1	na	

SOURCE: U.S. Bureau of the Census, Statistical Abstract of the United States, 1988, p. 16, table 17; 1989, p. 17, table 21. C 3.134:(year)
U.S. Bureau of the Census, Current Population Reports: Population Profile of the United States 1989, Series P-23, # 159, p. 31. C 3.186/8:989

NOTES: 'All Races' includes other races not shown separately. Data through 1940 excludes Alaska and Hawaii. 1985 and later data are based on estimates.

UNITS: Population in thousands of persons; median age in years.

Table 1.02 Population Projections, by Age and Sex, 1990, 2000, 2010

	Black	White	All Races
1990			
Persons, all ages, both sexes	31,148	210,616	250,410
under 5 years old	2,814	14,893	18,408
16 years old and older	22,226	164,465	192,989
75 years old and older	1,005	11,965	13,187
male	14,835	103,184	122,243
female	16,313	107,432	128,167
2000			
Persons, all ages, both sexes	35,129	221,514	268,266
under 5 years old	2,748	13,324	16,898
16 years old and older	25,708	175,579	210,134
75 years old and older	1,283	14,965	16,639
male	16,787	108,774	131,191
female	18,342	112,739	137,076
2010			
Persons, all ages, both sexes	38,833	228,978	282,575
under 5 years old	2,820	13,084	16,899
16 years old and older	29,467	186,417	227,390
75 years old and older	1,584	16,108	18,323
male	18,602	112,610	138,333
female	20,231	116,368	144,241

SOURCE: U.S. Bureau of the Census, Statistical Abstract of the United States, 1989, p. 15, table 17 (data from U.S. Bureau of the Census, *Current Population Reports*, Series P-25, forthcoming reports). C 3.134:989

NOTES: 'All races' includes other races not shown separately.

UNITS: Projected population in thousands of persons.

Table 1.03 Resident Population, by Age and Sex, 1980, 1985, 1987

	Black	White	All Races
1980			
Both sexes			
total	26,683	194,713	226,546
under 5 years old	2,459	13,414	16,348
16 years old and older	18,425	149,121	171,196
65 years old and older	2,092	23,162	25,549
male			
total	12,612	94,924	110,053
under 5 years old	1,240	6,882	8,362
16 years old and older	8,454	71,559	81,766
65 years old and older	849	9,316	10,305
female			
total	14,071	99,788	116,493
under 5 years old	1,220	6,532	7,986
16 years old and older	9,971	77,562	89,429
65 years old and older	1,243	13,846	15,245
1985			
Both sexes			
total	28,887	202,768	238,740
under 5 years old	2,706	14,636	18,037
16 years old and older	20,380	157,584	183,010
65 years old and older	2,343	25,743	28,530
male			
total	13,683	99,006	116,161
under 5 years old	1,370	7,509	9,230
16 years old and older	9,374	75,820	87,631
65 years old and older	940	10,390	11,529
female			
total	15,204	103,762	122,579
under 5 years old	1,335	7,127	8,806
16 years old and older	11,006	81,764	95,379
65 years old and older	1,403	15,353	17,002

continued on the next page

Table 1.03 continued

	Black	White	All Races
1987			
Both sexes			
total	29,736	205,820	243,400
under 5 years old	2,745	14,754	18,252
16 years old and older	20,116	160,733	187,463
65 years old and older	2,448	26,865	29,835
male			
total	14,103	100,589	118,531
under 5 years old	1,393	7,567	9,341
16 years old and older	9,729	77,454	89,892
65 years old and older	984	10,905	12,119
female			
total	15,633	105,231	124,869
under 5 years old	1,352	7,187	8,910
16 years old and older	11,386	83,279	97,572
65 years old and older	1,465	15,960	17,716

SOURCE: U.S. Bureau of the Census, Statistical Abstract of the United States, 1985, p. 28, table 30; 1987, p. 18, table 20; 1989, p. 17, table 21 (data from U.S. Bureau of the Census, *Current Population Reports*, Series P-25). C 3.134:(year)

NOTES: 'All races' includes other races not shown separately.

UNITS: Resident population in thousands of persons.

Table 1.04 Components of Population Change, 1980 and 1985; Projections, 1990, 2000, 2010

	Black	White	All Races
1980			
population on January 1	26,680	194,834	226,451
+ births during year	590	1,580	3,612
- deaths during year	233	1,739	1,990
+ net civilian immigration	75	431	845
net population increase	**452**	**1,580**	**2,582**
1985			
population on January 1	28,802	202,464	238,207
+ births during year	609	2,983	3,750
- deaths during year	244	1,816	2,083
+ net civilian immigration	58	352	648
net population increase	**422**	**1,521**	**2,316**
1990			
population on January 1	30,934	209,897	249,330
+ births during year	620	2,955	3,731
- deaths during year	254	1,888	2,180
+ net civilian immigration	60	340	575
net population increase	**426**	**1,408**	**2,125**
2000			
population on January 1	34,939	221,088	267,498
+ births during year	597	2,602	3,389
- deaths during year	272	2,038	2,368
+ net civilian immigration	54	273	500
net population increase	**379**	**838**	**1,522**
2010			
population on January 1	38,633	228,637	281,894
+ births during year	616	2,639	3,485
- deaths during year	312	2,238	2,635
+ net civilian immigration	54	273	500
net population increase	**358**	**674**	**1,351**

SOURCE: U.S. Bureau of the Census, Statistical Abstract of the United States, 1989 p. 9, table 6; p. 14, table 14. C 3.134:989

NOTES: 'All races' includes other races not shown separately.

UNITS: Population in thousands of persons.

Table 1.05 Population Projections, 2010 - 2080

	Black	White	All Races
2010	38,833	228,978	282,575
2015	40,564	232,081	288,997
2020	42,128	234,330	294,364
2025	43,473	235,369	298,252
2030	44,596	235,167	300,629
2035	45,513	233,941	301,725
2040	46,239	231,951	301,807
2045	46,780	229,429	301,100
2050	47,146	226,611	299,849
2055	47,386	223,746	298,369
2060	47,552	221,065	296,963
2065	47,660	218,668	295,744
2070	47,708	216,494	294,642
2075	47,684	214,401	293,500
2080	47,587	212,305	292,235

SOURCE: U.S. Bureau of the Census, Current Population Reports: Population Projections of the United States By Age, Sex and Race, 1988 - 2010, Series P-25, #1018, pp. 30-36, tables 1-3. C 3.186/8:989

NOTES: 'All Races' includes other races not shown separately. Population projections as of July 1, of the year shown.

UNITS: Estimates of the total population in thousands of persons, includes armed forces overseas. Based on Series 14 - Middle Series.

Table 1.06 Resident Population, by State, 1970 and 1980

	1970			1980		
	Black	White	All Races	Black	White	All Races
Alabama	903	2,534	3,444	996	2,873	3,894
Alaska	9	237	300	14	310	402
Arizona	53	1,605	1,771	75	2,241	2,718
Arkansas	352	1,566	1,923	374	1,890	2,286
California	1,400	17,761	19,953	1,819	18,031	23,668
Colorado	66	2,112	2,207	102	2,571	2,890
Connecticut	181	2,835	3,032	217	2,799	3,108
Delaware	78	466	548	96	488	594
District of Columbia	538	209	757	449	172	638
Florida	1,042	5,719	6,789	1,343	8,185	9,746
Georgia	1,187	3,391	4,590	1,465	3,947	5,463
Hawaii	8	298	769	17	319	965
Idaho	2	699	713	3	902	944
Illinois	1,426	9,600	11,114	1,675	9,233	11,427
Indiana	357	4,820	5,194	415	5,004	5,490
Iowa	33	2,783	2,824	42	2,839	2,914
Kansas	107	2,122	2,247	126	2,168	2,364
Kentucky	231	2,982	3,219	259	3,379	3,661
Louisiana	1,087	2,541	3,641	1,238	2,912	4,206
Maine	3	985	992	3	1,110	1,125
Maryland	699	3,195	3,922	958	3,159	4,217
Massachusetts	176	5,478	5,689	221	5,363	5,737
Michigan	991	7,833	8,875	1,199	7,872	9,262
Minnesota	35	3,736	3,805	53	3,936	4,076
Mississippi	816	1,393	2,217	887	1,615	2,521
Missouri	480	4,177	4,677	514	4,345	4,917
Montana	2	663	694	2	740	787
Nebraska	40	1,433	1,483	48	1,490	1,570
Nevada	28	448	489	51	700	800
New Hampshire	3	733	738	4	910	921
New Jersey	770	6,350	7,168	925	6,127	7,365
New Mexico	20	916	1,016	24	978	1,303
New York	2,169	15,834	18,237	2,402	13,961	17,558

continued on the next page

Table 1.06 continued

	1970			1980		
	Black	White	All Races	Black	White	All Races
North Carolina	1,126	3,902	5,082	1,319	4,458	5,882
North Dakota	2	599	618	3	626	653
Ohio	970	9,647	10,652	1,077	9,597	10,798
Oklahoma	172	2,280	2,559	205	2,598	3,025
Oregon	26	2,032	2,091	37	2,491	2,633
Pennsylvania	1,017	10,738	11,794	1,047	10,652	11,864
Rhode Island	25	915	947	28	897	947
South Carolina	789	1,794	2,591	949	2,147	3,122
South Dakota	2	630	666	2	640	691
Tennessee	621	3,294	3,924	726	3,835	4,591
Texas	1,399	9,717	11,197	1,710	11,198	14,229
Utah	7	1,032	1,059	9	1,383	1,461
Vermont	1	443	444	1	507	511
Virginia	861	3,762	4,648	1,009	4,230	5,347
Washington	71	3,251	3,409	106	3,779	4,132
West Virginia	67	1,673	1,744	65	1,875	1,950
Wisconsin	128	4,259	4,418	183	4,443	4,706
Wyoming	3	323	332	3	446	470

SOURCE: U.S. Bureau of the Census, Statistical Abstract of the United States, 1972, p. 12, table 12; p. 28, table 30. C 3.134:972
U.S. Bureau of the Census, Census of Population: General Population Characteristics: United State Summary PC80-1-B1, p. 1-125, table 62.

NOTES: 'All Races' includes other races not shown separately.

UNITS: Population in thousands of persons.

Table 1.07 Resident Population, by State, Projections for 1990 and 2000

	1990			2000		
	Black	White	All Races	Black	White	All Races
Alabama	1,071	3,076	4,181	1,136	3,225	4,410
Alaska	20	447	576	23	519	687
Arizona	99	3,369	3,752	123	4,108	4,618
Arkansas	387	2,011	2,427	398	2,093	2,529
California	2,392	23,920	29,126	2,909	26,641	33,500
Colorado	133	3,211	3,434	156	3,535	3,813
Connecticut	269	2,964	3,279	313	3,069	3,445
Delaware	126	528	666	155	561	734
District of Columbia	421	184	614	430	193	634
Florida	1,823	10,820	12,818	2,279	12,870	15,415
Georgia	1,789	4,803	6,663	2,151	5,698	7,957
Hawaii	21	385	1,141	24	432	1,345
Idaho	4	989	1,017	6	1,013	1,047
Illinois	1,869	9,443	11,612	2,029	9,173	11,580
Indiana	469	5,028	5,550	513	4,922	5,502
Iowa	53	2,681	2,758	58	2,462	2,549
Kansas	145	2,286	2,492	158	2,292	2,529
Kentucky	280	3,444	3,745	294	3,414	3,733
Louisiana	1,380	3,065	4,513	1,452	2,978	4,516
Maine	4	1,197	1,212	4	1,252	1,271
Maryland	1,233	3,352	4,729	1,469	3,597	5,274
Massachusetts	284	5,482	5,880	327	5,595	6,087
Michigan	1,355	7,774	9,293	1,497	7,543	9,250
Minnesota	67	4,138	4,324	77	4,250	4,490
Mississippi	962	1,717	2,699	1,037	1,812	2,877
Missouri	559	4,573	5,192	600	4,705	5,383
Montana	2	752	805	2	734	794
Nebraska	54	1,510	1,588	58	1,470	1,556
Nevada	74	944	1,076	94	1,125	1,303
New Hampshire	7	1,122	1,142	10	1,300	1,333
New Jersey	1,134	6,531	7,899	1,349	6,855	8,546
New Mexico	29	1,436	1,632	34	1,711	1,968

continued on the next page

Table 1.07 continued

	1990			2000		
	Black	White	All Races	Black	White	All Races
New York	2,858	14,338	17,773	3,180	14,062	17,986
North Carolina	1,480	5,071	6,690	1,641	5,653	7,483
North Dakota	3	627	660	4	592	629
Ohio	1,188	9,501	10,791	1,274	9,226	10,629
Oklahoma	223	2,789	3,285	231	2,810	3,376
Oregon	44	2,607	2,766	50	2,674	2,877
Pennsylvania	1,108	10,582	11,827	1,131	10,193	11,503
Rhode Island	38	943	1,002	45	974	1,049
South Carolina	1,067	2,451	3,549	1,170	2,694	3,906
South Dakota	2	642	708	2	635	714
Tennessee	810	3,076	4,972	887	4,331	5,266
Texas	2,104	15,272	17,712	2,439	17,311	20,211
Utah	12	1,692	1,776	13	1,879	1,991
Vermont	2	555	562	3	580	591
Virginia	1,171	4,840	6,157	1,332	5,346	6,877
Washington	114	4,251	4,657	116	4,488	4,991
West Virginia	54	1,792	1,856	45	1,164	1,722
Wisconsin	231	4,501	4,808	273	4,417	4,784
Wyoming	4	483	502	4	467	489

SOURCE: U.S. Bureau of the Census, Statistical Abstract of the United States, 1988, pp. 23-24, tables 27, 28 (data from U.S. Bureau of the Census, *Current Population Reports*, Series P-25). C 3.134:988

NOTES: 'All Races' includes other races not shown separately.

UNITS: Population in thousands of persons.

Table 1.08 Marital Status, Persons 15 Years Old and Older, 1980, 1985, 1988

	Black		White		All Races	
	number	percent	number	percent	number	percent
1980						
All marital statuses	17,896	100.0%	147,112	100.0%	168,198	100.0%
single	6,530	36.5	35,764	24.3	43,236	25.7
married, spouse present	6,753	37.7	88,962	60.5	97,531	58.0
married, spouse absent	1,644	9.2	3,499	2.4	5,269	3.1
widowed	1,596	8.9	10,698	7.3	12,451	7.4
divorced	1,373	7.7	8,199	5.6	9,711	5.8
1985						
All marital statuses	20,234	100.0%	157,090	100.0%	182,316	100.0%
single	8,057	39.8	38,177	24.3	47,744	26.2
married, spouse present	7,015	34.7	92,465	58.9	102,229	56.1
married, spouse absent	1,603	7.9	3,960	2.5	5,770	3.2
widowed	1,794	8.9	11,404	7.3	13,484	7.4
divorced	1,764	8.7	11,084	7.1	13,089	7.2
1988						
All marital statuses	21,221	100.0%	161,341	100.0%	188,452	100.0%
single	8,365	39.4	39,355	24.4	49,496	26.3
married, spouse present	7,434	35.0	94,457	58.5	105,226	55.8
married, spouse absent	1,710	8.1	4,279	2.7	6,230	3.3
widowed	1,758	8.3	11,522	7.1	13,532	7.2
divorced	1,954	9.2	11,728	7.3	13,968	7.4

SOURCE: U.S. Bureau of the Census, Current Population Reports: Marital Status and Living Arrangements, March, 1980, Series P-20, #365, p. 7, table 1, March, 1985, #410, p. 17, table 1; March,1988, #433, p. 3, table 1. C3.186/6:(year)

NOTES: 'All Races' includes other races not shown separately.

UNITS: Number in thousands of persons 15 years old and older; percent as a percent of total (percents not standardized for age).

Table 1.09 Marital Status, Men 15 Years Old and Older, 1980, 1985, 1988

	Black		White		All Races	
	number	percent	number	percent	number	percent
1980						
All marital statuses	8,067	100.0%	70,632	100.0%	80,218	100.0%
single	3,244	40.2	19,752	28.0	23,512	29.3
married, spouse present	3,416	42.3	44,490	63.0	48,765	60.8
married, spouse absent	577	7.2	1,458	2.1	2,093	2.6
widowed	316	3.9	1,629	2.3	1,972	2.5
divorced	515	6.4	3,303	4.7	3,875	4.8
1985						
All marital statuses	9,141	100.0%	75,487	100.0%	87,034	100.0%
single	3,965	43.3	21,276	28.2	26,108	30.0
married, spouse present	3,554	38.9	46,261	61.3	51,114	58.7
married, spouse absent	663	7.3	1,666	2.2	2,439	2.8
widowed	324	3.5	1,744	2.3	2,109	2.4
divorced	636	7.0	4,540	6.0	5,264	6.0
1988						
All marital statuses	9,603	100.0%	77,823	100.0%	90,284	100.0%
single	4,077	42.5	21,866	28.1	26,987	29.9
married, spouse present	3,765	39.2	47,271	60.7	52,613	58.3
married, spouse absent	603	6.3	1,901	2.4	2,620	2.9
widowed	343	3.6	1,921	2.5	2,293	2.5
divorced	814	8.5	4,844	6.2	5,771	6.4

SOURCE: U.S. Bureau of the Census, Current Population Reports: Marital Status and Living Arrangements, March 1980, Series P-20, #365, p. 7, table 1; March, 1985, #410, p. 17, table 1; March, 1988 #433, p. 3, table 1. C3.186/6:(year)

NOTES: 'All Races' includes other races not shown separately.

UNITS: Number in thousands of men 15 years old and older; percent as a percent of total (percents not standardized for age).

Table 1.10 Marital Status, Women 15 Years Old and Older, 1980, 1985, 1988

	Black		White		All Races	
	number	percent	number	percent	number	percent
1980						
All marital statuses	9,828	100.0%	76,480	100.0%	87,980	100.0%
single	3,286	33.4	16,012	20.9	19,724	22.4
married, spouse present	3,337	34.0	44,472	58.1	48,765	55.4
married, spouse absent	1,067	10.9	2,040	2.7	3,176	3.6
widowed	1,280	13.0	9,060	11.8	10,479	11.9
divorced	858	8.7	4,896	6.4	5,836	6.6
1985						
All marital statuses	11,092	100.0%	81,603	100.0%	95,282	100.0%
single	4,092	36.9	16,901	20.7	21,636	22.7
married, spouse present	3,461	31.2	46,205	56.6	51,114	53.6
married, spouse absent	940	8.5	2,294	2.8	3,331	3.5
widowed	1,471	13.3	9,660	11.8	11,375	11.9
divorced	1,128	10.2	6,544	8.0	7,826	8.2
1988						
All marital statuses	11,618	100.0%	83,518	100.0%	98,168	100.0%
single	4,288	36.9	17,470	20.9	22,509	22.9
married, spouse present	3,669	31.6	47,185	56.5	52,613	53.6
married, spouse absent	1,107	9.5	2,378	2.8	3,610	3.7
widowed	1,415	12.2	9,601	11.5	11,239	11.4
divorced	1,140	9.8	6,884	8.2	8,197	8.4

SOURCE: U.S. Bureau of the Census, Current Population Reports: Marital Status and Living Arrangements, March, 1980, Series P-20, #365, p. 7, table 1; March, 1985, #410, p. 17, table 1; March, 1988, #433, p. 3, table 1. C3.186/6:(year)

NOTES: 'All Races' includes other races not shown separately.

UNITS: Number in thousands of women 15 years old and older; percent as a percent of total (percents not standardized for age).

Table 1.11 Interracial Married Couples, 1970, 1980, 1988

	1970	1980	1988
All married couples	44,597	49,714	52,613
All interracial married couples	310	651	956
All Black-White married couples	65	167	218
husband black, wife white	41	122	149
wife black, husband white	24	45	69
Other interracial married couples	245	484	738
husband black	8	20	26
wife black	4	14	9
husband white	139	287	434
wife white	94	163	269

SOURCE: U.S. Bureau of the Census, Statistical Abstract of the United States, 1989, p. 44, table 55. C 3.134:989
U.S. Bureau of the Census, Current Population Reports: Household & Family Characteristics, March 1988, Series P-20, #437, p. 94, table 16. C3.186/6:989

NOTES: 1970 data includes persons 14 years old and older; 1980 and 1988 data includes persons 15 years old and older.

UNITS: Thousands of married couples.

Table 1.12 Age, Educational Attainment, and Residence, 1980

	thousands of persons			percent distribution		
	Black	White	All Races	Black	White	All Races
Age						
Persons of all ages	26,495	188,372	226,546	100.0%	100.0%	100.0%
persons:						
under 5 years old	2,436	12,634	16,348	9.2	6.7	7.2
5-14 years old	5,164	27,494	34,942	19.5	14.6	15.4
15-44 years old	12,629	86,468	105,203	47.7	45.9	46.4
45-64 years old	4,180	38,829	44,503	15.8	20.6	19.6
65 years old and over	2,087	22,948	25,549	7.9	12.2	11.3
Years of school completed						
All persons 25 years old and over	13,195	114,290	135,836	100.0%	100.0%	100.0%
persons completing:						
0-8 years of school	3,571	19,020	24,257	27.1	16.6	17.9
1-3 years high school	2,876	16,664	20,278	21.8	14.6	14.9
4 years high school	3,862	40,784	45,947	29.3	35.7	33.8
1-3 years college	1,786	18,264	20,795	13.5	16.0	15.3
4 or more years college	1,104	19,558	21,555	8.4	17.1	15.9
median years completed	12.0	12.5	12.5	-	-	-
Residence						
Northeast	4,848	42,326	49,135	9.7%	86.1%	100.0%
Midwest	5,337	52,195	58,866	9.1	88.7	100.0
South	14,048	58,960	75,372	18.6	78.2	100.0
West	2,262	34,890	43,172	5.2	80.8	100.0
nonfarm	25,145	182,520	221,982	99.0%	97.1%	97.3%
farm	240	5,528	5,865	0.9	2.9	2.7
inside metro areas	21,478	138,064	169,431	81.0%	73.3%	74.8%
outside metro areas	5,017	50,307	57,115	18.9	26.7	25.2

continued on the next page

Table 1.12 continued

SOURCE: U.S. Bureau of the Census, Census of Population: General Population Characteristics: United State Summary PC80-1-B1, p. 1-125, table 62; p. 1-50, table 1-53.
U.S. Bureau of the Census, Census of Population: General Social and Economic Characteristics: United State Summary PC80-1-C1, pp. 1-21 - 1-23, table 83.
U.S. Bureau of the Census, Current Population Reports: Characteristics of the Population Below the Poverty Level, 1979, Series P-60, #133, pp. 35-36, table 8. C3.186/P60/133
U.S. Bureau of the Census, Statistical Abstract of the United States, 1981, p. 143, table 226. C 3.134:981

NOTES: 'All Races' includes other races not shown separately. Data from the decennial census of population, differs from Current Population Survey data, hence the same totals under different categories may not match precisely.

UNITS: Population in thousands of persons; percent distribution as a percent of total, 100.0%.

Table 1.13 Age, Educational Attainment, and Residence, 1985

	thousands of persons			percent distribution		
	Black	White	All Races	Black	White	All Races
Age						
Persons of all ages	28,151	199,117	234,066	100.0%	100.0%	100.0%
persons:						
under 5 years old	2,699	14,610	17,958	9.6	7.3	7.7
5-14 years old	5,218	27,417	33,792	18.5	13.8	14.4
15-44 years old	13,590	93,852	110,948	48.3	47.1	47.4
45-64 years old	4,406	39,033	44,549	15.7	19.6	19.0
65 years old and over	2,238	24,205	26,818	7.9	12.2	11.5
Years of school completed						
All persons 25 years old and over	14,820	124,905	143,524	100.0%	100.0%	100.0%
persons completing:						
0-8 years of school	3,113	16,224	19,893	21.0	13.0	13.9
1-3 years high school	2,851	14,365	17,553	19.2	11.5	12.2
4 years high school	5,027	48,728	54,866	33.9	39.0	38.2
1-3 years college	2,188	20,652	23,405	14.8	16.5	16.3
4 or more years college	1,640	24,935	27,808	11.1	20.0	19.4
Residence						
Northeast	5,296	43,185	49,276	18.9%	21.7%	21.1%
Midwest	5,549	52,280	58,587	19.8	26.3	25.1
South	14,920	63,155	79,165	53.2	31.7	34.1
West	2,290	40,394	46,489	8.2	20.3	19.8
nonfarm	na	na	na			
farm	na	na	na			
inside metro areas	na	na	na			
outside metro areas	na	na	na			

continued on the next page

Table 1.13 continued

SOURCE: U.S. Bureau of the Census, Statistical Abstract of the United States, 1987, p. 35, table 39, (data from U.S. Bureau of the Census, *Current Population Reports*, Series P-25). C 3.134:987

U.S. Bureau of the Census, Current Population Reports: Money Income of Households, Families and Persons in the United States, 1984, Series P-60 (#151), pp. 10-15, table 4. C3.186/22:984

NOTES: 'All Races' includes other races not shown separately.

UNITS: Population in thousands of persons; percent distribution as a percent of total, 100.0%.

Table 1.14 Age, Educational Attainment, and Residence, 1987

	thousands of persons			percent distribution		
	Black	White	All Races	Black	White	All Races
Age						
Persons of all ages						
persons:	28,930	202,453	238,789	100.0%	100.0%	100.0%
under 5 years old	2,728	14,798	18,130	9.4	7.3	7.6
5-14 years old	5,283	27,441	33,972	18.3	13.6	14.2
15-44 years old	14,087	95,892	113,811	48.7	47.4	47.7
45-64 years old	4,501	39,149	44,901	15.6	19.3	18.8
65 years old and over	2,331	25,173	27,975	8.1	12.4	11.7
Years of school completed						
All persons 25 years old and over	15,580	129,170	149,144	100.0%	100.0%	100.0%
persons completing:						
0-8 years of school	2,863	15,478	18,941	18.4	12.0	12.7
1-3 years high school	2,835	14,233	17,417	18.2	11.0	11.7
4 years high school	5,773	50,690	57,669	37.1	39.2	38.7
1-3 years college	2,442	22,265	25,479	15.7	17.2	17.1
4 or more years college	1,667	26,505	29,637	10.7	20.5	19.9
Residence						
Northeast	4,877	43,524	49,572	16.9%	21.5%	20.8%
Midwest	5,485	52,306	58,702	19.0	25.9	24.6
South	16,039	64,441	81,646	55.5	31.9	34.2
West	2,470	42,012	48,634	8.6	20.8	20.4
nonfarm	28,699	197,399	233,475	99.4%	97.6%	97.9%
farm	172	4,884	5,079	0.6	2.4	2.1
inside metro areas	23,562	154,934	184,848	81.6%	76.6%	77.5%
outside metro areas	5,310	47,348	53,706	18.4	23.4	22.5

continued on the next page

Table 1.14 continued

SOURCE: U.S. Bureau of the Census, Statistical Abstract of the United States, 1989, p. 38, table 44 (data from U.S. Bureau of the Census, *Current Population Reports*, Series P-25). C 3.134:989
U.S. Bureau of the Census, Current Population Reports: Poverty in the United States, 1986, Series P-60, #160, pp. 15-25, tables 5, 6. C3.186/22:986

NOTES: 'All Races' includes other races not shown separately.

UNITS: Population in thousands of persons; percent distribution as a percent of total, 100.0%.

Table 1.15 Selected Characteristics of Households, 1980

	number			percent distribution		
	Black	White	All Races	Black	White	All Races
Marital status and sex of the householder						
All households, both sexes	8,405	69,454	79,108	100.0%	100.0%	100.0%
male householder	4,537	51,370	56,849	54.0	74.0	71.9
married, wife present	3,136	42,631	46,548	73.3	61.4	58.8
married, wife absent	324	941	1,296	3.9	1.4	1.6
widowed	207	1,324	1,550	2.5	1.9	2.0
divorced	307	2,300	2,638	3.7	3.3	3.3
single, never married	563	4,175	4,817	6.7	6.0	6.1
female householder	3,869	18,084	22,259	46.0	26.0	28.1
married, husband present	220	1,377	1,631	2.6	2.0	2.1
married, husband absent	870	1,477	2,390	10.4	2.1	3.0
widowed	1,064	7,773	8,912	12.7	11.2	11.3
divorced	737	3,977	4,783	8.8	5.7	6.0
single, never married	977	3,480	4,543	11.6	5.0	5.7
Age of the householder						
All ages	8,405	69,454	79,108	100.0%	100.0%	100.0%
15-24 years old	764	5,545	6,398	9.1	8.0	8.1
25-34 years old	2,122	15,398	17,900	25.3	22.2	22.6
35-44 years old	1,579	12,063	13,904	18.8	17.4	17.6
45-54 years old	1,380	10,969	12,581	16.4	15.8	15.9
55-64 years old	1,150	10,882	12,177	13.7	15.7	15.4
65 years old and over	1,410	14,597	16,149	16.8	21.0	20.4
Housing tenure						
All tenures	8,405	69,454	79,108	100.0%	100.0%	100.0%
own housing unit	4,085	49,026	53,830	48.6	70.6	68.0
rent housing unit	4,320	20,428	25,278	51.4	29.4	32.0

continued on the next page

Table 1.15 continued

	number			percent distribution		
	Black	White	All Races	Black	White	All Races
Size of the household						
All household sizes	8,405	69,454	79,108	100.0%	100.0%	100.0%
one person	2,038	15,568	17,816	24.2	22.4	22.5
two persons	2,046	22,403	24,734	24.3	32.3	31.3
three persons	1,517	12,098	13,845	18.0	17.4	17.5
four persons	1,306	10,953	12,470	15.5	15.8	15.8
five persons	665	5,191	5,996	7.9	7.5	7.6
six persons	405	2,013	2,499	4.8	2.9	3.2
seven or more persons	428	1,228	1,748	5.1	1.8	2.2
persons per household	3.01	2.71	2.75	-	-	-
Residence						
All residences	8,405	69,454	79,108	100.0%	100.0%	100.0%
Northeast	1,632	15,647	17,447	19.4	22.5	22.1
Midwest	1,808	18,969	20,933	21.5	27.3	26.5
South	4,125	21,213	25,523	49.1	30.5	32.3
West	840	13,625	15,205	10.0	19.6	19.2
inside metropolitan areas	6,659	46,416	54,051	79.2	66.8	88.3
outside metropolitan areas	1,746	23,038	25,057	20.8	33.2	11.7
nonfarm	8,347	67,635	77,210	99.3	97.4	97.6
farm	58	1,818	1,898	0.7	2.6	2.4

SOURCE: U.S. Bureau of the Census, Current Population Reports: Money Income of Households in the United States; March 1979, Series P-60, #126, pp. 13-18, table 3. C3.186/P-60/126
U.S. Bureau of the Census, Current Population Reports: Household & Family Characteristics, March 1980, Series P-20, #366, pp. 211-214, table 24. C3.186:980

NOTES: 'All Races' includes other races not shown separately.

UNITS: Number of households in thousands of households; persons per household, average; percent distribution in percent as a percent of the total, 100.0%.

Table 1.16 Selected Characteristics of Households, 1985

	number			percent distribution		
	Black	White	All Races	Black	White	All Races
Marital status and sex of the householder						
All households, both sexes	9,480	75,328	86,789	100.0%	100.0%	100.0%
male householder	4,665	53,868	60,025	49.2	71.5	69.2
married, wife present	3,077	43,444	47,683	32.5	57.7	54.9
married, wife absent	349	1,013	1,416	3.7	1.3	1.6
widowed	211	1,386	1,620	2.2	1.8	1.9
divorced	415	3,078	3,535	4.3	4.1	4.1
single, never married	623	4,947	5,772	6.6	6.6	6.7
female householder	4,815	21,461	26,763	50.8	28.5	30.8
married, husband present	392	2,199	2,667	4.1	2.9	3.1
married, husband absent	777	1,668	2,497	8.2	2.2	2.9
widowed	1,271	8,304	9,728	13.4	11.0	11.2
divorced	950	5,203	6,265	10.0	6.9	7.2
single, never married	1,425	4,087	5,606	15.0	5.4	6.5
Age of the householder						
All ages	9,480	75,328	86,789	100.0%	100.0%	100.0%
15-24 years old	669	4,626	5,438	7.1	6.1	6.3
25-34 years old	2,470	17,010	20,013	26.1	22.6	23.1
35-44 years old	1,947	15,024	17,481	20.5	19.9	20.1
45-54 years old	1,488	10,792	12,628	15.7	14.3	14.6
55-64 years old	1,350	11,471	13,073	14.2	15.2	15.1
65 years old and over	1,556	16,406	18,155	16.4	21.8	20.9
Housing tenure						
All tenures	9,480	75,328	86,789	100.0%	100.0%	100.0%
own housing unit	4,185	50,611	55,845	44.1	67.2	64.3
rent housing unit	5,295	24,667	30,943	55.9	32.7	35.7

continued on the next page

Table 1.16 continued

	number			percent distribution		
	Black	White	All Races	Black	White	All Races
Size of the household						
All household sizes	9,480	75,328	86,789	100.0%	100.0%	100.0%
one person	2,367	17,876	20,602	25.0	23.7	23.7
two persons	2,391	24,558	27,289	25.2	32.6	31.6
three persons	1,795	13,336	15,465	18.9	15.7	17.8
four persons	1,441	11,795	13,631	15.2	17.7	15.7
five persons	800	5,061	6,108	8.4	6.7	7.0
six persons	370	1,819	2,299	3.9	2.4	2.6
seven or more persons	317	882	1,296	3.3	1.2	1.5
persons per household	2.96	2.64	2.69	-	-	-
Residence						
All residences	9,480	75,328	86,789	100.0%	100.0%	100.0%
Northeast	1,860	16,244	18,348	19.6	21.6	21.1
Midwest	1,863	19,599	21,697	19.6	26.0	25.0
South	4,924	24,283	29,581	51.9	32.2	34.1
West	834	15,202	17,163	8.8	20.2	19.8
inside metropolitan areas	na	na	na			
outside metropolitan areas	na	na	na			
nonfarm	na	na	na			
farm	na	na	na			

SOURCE: U.S. Bureau of the Census, Current Population Reports: Money Income of Households Families and Persons in the United States; March 1984, Series P-60, #151, pp. 10-14, table 4. C3.186/2:984

U.S. Bureau of the Census, Current Population Reports: Household & Family Characteristics, March 1985, Series P-20, #411, pp. 107-112, table 22. C3.186/17:985

NOTES: 'All Races' includes other races not shown separately.

UNITS: Number of households in thousands of households; persons per household, average; percent distribution in percent as a percent of the total, 100.0%.

Table 1.17 Selected Characteristics of Households, 1988

	number			percent distribution		
	Black	White	All Races	Black	White	All Races
Marital status and sex of the householder						
All households, both sexes	10,186	78,469	91,066	100.0%	100.0%	100.0%
male householder	5,050	55,927	62,773	49.6%	71.3%	68.9
married, wife present	3,200	44,170	48,748	31.4	56.3	53.5
married, wife absent	378	1,208	1,671	3.7	1.5	1.8
widowed	270	1,626	1,920	2.7	2.1	2.1
divorced	472	3,398	3,957	4.6	4.3	4.3
single, never married	730	5,525	6,477	7.2	7.0	7.1
female householder	5,136	22,542	28,293	50.4%	28.7%	31.1%
married, husband present	482	2,474	3,061	4.7	3.2	3.4
married, husband absent	917	1,762	2,768	9.0	2.2	3.0
widowed	1,225	8,264	9,628	12.0	10.5	10.6
divorced	959	5,441	6,527	9.4	6.9	7.6
single, never married	1,554	4,601	6,310	15.3	5.9	6.9
Age of the householder						
All ages	10,186	78,469	91,066	100.0%	100.0%	100.0%
15-24 years old	673	4,397	5,228	6.6%	5.6%	5.7
25-34 years old	2,592	17,365	20,583	25.4	22.1	22.6
35-44 years old	2,266	16,426	19,323	22.2	20.9	21.2
45-54 years old	1,575	11,577	13,630	15.5	14.8	15.0
55-64 years old	1,323	11,270	12,846	13.0	14.4	14.1
65 years old and over	1,756	17,435	19,456	17.2	22.2	21.4
Housing tenure						
All tenures	10,186	78,469	91,066	100.0%	100.0%	100.0%
own housing unit	4,323	52,697	58,214	42.4%	67.2%	63.9
rent housing unit	5,863	25,772	32,852	57.6	32.8	36.1

continued on the next page

Table 1.17 continued

	number			percent distribution		
	Black	White	All Races	Black	White	All Races
Size of the household						
All household sizes	10,186	78,469	91,066	100.0%	100.0%	100.0%
one person	2,635	18,872	21,889	25.9%	24.0%	24.0
two persons	2,541	26,134	29,295	24.9	33.3	32.2
three persons	1,904	13,760	16,163	18.7	17.5	17.7
four persons	1,609	12,111	14,143	15.8	15.4	15.5
five persons	795	5,025	6,081	7.8	6.4	6.7
six persons	362	1,682	2,176	3.6	2.1	2.4
seven or more persons	341	886	1,320	3.3	1.1	1.4
persons per household	2.87	2.60	2.64	-	-	-
Residence						
All residences	10,186	78,469	91,066	100.0%	100.0%	100.0%
Northeast	1,768	16,953	19,137	17.4	21.6	21.0
Midwest	2,018	20,047	22,402	19.8	25.5	24.6
South	5,477	25,163	31,047	53.8	32.1	34.1
West	923	16,307	18,480	9.1	20.8	20.3
inside metropolitan areas	8,477	60,148	70,692	83.2	76.7	77.6
outside metropolitan areas	1,710	18,321	20,374	16.8	23.3	22.4
nonfarm	10,155	76,822	89,383	99.7	97.9	98.2
farm	31	1,648	1,684	0.3	2.1	1.8

SOURCE: U.S. Bureau of the Census, Current Population Reports: Money Income of Households Families and Persons in the United States; March 1987, Series P-60, #162, pp. 14-21, table 4. C3.186/2:989

U.S. Bureau of the Census, Current Population Reports: Household & Family Characteristics, March 1988, Series P-20, #437, pp. 121-125, table 24. C3.186/17:988

NOTES: 'All Races' includes other races not shown separately.

UNITS: Number of households in thousands of households; persons per household, average; percent distribution in percent as a percent of the total, 100.0%.

Table 1.18 Selected Characteristics of Family Households, 1980

	number			percent distribution		
	Black	White	All Races	Black	White	All Races
Type of family						
All families	6,042	51,389	58,428	100.0%	100.0%	100.0%
married couple families	3,355	44,008	48,180	55.5	85.6	82.5
male householder, no wife present	257	1,418	1,706	4.3	2.8	2.9
female householder, no husband present	2,429	5,963	8,540	40.2	11.6	14.6
Size of family						
All family sizes	6,042	51,389	58,426	100.0%	100.0%	100.0%
two persons	1,882	20,771	22,913	31.1	40.4	39.2
three persons	1,460	11,647	13,332	24.2	22.7	22.8
four persons	1,243	10,730	12,180	20.6	20.9	20.8
five persons	648	5,089	5,871	10.7	9.9	10.0
six persons	389	1,971	2,439	6.4	3.8	4.2
seven or more persons	419	1,181	1,691	6.9	2.3	2.9
average per family	3.67	3.22	3.28	-	-	-
Number of related children under 18 years old						
All families	6,042	51,389	58,426	100.0%	100.0%	100.0%
no children	2,311	25,227	27,909	38.2	49.1	47.8
one child	1,415	10,582	12,231	23.4	20.6	20.9
two children	1,213	9,849	11,280	20.0	19.2	19.3
three children	612	3,899	4,616	10.1	7.6	7.9
four children	297	1,277	1,613	4.9	2.5	2.8
five children	116	393	526	1.9	0.8	0.9
six or more children	78	161	251	1.2	0.3	0.4
average per family	1.28	0.95	0.99	-	-	-
average per family with children	2.07	1.86	1.89	-	-	-

continued on the next page

Table 1.18 continued

	number			percent distribution		
	Black	White	All Races	Black	White	All Races
Number of earners						
All families	5,937	50,787	57,702	100.0%	100.0%	100.0%
no earner	1,065	6,255	7,421	17.9	12.3	12.9
one earner	2,087	15,482	17,833	35.1	30.5	30.9
two earners	2,145	21,367	23,928	36.1	42.1	41.5
three earners	437	5,118	5,669	7.4	10.1	9.8
four earners or more	202	2,565	2,841	3.4	5.1	4.9
Housing tenure						
All tenures	6,042	51,389	58,426	100.0%	100.0%	100.0%
own housing unit	3,230	40,250	44,116	53.5	78.3	75.5
rent housing unit	2,812	11,139	14,310	46.5	21.7	24.5
Residence						
All residences	6,042	51,389	58,426	100.0%	100.0%	100.0%
Northeast	1,159	11,548	12,850	19.2	22.5	22.0
Midwest	1,253	14,200	15,568	20.7	27.6	26.6
South	3,072	16,143	19,367	50.8	31.4	33.1
West	558	9,499	10,641	9.2	18.5	18.2
nonfarm	5,995	49,790	56,760	99.2	96.9	97.1
farm	47	1,598	1,666	0.8	3.1	2.9
inside metropolitan areas	4,726	33,551	39,049	78.2	65.3	66.8
outside metropolitan areas	1,316	17,838	19,377	21.8	34.7	33.2

SOURCE: U.S. Bureau of the Census, Current Population Reports: Money Income of Families and Persons in the United States, 1979, Series P-60, #129, pp. 23-30, table 2; pp. 113-144, table 27. C3.186:/P60/129

U.S. Bureau of the Census, Current Population Reports: Household & Family Characteristics, March 1980, Series P-20, (#366), pp. 7-9, table 1; pp. 211-214, table 24. C3.186:/P20/366

NOTES: 'All Races' includes other races not shown separately. 'Number of earners' excludes families with members in the armed forces.

UNITS: Number of households in thousands of family households; percent distribution in percent as a percent of the total, 100.0%.

Table 1.19 Selected Characteristics of Family Households, 1985

	number			percent distribution		
	Black	White	All Races	Black	White	All Races
Type of family						
All families	6,778	54,400	62,706	100.0%	100.0%	100.0%
married couple families	3,469	45,643	50,350	51.2	83.9	80.3
male householder, no wife present	344	1,816	2,228	5.1	3.3	3.6
female householder, no husband present	2,964	6,941	10,129	43.7	12.8	16.1
Size of family						
All family sizes	6,778	54,400	62,706	100.0%	100.0%	100.0%
two persons	2,261	22,711	25,349	33.4	41.7	40.4
three persons	1,730	12,743	14,804	25.5	23.4	23.6
four persons	1,358	11,517	13,259	20.0	21.2	21.1
five persons	762	4,894	5,894	11.2	9.0	9.4
six persons	366	1,704	2,175	5.4	3.1	3.5
seven or more persons	300	831	1,225	4.4	1.5	2.0
average per family	3.60	3.16	3.23	-	-	-
Number of related children under 18 years old						
All families	6,778	54,400	62,706	100.0%	100.0%	100.0%
no children	2,887	28,169	31,594	42.6	51.8	50.4
one child	1,579	11,174	13,108	23.3	20.5	20.9
two children	1,330	9,937	11,645	19.6	18.3	18.6
three children	612	3,695	4,486	9.0	6.8	7.2
four children	223	1,049	1,329	3.3	1.9	2.1
five children	97	261	373	1.4	0.5	0.6
six or more children	50	115	171	0.7	0.3	0.3
average per family	1.14	0.88	0.92	-	-	-
average per family with children	1.99	1.83	1.85	-	-	-

continued on the next page

Table 1.19 continued

	number			percent distribution		
	Black	White	All Races	Black	White	All Races
Number of earners						
All families	6,671	53,777	61,930	100.0%	100.0%	100.0%
no earner	1,376	7,674	9,221	20.6	14.3	14.9
one earner	2,312	15,219	17,949	34.7	28.3	29.0
two earners	2,237	23,303	26,160	33.5	43.3	42.2
three earners	527	5,317	6,029	7.9	9.9	9.7
four earners or more	218	2,263	2,570	3.3	4.2	4.1
Housing tenure						
All tenures	6,778	54,400	62,706	100.0%	100.0%	100.0%
own housing unit	3,271	40,865	45,015	48.3	75.1	71.8
rent housing unit	3,508	13,535	17,691	51.8	24.9	28.2
Residence						
All residences	6,778	54,400	62,706	100.0%	100.0%	100.0%
Northeast	1,322	11,631	13,149	19.5	21.4	21.0
Midwest	1,345	14,309	15,839	19.8	26.3	25.3
South	3,561	17,953	21,781	52.5	33.0	34.7
West	550	10,507	11,938	8.1	19.3	19.0
nonfarm	na	na	na			
farm	na	na	na			
inside metropolitan areas	na	na	na			
outside metropolitan areas	na	na	na			

SOURCE: U.S. Bureau of the Census, Current Population Reports: Money Income of Households, Families, and Persons in the United States, 1984, Series P-60, #151, pp. 76-77, table 21. C3.186/2:984
U.S. Bureau of the Census, Current Population Reports: Household & Family Characteristics, March 1985, Series P-20, #437, pp. 13-45, table 1; pp. 107-111, table 22. C3.186/17:985

NOTES: 'All Races' includes other races not shown separately. 'Number of earners' excludes families with members in the armed forces.

UNITS: Number of households in thousands of family households; percent distribution in percent as a percent of the total, 100.0%.

Table 1.20 Selected Characteristics of Family Households, 1988

	number			percent distribution		
	Black	White	All Races	Black	White	All Races
Type of family						
All families	7,177	56,044	65,133	100.0%	100.0%	100.0%
married couple families	3,682	46,644	51,809	51.3	83.2	79.5
male householder, no wife present	421	2,165	2,715	5.9	3.9	4.2
female householder, no husband present	3,074	7,235	10,608	42.8	12.9	16.3
Size of family						
All family sizes	7,177	56,044	65,133	100.0%	100.0%	100.0%
two persons	2,395	23,919	26,871	33.4	42.7	41.3
three persons	1,826	13,116	15,410	25.4	23.4	23.7
four persons	1,549	11,756	13,729	21.6	21.0	21.1
five persons	749	4,845	5,844	10.4	8.6	8.9
six persons	339	1,596	2,057	4.7	2.8	3.2
seven or more persons	318	812	1,222	4.4	1.5	1.9
average per family	3.49	3.12	3.17	-	-	-
Number of related children under 18 years old						
All families	7,177	56,044	65,133	100.0%	100.0%	100.0%
no children	2,982	29,426	33,213	41.5	52.5	51.0
one child	1,803	11,299	13,578	25.1	20.2	20.8
two children	1,338	10,217	11,911	18.6	18.2	18.3
three children	655	3,728	4,581	9.1	6.7	7.0
four children	273	973	1,304	3.8	1.7	2.0
five children	69	262	342	1.0	0.5	0.5
six or more children	57	139	204	1.0	0.2	0.3
average per family	1.08	0.86	0.89	-	-	-
average per family with children	1.85	1.80	1.81	-	-	-

continued on the next page

Table 1.20 continued

	number			percent distribution		
	Black	White	All Races	Black	White	All Races
Number of earners						
All families	7,030	55,324	64,228	100.0%	100.0%	100.0%
no earner	1,396	7,803	9,440	19.9	14.1	14.7
one earner	2,396	15,064	18,009	34.1	27.2	28.0
two earners	2,442	24,559	27,748	34.7	44.4	43.2
three earners	569	5,545	6,329	8.1	10.0	9.9
four earners or more	227	2,353	2,703	3.2	4.3	4.2
Housing tenure						
All tenures	7,177	56,044	65,133	100.0%	100.0%	100.0%
own housing unit	3,406	42,237	46,680	47.5	75.4	71.7
rent housing unit	3,771	13,808	18,453	52.5	24.6	28.3
Residence						
All residences	7,177	56,044	65,133	100.0%	100.0%	100.0%
Northeast	1,189	11,855	13,382	16.6	21.2	20.5
Midwest	1,389	14,240	15,905	19.4	25.4	24.4
South	3,972	18,559	22,846	55.3	33.1	35.1
West	627	11,389	13,000	8.7	20.3	20.0
nonfarm	7,154	54,641	63,705	99.7%	97.5%	97.8
farm	22	1,403	1,428	0.3	2.5	2.2
inside metropolitan areas	5,934	42,386	49,967	82.7%	75.6%	76.7
outside metropolitan areas	1,243	13,658	15,166	17.3	24.4	23.3

SOURCE: U.S. Bureau of the Census, Current Population Reports: Money Income of Households, Families, and Persons in the United States, 1987, Series P-60, #162, pp. 31-33, table 4. C3.186/2:987
U.S. Bureau of the Census, Current Population Reports: Household & Family Characteristics, March 1989, Series P-20, #437, pp. 3-5, table 1; pp. 121- 124, table 24. C3.186/17:989

NOTES: 'All Races' includes other races not shown separately. 'Number of earners' excludes families with members in the armed forces.

UNITS: Number of households in thousands of family households; percent distribution in percent as a percent of the total, 100.0%.

Table 1.21 Families With Own Children Under 18 Years Old, 1980, 1985, 1988

	Black families	White families	All families
1980			
Total	6,042	51,389	58,426
all families with own children under 18 years old	3,731	26,162	30,517
- married couple families	1,884	22,153	24,568
- male householder families	102	494	609
- female householder families	1,745	3,514	5,340
all families with own children under 6 years old	1,688	11,115	13,121
- married couple families	905	9,896	11,082
- male householder families	37	113	153
- female householder families	747	1,106	1,886
all families with own children under 3 years old	982	6,743	7,926
- married couple families	552	6,181	6,913
- male householder families	18	64	84
- female householder families	412	498	929
1985			
Total	6,778	54,400	62,706
all families with own children under 18 years old	3,890	26,232	31,112
- married couple families	1,822	21,565	24,210
- male householder families	126	744	896
- female householder families	1,942	3,922	6,006
all families with own children under 6 years old	1,784	11,937	14,202
- married couple families	882	10,410	11,715
- male householder families	50	211	276
- female householder families	853	1,315	2,210
all families with own children under 3 years old	918	7,290	8,503
- married couple families	485	6,550	7,295
- male householder families	24	101	136
- female householder families	410	639	1,073

continued on the next page

Table 1.21 continued

	Black families	White families	All families
1988			
Total	7,177	56,044	65,133
all families with own children under 18 years old	4,195	26,618	31,920
- married couple families	2,016	21,699	24,600
- male householder families	160	852	1,047
- female householder families	2,020	4,066	6,273
all families with own children under 6 years old	1,881	12,247	14,656
- married couple families	972	10,486	11,915
- male householder families	66	274	347
- female householder families	843	1,486	2,394
all families with own children under 3 years old	1,098	7,276	8,691
- married couple families	596	6,374	7,251
- male householder families	41	151	199
- female householder families	461	750	1,241

SOURCE: U.S. Bureau of the Census, Current Population Reports: Household & Family Characteristics, March, 1980, Series P-20, #366, pp. 7-9, table 1; March, 1985 Series P-20, #411, pp. 13-14, table 1; March, 1989, Series P-20, #437, pp. 3-5, table 1. C3.186/17:989

NOTES: 'All families' includes families of other races not shown separately.

UNITS: Thousands of family households.

Table 1.22 Living Arrangements of Children Under 18 Years of Age by Selected Characteristic of the Parent 1980, 1985, 1988

	Black children	White children	All children
1980			
All children living with one or both parents	9,234	50,904	61,602
children living with both parents	3,917	42,187	47,286
- parents high school graduates	na	na	na
- at least one parent employed	na	na	na
-- both parents employed	na	na	na
children living with mother only	4,070	6,869	11,131
- mother high school graduate	na	na	na
- mother employed	na	na	na
-- mother employed full time	na	na	na
children living with father only	183	819	1,031
- father high school graduate	na	na	na
- father employed	na	na	na
-- father employed full time	na	na	na
1985			
All children living with one or both parents	8,854	49,829	60,784
children living with both parents	3,741	40,690	46,149
- parents high school graduates	71.5%	82.2%	81.3%
- at least one parent employed	2,945	36,075	40,306
-- both parents employed	1,925	19,872	22,595
children living with mother only	4,837	7,929	13,081
- mother high school graduate	61.7%	66.4%	64.7%
- mother employed	1,959	4,553	6,675
-- mother employed full time	1,554	3,539	5,227
children living with father only	276	1,210	1,554
- father high school graduate	66.0%	77.6%	75.0%
- father employed	179	976	1,199
-- father employed full time	153	901	1,089

continued on the next page

Table 1.22 continued

	Black children	White children	All children
1988			
All children living with one or both parents	8,986	49,911	61,271
children living with both parents	3,739	40,287	45,942
- parents high school graduates	78.1%	83.6%	83.0%
- at least one parent employed	2,937	36,005	40,386
-- both parents employed	2,062	34,388	24,366
children living with mother only	4,959	8,160	13,521
- mother high school graduate	60.5%	70.5%	66.7%
- mother employed	2,104	4,804	7,075
-- mother employed full time	1,702	3,881	5,737
children living with father only	288	1,464	1,808
- father high school graduate	69.8%	74.2%	74.1%
- father employed	183	1,149	1,381
-- father employed full time	171	1,048	1,263

SOURCE: U.S. Bureau of the Census, Current Population Reports: Marital Status and Living Arrangements, March, 1980, Series P-20, #365, pp. 27-29, table 4. C3.186:P-20/365
U.S. Bureau of the Census, Current Population Reports: Marital Status and Living Arrangements, March, 1985 Series P-20, #410, pp. 51-62, table 9; March, 1988, Series P-20, #437, pp. 42-53, table 9. C3.186/6:989

NOTES: 'All children' includes children of other races not shown separately.

UNITS: Thousands of children living in family households.

Table 2.01 Births and Birth Rates, by Age of the Mother, 1970 - 1986

	Black	White	All Races
1970			
Live births	572	3,091	3,731
Birth rate per 1,000 population	25.3	23.0	18.4
Birth rate per 1,000 women, by age group			
10-14 years old	5.2	0.5	1.2
15-17 years old	101.4	29.2	38.8
18-19 years old	204.9	101.5	114.7
20-24 years old	202.7	163.4	167.8
25-29 years old	136.3	145.9	145.1
30-34 years old	79.6	71.9	73.3
35-39 years old	41.9	30.0	31.7
40-44 years old	12.5	7.5	8.1
45-49 years old	1.0	0.4	0.5
1975			
Live births	512	2,552	3,144
Birth rate per 1,000 population	20.7	13.6	14.6
Birth rate per 1,000 women, by age group			
10-14 years old	5.1	0.6	1.3
15-17 years old	85.6	28.0	36.1
18-19 years old	152.4	74.0	85.0
20-24 years old	142.8	108.2	113.0
25-29 years old	102.2	108.1	108.2
30-34 years old	53.1	51.3	52.3
35-39 years old	25.6	18.2	19.5
40-44 years old	7.5	4.2	4.6
45-49 years old	0.5	0.2	0.3

continued on the next page

Table 2.01 continued

	Black	White	All Races
1980			
Live births	590	2,899	3,612
Birth rate per 1,000 population	22.1	14.9	15.9
Birth rate per 1,000 women, by age group			
10-14 years old	4.3	0.6	1.1
15-17 years old	73.6	25.2	32.5
18-19 years old	138.8	72.1	82.1
20-24 years old	146.3	109.5	115.1
25-29 years old	109.1	112.4	112.9
30-34 years old	62.9	60.4	61.9
35-39 years old	24.5	18.5	19.8
40-44 years old	5.8	3.4	3.9
45-49 years old	0.3	0.2	0.2
1986			
Live births	621	2,970	3,757
Birth rate per 1,000 population	21.2	14.5	15.6
Birth rate per 1,000 women, by age group			
10-14 years old	4.6	0.6	1.3
15-17 years old	70.0	23.4	30.6
18-19 years old	141.0	69.8	81.0
20-24 years old	143.7	101.5	108.2
25-29 years old	105.9	108.3	109.2
30-34 years old	62.2	68.9	69.3
35-39 years old	25.5	23.3	24.3
40-44 years old	5.1	3.7	4.1
45-49 years old	0.3	0.2	0.2

SOURCE: U.S. Department of Health and Human Services, Health United States, 1988, p. 42, table 2. HE 20.6223:988

NOTES: 'All Races' includes other races not shown separately. Data based on race of the child.

UNITS: Live births in thousands of births; rates as shown.

Table 2.02 Birth Rates for Women 15-44 Years of Age, by Live Birth Order, 1970 - 1986

	Black mothers	White mothers	mothers of All Races
1970			
All live births	115.4	84.1	87.9
first births	43.3	32.9	34.2
second births	27.1	23.7	24.2
third births	16.1	13.3	13.6
fourth births	10.0	6.8	7.2
fifth birth or higher	18.9	7.4	8.7
1975			
All live births	87.9	62.5	66.0
first births	36.9	26.7	28.1
second births	24.2	20.3	20.9
third births	12.6	8.8	9.4
fourth births	6.3	3.5	3.9
fifth birth or higher	8.0	3.1	3.7
1980			
All live births	88.1	64.7	68.4
first births	35.2	28.4	29.5
second births	25.7	21.0	21.8
third births	14.5	9.5	10.3
fourth births	6.7	3.4	3.9
fifth birth or higher	6.0	2.4	2.9
1986			
All live births	82.4	61.9	65.4
first births	32.5	26.0	27.2
second births	24.5	20.9	21.6
third births	14.1	9.6	10.3
fourth births	6.3	3.3	3.8
fifth birth or higher	4.9	1.9	2.5

SOURCE: U.S. Department of Health and Human Services, Health United States, 1988, p. 43, table 3. HE 20.6223:988

NOTES: Data based on race of the mother.

UNITS: Live births per 1,000 women 15-44 years of age.

Table 2.03 Selected Characteristics of Live Births, 1970 - 1986

	Black births	White births	births of All Races
1970			
birth weight under 2,500 grams	13.86%	6.84%	7.94%
birth weight under 1,500 grams	2.40	0.95	1.17
mother under 18 years old	14.7	4.18	6.3
mother 18-19 years old	16.6	10.4	11.3
births to unmarried mothers	37.4	5.7	10.7
mother with less than 12 years of school	51.0	27.0	30.8
mother with 16 years or more of school	2.8	9.5	8.6
prenatal care began in 1st trimester	44.4	72.4	68.0
prenatal care began in 3rd trimester or no prenatal care	16.6	6.2	7.9
1975			
birth weight under 2,500 grams	13.09%	6.26%	7.39%
birth weight under 1,500 grams	2.37	0.92	1.16
mother under 18 years old	16.1	6.0	7.6
mother 18-19 years old	16.8	10.3	11.3
births to unmarried mothers	49.0	7.3	14.3
mother with less than 12 years of school	45.1	25.0	28.6
mother with 16 years or more of school	4.4	12.7	11.4
prenatal care began in 1st trimester	55.8	75.9	72.4
prenatal care began in 3rd trimester or no prenatal care	10.5	5.0	6.0

continued on the next page

Table 2.03 continued

	Black births	White births	births of All Races
1980			
birth weight under 2,500 grams	12.49%	5.70%	6.84%
birth weight under 1,500 grams	2.44	0.90	1.15
mother under 18 years old	12.2	4.5	5.8
mother 18-19 years old	14.3	9.0	9.8
births to unmarried mothers	55.2	11.0	18.4
mother with less than 12 years of school	36.2	20.7	23.7
mother with 16 years or more of school	6.3	15.6	14.0
prenatal care began in 1st trimester	62.7	79.3	76.3
prenatal care began in 3rd trimester or no prenatal care	8.8	4.3	5.1
1986			
birth weight under 2,500 grams	12.53%	5.64%	6.81%
birth weight under 1,500 grams	2.66	0.93	1.21
mother under 18 years old	10.4	3.7	4.8
mother 18-19 years old	12.4	6.9	7.8
births to unmarried mothers	61.2	15.7	23.4
mother with less than 12 years of school	31.7	17.6	20.4
mother with 16 years or more of school	7.3	19.2	17.1
prenatal care began in 1st trimester	61.6	79.2	75.9
prenatal care began in 3rd trimester or no prenatal care	10.6	5.0	6.0

SOURCE: U.S. Department of Health and Human Services, Health United States, 1988, p. 47, table 7. HE 20.6223:988

NOTES: Data based on race of the child.

UNITS: Percent, as a percent of all live births, 100.0%.

Table 2.04 Lifetime Births Expected by Currently Married Women Age 18-34 Years Old, by Age of the Woman, 1975 - 1987

	Black women	White women	women of All Races
Lifetime births expected by currently married women			
1975			
all women 18-34 years old	2.8	2.3	2.3
women 18-19 years old	na	2.2	2.2
women 20-21 years old	2.6	2.1	2.2
women 22-24 years old	2.5	2.1	2.2
women 25-29 years old	2.6	2.2	2.3
women 30-34 years old	3.2	2.6	2.6
1980			
all women 18-34 years old	2.4	2.2	2.2
women 18-19 years old	na	2.1	2.1
women 20-21 years old	2.2	2.2	2.2
women 22-24 years old	2.1	2.1	2.1
women 25-29 years old	2.4	2.1	2.2
women 30-34 years old	2.5	2.2	2.2
1985			
all women 18-34 years old	2.4	2.2	2.2
women 18-19 years old	na	2.0	2.1
women 20-21 years old	na	2.2	2.2
women 22-24 years old	2.3	2.2	2.2
women 25-29 years old	2.3	2.2	2.2
women 30-34 years old	2.5	2.1	2.2

continued on the next page

Table 2.04 continued

	Black women	White women	women of All Races
Lifetime births expected by currently married women			
1987			
all women 18-34 years old	2.3	2.2	2.2
women 18-19 years old	na	2.0	2.1
women 20-21 years old	na	2.2	2.2
women 22-24 years old	2.2	2.2	2.2
women 25-29 years old	2.3	2.2	2.2
women 30-34 years old	2.3	2.2	2.2

SOURCE: U.S. Department of Health and Human Services, Health United States, 1988, p. 45, table 5 (data from U.S. Bureau of the Census, *Current Population Reports*, series P-20). HE 20.6223:988

NOTES: 'Women of All Races' includes women of other races not shown separately.

UNITS: Expected births by currently married women, in births expected per woman.

Table 2.05 Percent of Expected Lifetime Births Already Born to Currently Married Women 18-34 Years Old, by Age of the Woman, 1975 - 1987

	Black women	White women	women of All Races
Percent of expected lifetime births already born			
1975			
all women 18-34 years old	76.4%	68.2%	68.8%
women 18-19 years old	na	24.9	27.5
women 20-21 years old	43.3	29.4	30.7
women 22-24 years old	61.0	42.3	43.9
women 25-29 years old	78.2	70.5	70.9
women 30-34 years old	91.8	93.2	93.0
1980			
all women 18-34 years old	74.4%	66.3%	67.0%
women 18-19 years old	na	28.6	29.5
women 20-21 years old	46.1	31.8	32.9
women 22-24 years old	58.9	43.5	44.9
women 25-29 years old	73.8	64.0	64.7
women 30-34 years old	90.9	90.0	89.7
1985			
all women 18-34 years old	77.1%	63.3%	64.2%
women 18-19 years old	na	25.7	27.0
women 20-21 years old	na	30.6	30.9
women 22-24 years old	62.3	40.4	41.8
women 25-29 years old	72.8	59.4	60.2
women 30-34 years old	91.4	84.1	84.4

continued on the next page

Table 2.05 continued

	Black women	White women	women of All Races
Percent of expected lifetime births already born - continued			
1987			
all women 18-34 years old	77.8%	65.6%	66.5%
women 18-19 years old	na	27.0	27.8
women 20-21 years old	na	36.0	36.4
women 22-24 years old	55.4	42.0	43.0
women 25-29 years old	76.6	60.9	62.0
women 30-34 years old	89.7	83.6	83.8

SOURCE: U.S. Department of Health and Human Services, Health United States, 1988, p. 45, table 5 (data from U.S. Bureau of the Census, *Current Population Reports*, series P-20). HE 20.6223:988

NOTES: 'Women of All Races' includes women of other races not shown separately.

UNITS: Percent of expected lifetime births already born to currently married woman.

Table 2.06 Legal Abortions, Women 15-44 Years Old, 1975, 1980, 1985

	Black	White	All Races
1975			
All women, 15-44 years old	6,749	40,857	47,606
abortions			
number	333.0	701.2	1,034.2
rate per 1,000 women	49.3	17.2	21.7
ratio per 1,000 live births	565	276	331
1980			
All women, 15-44 years old	8,106	44,942	53,048
abortions			
number	460.3	1,093.6	1,553.9
rate per 1,000 women	56.5	24.3	29.3
ratio per 1,000 live births	642	376	428
1985			
All women, 15-44 years old	9,242	47,512	56,754
abortions			
number	na	na	1,588.6
rate per 1,000 women	na	na	28.0
ratio per 1,000 live births	na	na	425

SOURCE: U.S. Bureau of the Census, Statistical Abstract of the United States, 1989, p. 70, table 103. C 3.134:989

NOTES: 'All Races' includes women of other races not shown separately. Data based on estimates.

UNITS: Number of women and number of abortions in thousands; rates and ratios as shown.

Table 2.07 Life Expectancy at Birth, by Sex, 1970 - 1987

	Black		White		All Races	
	male	female	male	female	male	female
1970	60.0	68.3	68.0	75.6	67.1	74.7
1975	62.4	62.4	69.5	77.3	68.8	77.3
1980	64.0	72.5	70.7	78.1	70.0	77.4
1985	65.3	73.5	71.9	78.7	71.2	78.2
1987	65.4	73.8	72.1	78.8	71.5	78.3

SOURCE: U.S. Bureau of the Census, Statistical Abstract of the United States, 1989, p. 71, table 106. C 3.134:989

NOTES: 'All Races' includes other races not shown separately.

UNITS: Life expectancy in years.

Table 2.08 Life Expectancy by Sex, by Age in 1986

	Black		White		All Races
	male	female	male	female	both sexes
at birth in 1986	65.2	73.5	72.0	78.8	74.8
age 10 in 1986	56.8	65.0	62.9	69.6	65.8
age 20 in 1986	47.3	55.3	53.4	59.9	56.2
age 30 in 1986	38.5	45.7	44.2	50.1	46.8
age 40 in 1986	30.3	36.6	34.9	40.5	37.4
age 50 in 1986	22.7	28.0	26.1	31.2	28.5
age 60 in 1986	16.1	20.3	18.2	22.6	20.4
age 70 in 1986	10.8	13.9	11.7	15.1	13.6
age 80 in 1986	6.8	8.5	6.9	8.8	8.1
age 85 and over in 1986	5.5	6.7	5.1	6.4	6.0

SOURCE: U.S. Bureau of the Census, Statistical Abstract of the United States, 1989, p. 73, table 109. C 3.134:989

NOTES: 'All Races' includes other races not shown separately.

UNITS: Life expectancy in years.

Table 2.09 Infant Mortality, Fetal Deaths, and Perinatal Mortality Rates, 1970 - 1986

	Black	White	All Races
1970			
infant mortality rate	32.6	17.8	20.0
neonatal mortality rates:			
- under 28 days	22.8	13.8	15.1
- under 7 days	20.3	12.5	13.6
post neonatal mortality rate	9.9	4.0	4.9
fetal death rate	23.2	12.3	14.0
late fetal death rate	na	8.6	9.5
perinatal mortality rate	na	12.1	23.0
1975			
infant mortality rate	26.2	14.2	16.1
neonatal mortality rates:			
- under 28 days	18.3	10.4	11.6
- under 7 days	15.7	9.0	10.0
post neonatal mortality rate	7.9	3.8	4.5
fetal death rate	16.8	9.4	10.6
late fetal death rate	11.4	7.1	7.8
perinatal mortality rate	26.9	16.0	17.7
1980			
infant mortality rate	21.4	11.0	12.6
neonatal mortality rates:			
- under 28 days	14.1	7.5	8.5
- under 7 days	11.9	6.2	7.1
post neonatal mortality rate	7.3	3.5	4.1
fetal death rate	14.4	8.1	9.1
late fetal death rate	8.9	5.7	6.2
perinatal mortality rate	20.7	11.9	13.2

continued on the next page

Table 2.09 continued

	Black	White	All Races
1985			
infant mortality rate	18.2	9.3	10.6
neonatal mortality rates:			
- under 28 days	12.1	6.1	7.0
- under 7 days	10.3	5.0	5.8
post neonatal mortality rate	6.1	3.2	3.7
fetal death rate	12.6	7.0	7.8
late fetal death rate	7.1	4.5	4.9
perinatal mortality rate	17.4	9.6	10.7
1986			
infant mortality rate	18.0	8.9	10.4
neonatal mortality rates:			
- under 28 days	11.7	5.8	6.7
- under 7 days	10.1	4.8	5.6
post neonatal mortality rate	6.3	3.1	3.6
fetal death rate	12.5	6.7	7.7
late fetal death rate	7.0	4.3	4.7
perinatal mortality rate	17.0	9.1	10.3

SOURCE: U.S. Department of Health and Human Services, Health United States, 1988, p. 54, table 14. HE 20.6223:988

NOTES: 'All Races' includes other races not shown separately. Data based on race of the child. Infant mortality rate is the number of deaths of infants under one year; neonatal deaths occur within 28 days of birth; post-neonatal deaths occur 28-365 days after birth; deaths within 7 days of birth are early neonatal deaths; fetal deaths are deaths of fetuses of more than 20 weeks gestation; late fetal deaths are deaths of fetuses of more than 28 weeks of gestation; perinatal mortality is the sum of late fetal deaths and infant deaths within the first 7 days of life.

UNITS: All rates per 1,000 live births, as shown.

Table 2.10 Death Rates by Age and Sex, 1980 - 1987

	Black		White		All Races	
	male	female	male	female	male	female
1980						
All ages	1,034	733	983	806	977	785
under 1 year old	2,587	2,124	1,230	963	1,429	1,142
1-4 years old	111	84	66	49	73	55
5-14 years old	47	31	35	23	37	24
15-24 years old	209	71	167	56	172	58
25-34 years old	407	150	171	65	196	76
35-44 years old	690	324	257	138	299	159
45-54 years old	1,480	768	699	373	767	413
55-64 years old	2,873	1,561	1,729	876	1,815	934
65-74 years old	5,131	3,057	4,036	2,067	4,105	2,145
75-84 years old	9,232	6,212	8,830	5,402	8,817	5,440
85 years old and over	16,099	12,367	19,097	14,980	18,801	14,747
1985						
All ages	977	728	960	837	945	807
under 1 year old	2,135	1,757	1,039	787	1,197	932
1-4 years old	89	71	52	40	58	45
5-14 years old	41	28	30	19	32	21
15-24 years old	174	60	136	48	141	50
25-34 years old	347	136	157	59	178	69
35-44 years old	642	278	241	121	278	138
45-54 years old	1,283	654	609	340	669	373
55-64 years old	2,623	1,502	1,614	864	1,693	919
65-74 years old	4,889	2,926	3,717	2,028	3,788	2,095
75-84 years old	9,298	6,252	8,500	5,171	8,504	5,220
85 years old and over	15,046	12,155	18,789	14,579	18,325	14,343

continued on the next page

Table 2.10 continued

	Black		White		All Races	
	male	female	male	female	male	female
1987						
All ages	973	727	952	851	935	816
under 1 year old	2,218	1,781	939	730	1,123	884
1-4 years old	85	51	54	44	58	44
5-14 years old	46	26	30	18	32	19
15-24 years old	195	64	145	50	151	52
25-34 years old	370	140	167	64	189	74
35-44 years old	674	295	251	116	290	135
45-54 years old	1,244	644	578	335	638	367
55-64 years old	2,474	1,466	1,555	858	1,626	910
65-74 years old	4,592	2,879	3,586	2,012	3,636	2,070
75-84 years old	9,239	5,980	8,200	5,076	8,206	5,102
85 years old and over	14,957	11,921	18,456	14,642	18,037	14,377

SOURCE: U.S. Bureau of the Census, Statistical Abstract of the United States, 1989, p. 74, table 111. C 3.134:989

NOTES: 'All Races' includes other races not shown separately. Rates are crude rates (not age adjusted). 1987 data, preliminary.

UNITS: Rates per 100,000 of population in specified age groups, as shown.

Table 2.11 Death Rates by Selected Cause of Death, 1980, 1985, 1986

	Black		White		All Races	
	male	female	male	female	male	female
1980						
All causes	1,112.8	631.1	745.3	411.1	777.2	432.6
diseases of the heart	327.3	201.1	277.5	134.6	280.4	140.3
malignant neoplasms	229.9	129.7	160.5	107.7	165.5	109.2
accidents and adverse affects	82.0	25.1	62.3	21.4	64.0	21.8
cerebrovascular diseases	75.5	61.7	41.9	35.2	44.9	37.6
chronic obstructive pulmonary diseases	20.9	6.3	16.2	9.2	26.1	8.9
pneumonia	28.0	12.7	26.7	9.4	17.4	9.8
suicide	11.1	2.4	18.9	5.7	18.0	5.4
diabetes	17.7	22.1	9.5	8.7	10.2	10.0
chronic liver disease	30.6	14.4	15.7	7.0	17.1	7.9
1985						
All causes	1,024.0	589.1	688.7	390.6	716.8	409.4
diseases of the heart	301.0	186.8	244.5	121.7	247.7	127.3
malignant neoplasms	231.6	130.4	159.2	110.3	164.5	111.4
accidents and adverse affects	66.7	20.7	50.4	18.4	51.8	18.6
cerebrovascular diseases	60.8	50.3	32.8	27.9	35.2	30.0
chronic obstructive pulmonary diseases	23.9	8.7	28.5	12.9	27.9	12.5
pneumonia	26.8	12.4	17.4	9.8	18.2	10.1
suicide	11.3	2.1	19.9	5.3	18.8	4.9
diabetes	17.7	21.1	9.2	8.1	9.9	9.4
chronic liver disease	23.4	10.1	12.6	5.6	13.6	6.1

continued on the next page

Table 2.11 continued

	Black		White		All Races	
	male	female	male	female	male	female
1986						
All causes	1,026.9	588.2	679.8	387.7	709.1	406.6
diseases of the heart	294.3	185.1	235.8	119.0	238.2	124.6
malignant neoplasms	229.0	132.1	158.8	110.1	163.6	111.4
accidents and adverse affects	66.9	21.0	51.1	18.4	52.5	18.7
cerebrovascular diseases	58.9	47.6	31.1	27.1	33.5	29.0
chronic obstructive pulmonary diseases	24.6	8.9	28.1	13.3	27.6	12.8
pneumonia	27.2	13.1	17.5	9.9	18.4	10.3
suicide	11.5	2.4	20.5	5.4	19.3	5.1
diabetes	17.9	21.4	9.1	8.1	9.9	9.3
chronic liver disease	20.8	9.3	12.2	5.4	13.0	5.9

SOURCE: U.S. Bureau of the Census, Statistical Abstract of the United States, 1989, p. 80, table 119. C 3.134:989

NOTES: 'All Races' includes other races not shown separately. Rates are age adjusted.

UNITS: Rates per 100,000 of population.

Table 2.12 Maternal Mortality Rates, by Age of the Mother, 1970 - 1986

	Black mothers	White mothers	mothers of All Races
1970			
All ages, age adjusted rate	64.2	14.5	21.5
All ages, crude rate	59.8	14.4	21.5
women under 20 years old	31.8	13.9	18.9
women 20-24 years old	41.0	8.4	13.0
women 25-29 years old	63.8	11.2	17.0
women 30-34 years old	115.6	18.8	31.6
women 35 years old and over	204.7	59.6	81.9
1980			
All ages, age adjusted rate	24.0	7.0	9.6
All ages, crude rate	21.5	6.7	9.2
women under 20 years old	12.8	5.9	7.6
women 20-24 years old	13.4	4.3	5.8
women 25-29 years old	21.4	5.5	7.7
women 30-34 years old	41.9	9.4	13.6
women 35 years old and over	96.5	25.8	36.3
1985			
All ages, age adjusted rate	22.2	5.1	7.9
All ages, crude rate	20.4	5.2	7.8
women under 20 years old	12.1*	4.3*	6.9
women 20-24 years old	14.0	3.4	5.4
women 25-29 years old	18.4	4.7	6.4
women 30-34 years old	35.8	5.2	8.9
women 35 years old and over	72.6	17.8	25.0

continued on the next page

Table 2.12 continued

	Black mothers	White mothers	mothers of All Races
1986			
All ages, age adjusted rate	19.3	4.7	7.0
All ages, crude rate	18.8	4.9	7.2
women under 20 years old	10.6*	4.1*	5.9
women 20-24 years old	13.9	3.7	5.7
women 25-29 years old	19.3	3.6	5.8
women 30-34 years old	29.0	5.2	7.8
women 35 years old and over	58.6*	16.1	21.4

SOURCE: U.S. Department of Health and Human Services, Health United States, 1988, p. 71, table 29. HE 20.6223:988

NOTES: 'Mothers of All Races' include mothers of other races not shown separately. Data for maternal mortality cover complications of pregnancy, childbirth and the puerperium. Rates for women 35 years old and over computed by relating deaths to live births to women in this age group. *Indicates data based on fewer than 20 deaths.

UNITS: Rate is the number of deaths of mothers, per 100,000 live births.

Table 2.13 Death Rates for Malignant Neoplasms of the Breast, for Females, by Age 1970 - 1986

	Black women	White women	women of All Races
1970			
All ages, age adjusted rate	21.5	23.4	23.1
All ages, crude rate	19.7	29.9	28.4
under 25 years old	0.1	0.0	0.0
25-34 years old	5.9	3.7	3.9
35-44 years old	24.4	20.2	20.4
45-54 years old	52.0	53.0	52.6
55-64 years old	64.7	79.3	77.6
65-74 years old	77.3	95.9	93.8
75-84 years old	101.8	129.6	127.4
85 years old and over	112.1	161.9	157.1
1980			
All ages, age adjusted rate	23.3	22.8	22.7
All ages, crude rate	22.9	32.3	30.6
under 25 years old	0.0	0.0	0.0
25-34 years old	5.3	3.0	3.3
35-44 years old	24.1	17.3	17.9
45-54 years old	52.7	48.1	48.1
55-64 years old	79.9	81.3	80.5
65-74 years old	84.3	103.7	101.1
75-84 years old	114.1	128.4	126.4
85 years old and over	149.9	171.7	169.3

continued on the next page

Table 2.13 continued

	Black women	White women	women of All Races
1985			
All ages, age adjusted rate	25.3	23.3	23.2
All ages, crude rate	25.6	34.6	32.7
under 25 years old	0.1	0.0	0.0
25-34 years old	4.4	2.8	3.0
35-44 years old	26.3	16.7	17.5
45-54 years old	54.4	46.5	46.7
55-64 years old	88.5	84.2	83.6
65-74 years old	99.3	110.0	107.7
75-84 years old	121.0	140.4	137.7
85 years old and over	152.5	178.9	175.9
1986			
All ages, age adjusted rate	25.8	23.0	23.1
All ages, crude rate	26.2	34.6	32.8
under 25 years old	0.1	0.0	0.0
25-34 years old	5.6	2.7	3.1
35-44 years old	28.3	17.3	18.3
45-54 years old	59.1	44.4	45.4
55-64 years old	83.6	81.8	80.9
65-74 years old	100.5	112.4	109.9
75-84 years old	112.1	139.7	136.2
85 years old and over	162.1	182.7	180.0

SOURCE: U.S. Department of Health and Human Services, Health United States, 1988, p. 70, table 28. HE 20.6223:988

NOTES: 'Women of All Races' includes women of other races not shown separately. Data excludes deaths of nonresidents of the United States.

UNITS: Rate is the number of deaths per 100,000 resident female population, by age group.

Table 2.14 Death Rates for Motor Vehicle Accidents, by Sex and Age, 1970 - 1986

	Black		White		All Races
	male	female	male	female	both sexes
1970					
All ages, age adjusted	50.1	13.8	40.1	14.4	27.4
All ages, crude	44.2	13.4	39.1	14.8	26.9
under 1 year	10.6	11.9	9.1	10.2	9.8
1-4 years old	16.9	12.6	12.2	9.6	11.5
5-14 years old	16.1	9.3	12.6	6.9	10.2
15-24 years old	58.1	13.4	75.2	22.7	47.2
25-34 years old	70.4	13.3	47.0	12.7	30.9
35-44 years old	59.5	16.1	35.2	12.3	24.9
45-54 years old	61.4	16.4	34.6	14.3	25.5
55-64 years old	62.1	17.1	39.0	16.1	27.9
65-74 years old	54.9	16.3	46.2	22.1	32.8
75-84 years old	51.5	14.3	69.2	28.1	43.5
85 years old and over	53.8	17.5	72.0	18.9	36.6
1980					
All ages, age adjusted	32.9	8.4	34.8	12.3	22.9
All ages, crude	31.1	8.3	35.9	12.8	23.5
under 1 year	7.8	5.3	7.0	7.1	7.0
1-4 years old	13.7	9.5	9.5	7.7	9.2
5-14 years old	10.5	5.2	9.8	5.7	7.9
15-24 years old	34.9	8.0	73.8	23.0	44.8
25-34 years old	44.9	10.6	46.6	12.2	29.1
35-44 years old	41.2	8.3	30.7	10.6	20.9
45-54 years old	39.1	9.1	26.3	10.2	18.6
55-64 years old	40.3	9.3	23.9	10.5	17.4
65-74 years old	41.8	8.5	25.8	13.4	19.2
75-84 years old	46.5	11.1	43.6	19.0	28.1
85 years old and over	34.0	12.3	57.3	15.3	27.6

continued on the next page

Table 2.14 continued

	Black		White		All Races
	male	female	male	female	both sexes
1985					
All ages, age adjusted	27.7	8.2	27.6	10.8	18.8
All ages, crude	26.7	8.3	28.2	11.4	19.2
under 1 year	5.9	7.8	4.5	3.9	4.8
1-4 years old	10.7	6.8	7.6	5.7	7.1
5-14 years old	8.9	4.3	8.5	5.2	6.8
15-24 years old	32.1	9.1	57.4	20.1	36.1
25-34 years old	37.2	9.2	35.5	10.0	22.8
35-44 years old	35.4	9.1	24.1	9.4	17.1
45-54 years old	29.9	8.2	20.9	8.9	15.2
55-64 years old	34.3	9.5	20.6	9.9	15.5
65-74 years old	30.0	9.6	21.7	14.3	17.7
75-84 years old	42.2	15.0	41.2	19.9	27.6
85 years old and over	36.9	9.4	56.4	15.1	26.1
1986					
All ages, age adjusted	29.2	8.5	28.7	11.0	19.4
All ages, crude	28.6	8.5	29.2	11.5	19.9
under 1 year	8.0	5.3	4.1	4.6	4.9
1-4 years old	10.7	6.9	7.0	6.0	7.0
5-14 years old	9.6	4.8	8.7	4.9	6.9
15-24 years old	35.3	9.1	52.6	21.5	39.0
25-34 years old	41.7	10.3	37.3	10.8	24.2
35-44 years old	35.1	8.7	23.7	8.4	16.6
45-54 years old	31.4	8.7	20.8	8.5	15.1
55-64 years old	31.9	10.9	19.9	9.6	15.1
65-74 years old	27.2	9.7	22.4	14.4	17.9
75-84 years old	53.1	10.0	42.9	20.5	28.8
85 years old and over	62.7	11.0	51.6	14.7	25.3

SOURCE: U.S. Department of Health and Human Services, Health United States, 1988, p. 72, table 30. HE 20.6223:988

NOTES: 'All Races' includes other races not shown separately. Excludes deaths of nonresidents of the United States.

UNITS: Rate is the number of deaths per 100,000 resident population.

Table 2.15 Death Rates for Homicide and Legal Intervention, by Sex and Age, 1970 - 1986

	Black		White		All Races
	male	female	male	female	both sexes
1970					
All ages, age adjusted	82.1	15.0	7.3	2.2	9.1
All ages, crude	67.5	13.2	6.8	2.1	8.3
under 1 year	14.3	10.7	2.9	2.9	4.3
1-4 years old	5.1	6.3	1.4	1.2	1.9
5-14 years old	4.2	2.0	0.5	0.5	0.9
15-24 years old	102.5	17.7	7.9	2.7	11.7
25-34 years old	158.5	25.6	13.0	3.4	16.6
35-44 years old	126.2	25.1	11.0	3.2	13.7
45-54 years old	100.6	17.5	9.0	2.2	10.1
55-64 years old	59.8	8.1	7.7	2.0	7.1
65-74 years old	40.6	7.7	5.6	1.7	5.0
75-84 years old	18.9	5.7	5.1	2.5	4.0
85 years old and over	23.1	11.1	7.0	2.0	4.5
1980					
All ages, age adjusted	71.9	13.7	10.9	3.2	10.8
All ages, crude	66.6	13.5	10.9	3.2	10.7
under 1 year	18.6	12.8	4.3	4.3	5.9
1-4 years old	7.2	6.4	2.0	1.5	2.5
5-14 years old	2.9	2.2	0.9	1.0	1.2
15-24 years old	84.3	18.4	15.5	4.7	15.6
25-34 years old	145.1	25.8	18.9	4.3	19.6
35-44 years old	110.3	17.7	15.5	4.1	15.1
45-54 years old	83.8	12.5	11.9	3.0	11.1
55-64 years old	55.6	8.9	7.8	2.1	7.0
65-74 years old	33.9	8.6	6.9	2.5	5.7
75-84 years old	27.6	6.7	6.3	3.3	5.2
85 years old and over	17.0	8.5	6.4	4.0	5.3

continued on the next page

Table 2.15 continued

	Black		White		All Races
	male	female	male	female	both sexes
1985					
All ages, age adjusted	49.9	10.8	8.1	2.9	8.3
All ages, crude	48.4	11.0	8.2	2.9	8.3
under 1 year	16.0	10.3	3.7	4.3	5.3
1-4 years old	6.5	6.3	1.9	1.6	2.4
5-14 years old	3.2	2.0	1.1	0.8	1.2
15-24 years old	66.1	14.2	11.2	3.6	12.1
25-34 years old	94.3	19.8	13.9	4.4	14.7
35-44 years old	76.3	14.8	11.5	3.6	11.3
45-54 years old	51.1	9.0	8.6	2.9	8.1
55-64 years old	37.8	6.4	6.3	2.3	5.7
65-74 years old	27.6	7.2	4.5	2.2	4.3
75-84 years old	21.5	7.6	4.5	3.1	4.3
85 years old and over	16.9	11.5	3.9	3.2	4.1
1986					
All ages, age adjusted	55.9	11.8	8.4	2.9	9.0
All ages, crude	55.0	12.1	8.6	3.0	9.0
under 1 year	22.5	17.0	5.4	5.1	7.4
1-4 years old	9.3	6.8	1.9	1.4	2.7
5-14 years old	3.2	2.3	0.9	0.8	1.1
15-24 years old	79.2	16.2	12.5	4.3	14.2
25-34 years old	108.0	21.9	14.6	4.4	16.1
35-44 years old	79.4	14.8	11.6	3.5	11.4
45-54 years old	56.3	8.5	8.6	2.8	8.3
55-64 years old	35.4	6.8	6.0	1.9	5.4
65-74 years old	30.0	8.7	4.3	2.2	4.4
75-84 years old	27.9	8.6	4.6	3.1	4.6
85 years old and over	25.4	13.1	4.4	3.3	4.7

SOURCE: U.S. Department of Health and Human Services, Health United States, 1988, p. 73, table 31. HE 20.6223:988

NOTES: 'All Races' includes other races not shown separately. Excludes deaths of nonresidents of the United States.

UNITS: Rate is the number of deaths per 100,000 resident population.

Table 2.16 Death Rates for Suicide, by Sex and Age, 1970 - 1986

	Black		White		All Races
	male	female	male	female	both sexes
1970					
All ages, age adjusted	8.9	2.9	18.2	7.2	11.8
All ages, crude	9.0	2.6	18.0	7.1	11.6
under 1 year	-	-	-	-	-
1-4 years old	-	-	-	-	-
5-14 years old	0.1	0.2	0.5	0.1	0.3
15-24 years old	10.5	3.8	13.9	4.2	8.8
25-34 years old	19.2	5.7	19.9	9.0	14.1
35-44 years old	12.6	3.7	23.3	13.0	16.9
45-54 years old	13.8	3.7	29.5	13.5	20.0
55-64 years old	10.6	2.0	35.0	12.3	21.4
65-74 years old	8.7	2.9	38.7	9.6	20.8
75-84 years old	8.9	1.7	45.5	7.2	21.2
85 years old and over	10.3	3.2	50.3	6.1	20.4
1980					
All ages, age adjusted	11.1	2.4	18.9	5.7	11.4
All ages, crude	10.3	2.2	19.9	5.9	11.9
under 1 year	-	-	-	-	-
1-4 years old	-	-	-	-	-
5-14 years old	0.3	0.1	0.7	0.2	0.4
15-24 years old	12.3	2.3	21.4	4.6	12.3
25-34 years old	21.8	4.1	25.6	7.5	16.0
35-44 years old	15.6	4.6	23.5	9.1	15.4
45-54 years old	12.0	2.8	24.2	10.2	15.9
55-64 years old	11.7	2.3	25.8	9.1	15.9
65-74 years old	11.1	1.7	32.5	7.0	16.9
75-84 years old	10.5	1.4	45.5	5.7	19.1
85 years old and over	18.9	-	52.8	5.8	19.2

continued on the next page

Table 2.16 continued

	Black		White		All Races
	male	female	male	female	both sexes
1985					
All ages, age adjusted	11.3	2.1	19.9	5.3	11.5
All ages, crude	10.8	2.1	21.5	5.6	12.3
under 1 year	-	-	-	-	-
1-4 years old	-	-	-	-	-
5-14 years old	0.6	0.2	1.3	0.5	0.8
15-24 years old	13.3	2.0	22.7	4.7	12.9
25-34 years old	19.6	3.0	25.4	6.4	15.2
35-44 years old	14.9	3.6	23.5	7.7	14.6
45-54 years old	13.5	3.2	25.1	9.0	15.6
55-64 years old	11.5	2.2	28.6	8.4	16.7
65-74 years old	15.8	2.0	35.3	7.3	18.5
75-84 years old	15.6	4.5	57.1	7.0	24.1
85 years old and over	7.7	1.4	60.3	4.7	19.1
1986					
All ages, age adjusted	11.5	2.4	20.5	5.4	11.9
All ages, crude	11.1	2.3	22.3	5.9	12.8
under 1 year	-	-	-	-	-
1-4 years old	-	-	-	-	-
5-14 years old	0.8	0.2	1.2	0.3	0.8
15-24 years old	11.5	2.3	23.6	4.7	13.1
25-34 years old	21.3	3.8	26.4	6.2	15.7
35-44 years old	17.5	2.8	23.9	8.3	15.2
45-54 years old	12.8	3.2	26.3	9.6	16.4
55-64 years old	9.9	4.2	28.7	9.0	17.0
65-74 years old	16.1	2.8	37.6	7.7	19.7
75-84 years old	16.0	2.6	58.9	8.0	25.2
85 years old and over	17.9	-	66.3	5.0	20.8

SOURCE: U.S. Department of Health and Human Services, Health United States, 1988, p. 74, table 32. HE 20.6223:988

NOTES: 'All Races' includes other races not shown separately. Excludes deaths of nonresidents of the United States.

UNITS: Rate is the number of deaths per 100,000 resident population.

Table 2.17 AIDS (Acquired Immunodeficiency Syndrome) Cases, by Sex and Age, 1982 - 1988

	number			percent distribution		
	Black	White	All Races	Black	White	All Races
All years*						
children under 13 years old	675	294	1,221	55.3%	24.1%	100.0%
persons over 13 years old						
male	16,950	43,696	70,239	24.1	62.2	100.0
female	3,467	1,856	6,423	53.8	28.9	100.0
1982						
children under 13 years old	5	5	13	38.5%	38.5%	100.0%
persons over 13 years old						
male	173	345	603	28.7	57.2	100.0
female	32	9	48	66.7	18.8	100.0
1983						
children under 13 years old	22	6	34	64.7%	17.6%	100.0%
persons over 13 years old						
male	475	1,141	1,898	25.0	60.1	100.0
female	66	34	141	46.8	24.1	100.0
1984						
children under 13 years old	29	10	50	58.0%	20.0%	100.0%
persons over 13 years old						
male	945	2,610	4,122	22.9	63.3	100.0
female	141	79	277	50.9	28.5	100.0
1985						
children under 13 years old	86	25	129	66.7%	19.4%	100.0%
persons over 13 years old						
male	1,722	4,846	7,581	22.7	63.9	100.0
female	283	141	523	54.1	27.0	100.0

continued on the next page

Table 2.17 continued

	number			percent distribution		
	Black	White	All Races	Black	White	All Races
1986						
children under 13 years old	106	42	186	57.0%	22.6%	100.0%
persons over 13 years old						
male	2,757	7,577	12,025	22.9	63.0	100.0
female	520	271	963	54.0	28.1	100.0
1987						
children under 13 years old	162	81	319	50.8%	25.4%	100.0%
persons over 13 years old						
male	4,316	12,377	19,136	22.6	64.7	100.0
female	883	545	1,668	52.9	32.6	100.0
1988**						
children under 13 years old	265	125	490	54.1%	25.5%	100.0%
persons over 13 years old						
male	6,521	14,680	24,688	26.4	59.5	100.0
female	1,540	776	2,797	55.1	27.7	100.0

SOURCE: U.S. Department of Health and Human Services, Health United States, 1988, p. 82, table 40 (data from Centers for Disease Control, Center for Infectious Diseases, AIDS Program). HE 20.6223:988

NOTES: 'All Races' includes other races not shown separately. 'Black' excludes Black hispanics, 'White' excludes White hispanics. Data excludes residents of U.S. Territories. *'All years' includes cases prior to 1982 through November, 1988. **1988 data as of November, 1988.

UNITS: Number of cases known to the Centers for Disease Control, by year of report; percent distribution as a percent of total (100.0%).

Table 2.18 AIDS (Acquired Immunodeficiency Syndrome) Deaths, by Sex and Age, 1982 - 1988

	number			percent distribution		
	Black	White	All Races	Black	White	All Races
All years*						
children under 13 years old	368	183	697	52.8%	26.3%	100.0%
persons over 13 years old						
male	9,957	24,408	39,551	25.2	61.7	100.0
female	1,932	1,072	3,542	54.5	30.3	100.0
1982						
children under 13 years old	6	4	11	54.5%	36.4%	100.0%
persons over 13 years old						
male	121	197	384	31.5	51.3	100.0
female	20	9	36	55.6	25.0	100.0
1983						
children under 13 years old	19	6	29	65.5%	20.7%	100.0%
persons over 13 years old						
male	368	716	1,271	29.0	56.3	100.0
female	54	23	102	52.9	22.5	100.0
1984						
children under 13 years old	26	8	45	57.8%	17.8%	100.0%
persons over 13 years old						
male	691	1,751	2,849	24.3	61.5	100.0
female	129	53	228	56.6	23.2	100.0
1985						
children under 13 years old	56	26	96	58.3%	27.1%	100.0%
persons over 13 years old						
male	1,331	3,456	5,510	24.2	62.7	100.0
female	194	130	404	48.0	32.2	100.0

continued on the next page

Table 2.18 continued

	number			percent distribution		
	Black	White	All Races	Black	White	All Races
1986						
children under 13 years old	73	30	136	53.7%	22.1%	100.0%
persons over 13 years old						
male	2,123	5,765	9,107	23.3	63.3	100.0
female	408	230	767	53.2	30.0	100.0
1987						
children under 13 years old	111	63	230	48.3%	27.4%	100.0%
persons over 13 years old						
male	2,936	7,031	11,514	25.5	61.1	100.0
female	608	356	1,099	55.3	32.4	100.0
1988**						
children under 13 years old	71	42	136	52.2%	30.9%	100.0%
persons over 13 years old						
male	2,294	5,354	8,651	26.5	61.9	100.0
female	496	263	870	57.0	30.2	100.0

SOURCE: U.S. Department of Health and Human Services, Health United States, 1988, p. 83, table 41 (data from Centers for Disease Control, Center for Infectious Diseases, AIDS Program). HE 20.6223:988

NOTES: 'All Races' includes other races not shown separately. 'Black' excludes Black hispanics, 'White' excludes White hispanics. Data excludes deaths of residents of U.S. Territories. *'All years' include deaths prior to 1982 through November, 1988. **1988 data as of November, 1988.

UNITS: Number of deaths known to the Centers for Disease Control, by year of report of death.

Table 2.19 AIDS (Acquired Immunodeficiency Syndrome) Cases, by Transmission Category, 1982 - 1988

	Black	White	All Races
All years*			
all transmission categories	20,417	45,552	76,662
male homosexual/bisexual	7,616	35,451	48,198
intravenous drug use	7,796	3,041	14,542
male homosexual and intravenous drug use	1,416	3,388	5,421
hemophilia	50	631	744
born in Caribbean/African countries	1,210	5	1,226
heterosexual	1,038	647	2,123
heterosexual contact with intravenous drug user	799	349	1,505
transfusion	313	1,446	1,937
undetermined	978	943	2,471
1982			
all transmission categories	205	354	651
male homosexual/bisexual	77	279	394
intravenous drug use	55	31	121
male homosexual and intravenous drug use	17	25	56
hemophilia	0	7	7
born in Caribbean/African countries	44	0	45
heterosexual	4	1	7
heterosexual contact with intravenous drug user	4	1	6
transfusion	0	5	6
undetermined	8	6	15

continued on the next page

Table 2.19 continued

	Black	White	All Races
1984			
all transmission categories	1,086	2,689	4,399
male homosexual/bisexual	399	2,162	2,869
intravenous drug use	404	145	773
male homosexual and intravenous drug use	94	265	408
hemophilia	5	25	35
born in Caribbean/African countries	109	1	110
heterosexual	23	16	57
heterosexual contact with intravenous drug user	18	9	43
transfusion	10	40	53
undetermined	42	35	94
1986			
all transmission categories	3,277	7,848	12,988
male homosexual/bisexual	1,321	6,253	8,541
intravenous drug use	1,191	406	2,222
male homosexual and intravenous drug use	228	646	972
hemophilia	5	113	125
born in Caribbean/African countries	214	1	217
heterosexual	160	93	333
heterosexual contact with intravenous drug user	116	39	224
transfusion	44	232	300
undetermined	114	104	278

continued on the next page

Table 2.19 continued

	Black	White	All Races
1987			
all transmission categories	5,199	12,922	20,804
male homosexual/bisexual	2,083	10,033	13,501
intravenous drug use	1,853	816	3,502
male homosexual and intravenous drug use	380	971	1,505
hemophilia	12	187	218
born in Caribbean/African countries	262	1	266
heterosexual	293	196	594
heterosexual contact with intravenous drug user	223	99	398
transfusion	92	469	621
undetermined	224	249	597
1988**			
all transmission categories	8,061	15,456	27,485
male homosexual/bisexual	2,727	11,603	16,033
intravenous drug use	3,355	1,317	6,142
male homosexual and intravenous drug use	507	974	1,680
hemophilia	24	225	273
born in Caribbean/African countries	351	1	356
heterosexual	474	308	979
heterosexual contact with intravenous drug user	373	185	721
transfusion	138	552	766
undetermined	485	476	1,256

continued on the next page

Table 2.19 continued

SOURCE: U.S. Department of Health and Human Services, Health United States, 1988, p. 84, table 42 (data from Centers for Disease Control, Center for Infectious Diseases, AIDS Program). HE 20.6223:988

NOTES: 'All Races' includes other races not shown separately. 'Black' excludes Black hispanics, 'White' excludes White hispanics. Data excludes deaths of residents of U.S. Territories. 'Hemophilia' includes coagulation disorders. 'Heterosexual' includes persons who have had heterosexual contact with a person with AIDS, or at risk of AIDS, and persons without other identified risks who were born in countries where heterosexual transmission is believed to play a major role although precise means of transmission have not yet been fully determined. *'All years' includes cases prior to 1982 through November, 1988. **1988 data as of November, 1988.

UNITS: Number of cases known to the Centers for Disease Control, by year of report.

Table 2.20 AIDS (Acquired Immunodeficiency Syndrome) Deaths, by Transmission Category, 1982 - 1988

	Black	White	All Races
All years*			
all transmission categories	11,889	25,480	43,093
male homosexual/bisexual	4,551	19,676	27,053
intravenous drug use	4,459	1,587	7,947
male homosexual and intravenous drug use	889	1,986	3,254
hemophilia	29	392	452
born in Caribbean/African countries	671	1	676
heterosexual	558	312	1,061
heterosexual contact with intravenous drug user	419	152	728
transfusion	195	1,035	1,349
undetermined	537	491	1,301
1982			
all transmission categories	141	206	420
male homosexual/bisexual	54	159	244
intravenous drug use	41	14	82
male homosexual and intravenous drug use	11	14	38
hemophilia	0	6	6
born in Caribbean/African countries	29	0	29
heterosexual	1	1	3
heterosexual contact with intravenous drug user	1	1	3
transfusion	0	3	3
undetermined	5	9	15

continued on the next page

Table 2.20 continued

	Black	White	All Races
1984			
all transmission categories	820	1,804	3,077
male homosexual/bisexual	287	1,409	1,915
intravenous drug use	321	101	588
male homosexual and intravenous drug use	72	184	294
hemophilia	1	21	24
born in Caribbean/African countries	73	1	74
heterosexual	24	5	42
heterosexual contact with intravenous drug user	19	4	35
transfusion	10	51	64
undetermined	32	32	76
1986			
all transmission categories	2,531	5,995	9,874
male homosexual/bisexual	1,013	4,709	6,409
intravenous drug use	950	306	1,684
male homosexual and intravenous drug use	182	480	744
hemophilia	3	85	96
born in Caribbean/African countries	122	0	123
heterosexual	97	70	221
heterosexual contact with intravenous drug user	72	34	151
transfusion	39	250	320
undetermined	125	95	277

continued on the next page

Table 2.20 continued

	Black	White	All Races
1987			
all transmission categories	3,544	7,387	12,613
male homosexual/bisexual	1,352	5,594	7,774
intravenous drug use	1,338	513	2,419
male homosexual and intravenous drug use	252	569	921
hemophilia	12	120	140
born in Caribbean/African countries	158	0	160
heterosexual	206	98	353
heterosexual contact with intravenous drug user	153	52	243
transfusion	70	338	446
undetermined	156	155	400
1988**			
all transmission categories	2,790	5,617	9,521
male homosexual/bisexual	1,074	4,288	5,917
intravenous drug use	1,052	365	1,759
male homosexual and intravenous drug use	211	376	660
hemophilia	7	97	109
born in Caribbean/African countries	98	0	98
heterosexual	165	109	319
heterosexual contact with intravenous drug user	125	52	214
transfusion	48	249	324
undetermined	135	133	335

continued on the next page

Table 2.20 continued

SOURCE: U.S. Department of Health and Human Services, Health United States, 1988, p. 86, table 43 (data from Centers for Disease Control, Center for Infectious Diseases, AIDS Program) HE 20.6223:988

NOTES: 'All Races' includes other races not shown separately. 'Black' excludes Black hispanics, 'White' excludes White hispanics. Data excludes deaths of residents of U.S. Territories. 'Hemophilia' includes coagulation disorders. 'Heterosexual' includes persons who have had heterosexual contact with a person with AIDS, or at risk of AIDS, and persons without other identified risks who were born in countries where heterosexual transmission is believed to play a major role although precise means of transmission have not yet been fully determined. *'All years' includes cases prior to 1982 through November, 1988. **1988 data as of November, 1988.

UNITS: Number of deaths known to the Centers for Disease Control, by year of report.

Table 2.21 Five Year Relative Cancer Survival Rates for Selected Cancer Sites, 1974-76 and 1980-85

	Black		White		All Races	
	male	female	male	female	male	female
1974-76						
All cancer sites	31.0%	46.5%	41.6%	57.1%	40.5%	56.3%
prostrate gland	57.6	-	67.4	-	66.4	-
lung and bronchus	10.8	12.9	10.9	15.6	10.9	15.4
breast	-	62.6	-	74.6	-	74.0
colon	43.4	46.4	49.6	50.4	49.2	50.2
rectum	34.2	48.2	47.5	49.4	47.2	49.1
corpus uteri	-	62.2	-	89.0	-	88.1
ovary	-	40.8	-	36.1	-	36.4
cervix uteri	-	63.0	-	69.0	-	68.2
urinary bladder	53.5	-	74.3	-	73.4	-
oral cavity and pharynx	30.8	-	54.0	-	51.8	-
stomach	15.6	-	12.8	-	13.6	-
esophagus	2.2	-	4.3	-	3.6	-
leukemia	31.1	-	32.9	-	32.4	-
non-Hodgkin's lymphoma	43.5	52.7	47.5	47.1	46.8	47.0
pancreas	1.1	3.4	3.2	2.3	3.0	2.4
melanoma of skin	-	-	-	84.1	-	84.0

continued on the next page

Table 2.21 continued

	Black		White		All Races	
	male	female	male	female	male	female
1980-85						
All cancer sites	32.7%	44.3%	45.6%	56.1%	44.2%	55.2%
prostrate gland	62.8	-	73.4	-	72.1	-
lung and bronchus	10.4	14.7	11.7	15.7	11.6	15.5
breast	-	63.5	-	76.3	-	75.4
colon	46.9	48.6	55.0	55.3	54.7	54.8
rectum	35.9	42.9	51.4	54.6	50.3	53.9
corpus uteri	-	52.0	-	83.4	-	88.9
ovary	-	38.3	-	33.4	-	38.6
cervix uteri	-	59.3	-	66.9	-	66.0
urinary bladder	59.6	-	78.7	-	78.1	-
oral cavity and pharynx	25.5	-	52.9	-	49.7	-
stomach	18.1	-	14.2	-	15.5	-
esophagus	4.7	-	5.3	-	6.6	-
leukemia	25.2	-	35.1	-	33.2	-
non-Hodgkin's lymphoma	38.7	50.9	45.6	52.4	48.4	52.1
pancreas	3.6	-	2.0	2.6	2.8	3.1
melanoma of skin	-	-	-	86.6	-	86.5

SOURCE: U.S. Department of Health and Human Services, Health United States, 1988, p. 92, table 47 (data from National Cancer Institute, National Institutes of Health, *1988 Annual Cancer Statistics Review, Including a Report of the Status of Cancer Control*). HE 20.6223:988

NOTES: 'All Races' includes other races not shown separately. Data are based on the Surveillance, Epidemiology, and End Results program's population-based registries in Atlanta, Detroit, Seattle-Puget Sound, San Francisco-Oakland, Connecticut, Iowa, New Mexico, Utah, and Hawaii. Rates are based on follow-up of patients through 1986.

UNITS: The five year cancer relative survival rate is the ratio of the observed survival rate for the patient group to the expected survival rate for persons in the general population similar to the patient group with respect to age, sex, race, and calendar year of observation. It estimates the chance of surviving cancer. Percent of patients surviving is shown.

Table 2.22 Cigarette Smoking by Persons 20 Years Old and Older, by Sex and Age, 1976, 1980, 1987

	current smoker			former smoker		
	Black	White	All Races	Black	White	All Races
1976						
males 20 years older and older-age adjusted rate	50.1%	41.0%	41.6%	20.2%	30.7%	29.6%
males 20-44 years old	57.4	46.8	na	10.2	20.5	na
males 45 years old and over	42.3	35.0	na	30.0	40.5	na
females 20 years older and older-age adjusted rate	34.7%	32.4%	32.5%	10.2%	14.6%	13.9%
females 20-44 years old	40.1	36.8	na	12.1	14.2	na
females 45 years old and over	28.3	26.7	na	8.4	14.6	na
1980						
males 20 years older and older-age adjusted rate	44.9%	37.1%	37.9%	20.6%	31.9%	30.5%
males 20-44 years old	47.9	41.4	na	14.2	21.7	na
males 45 years old and over	42.2	32.4	na	24.6	42.2	na
females 20 years older and older-age adjusted rate	30.6%	30.0%	29.8%	11.8%	16.3%	15.7%
females 20-44 years old	34.3	33.3	na	9.3	15.9	na
females 45 years old and over	25.6	25.5	na	14.1	16.2	na

continued on the next page

Table 2.22 continued

	current smoker			former smoker		
	Black	White	All Races	Black	White	All Races
1987						
males 20 years older and older-age adjusted rate	40.3%	30.7%	31.5%	22.9%	32.6%	31.4%
males 20-44 years old	41.3	34.3	na	12.9	20.4	na
males 45 years old and over	39.5	26.3	na	32.0	46.6	na
females 20 years older and older-age adjusted rate	27.9%	27.3%	27.0%	13.2%	18.9%	18.0%
females 20-44 years old	32.7	30.5	na	8.9	17.2	na
females 45 years old and over	22.7	22.7	na	17.4	20.9	na

SOURCE: U.S. Department of Health and Human Services, Health United States, 1987, p. 92, table 46; 1988, p 96, table 51 (data from the National Health Interview Survey). HE 20.6223:(year)

NOTES: 'All Races' includes other races not shown separately. A current smoker is a person who has smoked at least 100 cigarettes and now smokes, including occasional smokers.

UNITS: Percent as a percent of total U.S. civilian non-institutionalized population, 100.0%.

Table 2.23 Cigarettes Smoked Per Day by Persons 20 Years Old and Older, by Sex and Age, 1976, 1980, 1985

	less than 15 cigarettes per day			more than 25 cigarettes per day		
	Black	White	All Races	Black	White	All Races
1976						
males 20 years older and older-age adjusted rate	43.7%	22.3%	24.9%	10.8%	33.3%	30.7%
males 20-44 years old	46.5	21.9	na	12.0	31.9	na
males 45 years old and over	39.4	20.6	na	10.6	36.3	na
females 20 years older and older-age adjusted rate	64.5%	34.3%	37.6%	5.6%	20.9%	19.0%
females 20-44 years old	61.0	32.3	na	4.6	22.0	na
females 45 years old and over	58.3	34.5	na	9.0	21.1	na
1980						
males 20 years older and older-age adjusted rate	48.4%	20.0%	24.2%	13.8%	37.3%	34.2%
males 20-44 years old	48.5	19.0	na	10.3	34.6	na
males 45 years old and over	48.6	19.3	na	16.3	42.7	na
females 20 years older and older-age adjusted rate	61.1%	30.7%	34.7%	8.6%	25.2%	23.2%
females 20-44 years old	64.1	29.1	na	10.2	27.4	na
females 45 years old and over	56.9	31.3	na	9.3	23.3	na

continued on the next page

Table 2.23 continued

	less than 15 cigarettes per day			more than 25 cigarettes per day		
	Black	White	All Races	Black	White	All Races
1985						
males 20 years older and older-age adjusted rate	52.9%	21.7%	26.2%	10.7%	36.6%	32.8%
males 20-44 years old	51.0	23.0	na	11.6	34.6	na
males 45 years old and over	52.8	19.1	na	11.3	40.4	na
females 20 years older and older-age adjusted rate	61.2	32.8%	36.5%	6.6%	22.7%	20.5%
females 20-44 years old	56.0	33.5	na	8.3	23.6	na
females 45 years old and over	62.9	31.4	na	6.0	22.5	na

SOURCE: U.S. Department of Health and Human Services, Health United States, 1987, p. 93, table 47 (data from the National Health Interview Survey). HE 20.6223:987

NOTES: 'All Races' includes other races not shown separately.

UNITS: Percent as a percent of current smokers, 100.0%.

Table 2.24 Current Users of Alcohol, Marijuana, and Cocaine, by Age, 1985

	Black	White	All Races
Alcohol			
Total	47.6%	61.8%	59.2%
persons 12-17 years old	21.3	34.6	31.5
persons 18-25 years old	57.8	75.8	71.5
persons 26-34 years old	65.9	75.2	70.0
persons 35 years old and over	43.9	59.3	57.3
Marijuana			
Total	13.2%	9.1%	9.4%
persons 12-17 years old	8.2	13.2	12.3
persons 18-25 years old	24.1	22.2	21.9
persons 26-34 years old	22.8	16.9	16.8
persons 35 years old and over	5.8	1.8	2.2
Cocaine			
Total	3.2%	3.0%	2.9%
persons 12-17 years old	1.1	1.8	1.8
persons 18-25 years old	6.5	8.0	7.7
persons 26-34 years old	5.6	6.6	6.1
persons 35 years old and over	1.4	0.4	0.5

SOURCE: U.S. Bureau of the Census, Statistical Abstract of the United States, 1988, p. 112, table 181 (data from, U.S. National Institute on Drug Abuse Main Findings From the National Household Survey on Drug Abuse). C 3.134:988

NOTES: 'All Races' includes other races not shown separately. Both 'Black' and 'White' exclude hispanic persons.

UNITS: Percent as a percent of population by age.

Table 2.25 Limitation of Activity Caused by Chronic Health Conditions, 1983, 1987, 1988

	Black	White	All Races
1983			
Total with any limitation of activity	17.5%	13.4%	13.8%
persons limited, but not in a major activity	3.8%	4.2	4.1
persons limited in amount or kind of major activity	7.5	5.9	6.0
persons unable to carry on a activity	6.2	3.3	3.6
1987			
Total with any limitation of activity	16.0%	12.7%	12.9%
persons limited, but not in a major activity	3.5	4.1	4.0
persons limited in amount or kind of major activity	6.2	5.2	5.2
persons unable to carry on a activity	6.2	3.4	3.7

continued on the next page

Table 2.25 continued

	Black	White	All Races
1988			
Total with any limitation of activity	14.7%	13.7%	12.9%
persons limited, but not in a major activity	3.4	4.3	4.0
persons limited in amount or kind of major activity	5.5	5.4	5.2
persons unable to carry on a activity	5.8	4.0	3.7

SOURCE: U.S. Department of Health and Human Services, Health United States, 1988, p. 93, table 48 (data from the National Health Interview Survey). HE 20.6223:988
U.S. Department of Health and Human Services, Vital and Health Statistics, Series 10, #173, p. 108, table 67 (data from the National Health Interview Survey). HE 20.6209/4:988

NOTES: 'All Races' includes other races not shown separately. Each person identified by the National Health Interview Survey as having a chronic condition (a chronic condition is one lasting three months or more: a health condition is a departure from a state of physical or mental well being) is classified to the extent according to which his or her activities are limited because of the condition. A major activity is the principal activity of a person or of his or her sex-age group. For persons 1-5 years of age, it refers to ordinary play with other children; for persons 6-16 years of age it refers to school attendance; for persons 17 years of age and over, it usually refers to a job, housework, or school attendance.

UNITS: Percent as a percent of the civilian non-institutionalized population.

Table 2.26 Selected Characteristics of Persons With a Work Disability, 1988

	Black	White	All Races
Persons with a work disability by age			
Total	2,512	10,544	13,420
persons 16-24 years old	291	963	1,285
persons 25-34 years old	464	1,874	2,414
persons 35-44 years old	433	1,957	2,455
persons 45-54 years old	502	1,852	2,443
persons 55-64 years old	822	3,898	4,825
Work disabled as a percent of total population, by age			
Total	13.7%	7.9%	8.6%
persons 16-24 years old	6.1	3.5	3.8
persons 25-34 years old	8.8	5.2	5.6
persons 35-44 years old	11.7	6.6	7.1
persons 45-54 years old	20.1	9.1	10.3
persons 55-64 years old	39.6	20.4	22.3
Percent of work disabled:			
receiving Social Security Income	30.0%	29.7%	29.5%
receiving Food Stamps	37.0	14.4	18.8
covered by Medicare	37.0	17.8	21.6
residing in public housing	12.7	2.5	4.6
residing in subsidized housing	4.5	2.5	2.9

continued on the next page

Table 2.26 continued

SOURCE: U.S. Bureau of the Census, Statistical Abstract of the United States, 1989, p. 360 table 592 (data from the Current Population Survey). C 3.134:989

NOTES: 'All Races' includes other races not shown separately. Covers the civilian noninstitutional population and members of the armed forces living off post or with members of their families on post. Persons are classified as having a work disability if they (1) have a health problem or disability which prevents them from or which limits the kind or amount of work they can do; (2) have a service disability or ever retired or left a job for health reasons; (3) did not work in survey reference week or previous year because of long-term illness or disability; or, (4) are under age 65 and are covered by Medicare or receive Supplemental Security Income.

UNITS: Persons with a work disability in thousands of persons; work disabled as a percent of total population in percent; percent of the work disabled by characteristic as a percent of the work disabled.

Table 2.27 Work-Loss Days Associated With an Acute Condition, by Type of Condition, 1985 and 1988

	Black	White	All Races
1985			
All acute conditions	426.5	297.3	309.6
infective and parasitic diseases	16.3*	26.3	24.7
respiratory conditions	135.8	106.3	108.0
digestive system conditions	31.1*	16.8	18.4
injuries	166.1	98.0	104.4
all other acute conditions	77.2*	49.8	54.1
1988			
All acute conditions	370.7	305.3	311.4
infective and parasitic diseases	25.5*	25.5	25.2
respiratory conditions	104.7	110.2	110.5
digestive system conditions	16.1*	12.6	12.7
injuries	153.2	88.4	95.1
all other acute conditions	71.1*	68.6	67.8

SOURCE: U.S. Department of Health and Human Services, Vital and Health Statistics, Series 10, #160, p. 55, table 36; p. 57, table 38 (data from the National Health Interview Survey). HE 20.6209/4:985
U.S. Department of Health and Human Services, Vital and Health Statistics, Series 10, #173, p. 57, table 36; p. 59, table 38 (data from the National Health Interview Survey). HE 20.6209/4:988

NOTES: 'All Races' includes other races not shown separately. Covers the civilian noninstitutional population and members of the armed forces living off post or with members of their families on post.
*Relative standard error is greater than 30%

UNITS: Number of work-loss days per 100 persons 18 years old and over, currently employed

Table 2.28 School-Loss Days Associated With an Acute Condition, by Type of Condition, 1985 and 1988

	Black	White	All Races
1985			
All acute conditions	339.8	399.7	386.9
infective and parasitic diseases	125.7	91.3	93.9
respiratory conditions	143.7	229.2	215.6
digestive system conditions	16.6*	12.1*	12.9*
injuries	27.6*	22.9	23.6
all other acute conditions	26.3*	44.0*	40.8*
1988			
All acute conditions	322.0	427.2	405.9
infective and parasitic diseases	97.1	113.1	106.5
respiratory conditions	147.8	230.8	217.2
digestive system conditions	16.7*	14.1	14.4
injuries	20.6*	28.4	26.6
all other acute conditions	39.9*	40.8*	41.3*

SOURCE: U.S. Department of Health and Human Services, Vital and Health Statistics, Series 10, #160, p. 65, table 46 (data from the National Health Interview Survey). HE 20.6209/4:985
U.S. Department of Health and Human Services, Vital and Health Statistics, Series 10, #173, p. 67, table 46 (data from the National Health Interview Survey). HE 20.6209/4:988

NOTES: 'All Races' includes other races not shown separately. Covers the civilian noninstitutional population and members of the armed forces living off post or with members of their families on post.
*Relative standard error is greater than 30%

UNITS: Number of school-loss days per 100 persons 5-17 years old.

Table 2.29 Injuries, by Selected Characteristic, 1985 and 1988

	Black	White	All Races
1985			
All episodes of injury	23.4	27.1	26.8
involving a motor vehicle	1.7*	2.2	2.2
happened while at work	6.4	6.6	6.6
by place of occurrence			
- at home	7.3	9.5	9.3
- on a street or highway	3.1*	3.1	3.1
- at an industrial place	3.9	3.3	3.4
- other	6.1	7.4	7.3
1988			
All episodes of injury	18.7	24.9	24.0
involving a motor vehicle	1.6*	1.7	1.7
happened while at work	3.9	5.8	5.7
by place of occurrence	7.6	8.9	8.5
- at home	2.4	2.5	2.5
- on a street or highway	1.5*	3.0	3.0
- at an industrial place	4.8	6.7	6.4
- other			

SOURCE: U.S. Department of Health and Human Services, Vital and Health Statistics, Series 10, #160, p. 70, table 51 (data from the National Health Interview Survey). HE 20.6209/4:985
U.S. Department of Health and Human Services, Vital and Health Statistics, Series 10, #173, p. 72, table 51 (data from the National Health Interview Survey). HE 20.6209/4:988

NOTES: 'All Races' includes other races not shown separately. Covers the civilian noninstitutional population and members of the armed forces living off post or with members of their families on post.
*Relative standard error is greater than 30%

UNITS: Number of episodes of injuries per 100 persons per year.

Table 2.30 Restricted Activity Days, 1970 - 1988

	total number of days			days per person		
	Black	White	All Races	Black	White	All Races
1970	365	2,526	2,913	16.2	14.4	14.6
1980	580	3,518	4,165	22.7	18.7	19.1
1985	489	2,899	3,453	17.4	14.5	14.8
1988	487	2,969	3,536	16.6	14.6	14.7

SOURCE: U.S. Bureau of the Census, Statistical Abstract of the United States, 1988, p. 105, table 166 (data from the National Health Interview Survey). C 3.134:988

U.S. Department of Health and Human Services, Vital and Health Statistics, Series 10, #173, p. 112, table 69 (data from the National Health Interview Survey). HE 20.6209/4:988

NOTES: 'All Races' includes other races not shown separately. A restricted activity day is a day when a person cuts down on his or her usual activities for the whole day because of illness or injury. Restricted activity days include bed disability days, work-loss days, and school loss days.

UNITS: Total number of days in millions of days; days per person.

Table 2.31 Personal Health Practices, 1985

	Black	White	All Races
Persons who:			
sleep 6 hours or less	27.8%	21.3%	22.0%
never eat breakfast	23.6	24.5	24.3
snack every day	37.2	39.4	39.0
are less physically active than their contemporaries	13.9	16.7	16.4
had more than 5 drinks in one day during the past year	29.3	38.3	37.5
are current smokers	34.9	29.6	30.1
are 30% or more above their desireable weight	18.7	12.4	13.0

SOURCE: U.S. Bureau of the Census, Statistical Abstract of the United States, 1988, p. 111, table 178 (data from the National Health Interview Survey). C 3.134:988

NOTES: 'All Races' includes other races not shown separately. Data are self-reported. Excludes persons whose health practices are unknown.

UNITS: Percent as a percent of the civilian non-institutionalized population. Persons having more than five drinks in one day during the past year, as a percent of all persons who drink.

Table 2.32 Characteristics of Physicians Visits, 1982, 1983, 1987

	Black	White	All Races
Physician visits by site of visit			
1983			
all physicians visits (per person)	4.9	5.2	5.1
- at doctor's offices	44.3%	57.6%	56.1%
- at hospital outpatient department	26.8	13.4	14.9
- by telephone	9.7	16.3	15.5
- home	1.	1.5	1.5
- other	18.2	11.1	12.0
1987			
all physicians visits (per person)	5.1	5.5	5.4
- at doctor's offices	47.2%	58.6%	57.1%
- at hospital outpatient department	23.5	12.8	14.1
- by telephone	7.8	14.1	13.4
- home	3.1	2.0	2.1
- other	18.3	12.5	13.4
Interval since last physician visit			
1982			
less than one year	74.9%	76.1%	75.8
1 year to 2 years	12.4	10.8	11.0
more than 2 years	12.7	13.1	13.2
1987			
less than one year	75.1%	77.1%	76.6%
1 year to 2 years	11.8	10.4	10.6
more than 2 years	13.1	12.6	12.8

SOURCE: U.S. Department of Health and Human Services, Health United States, 1988, pp. 106-107, tables 61-62 (data from the National Health Interview Survey). HE 20.6223:988

NOTES: 'All Races' includes other races not shown separately. 'Hospital outpatient department' includes outpatient clinics and emergency rooms; 'other' includes clinics and other places outside a hospital.

UNITS: Physicians visits in visits per person; data by place of visit as a percent of all visits to physicians; interval since last physician visit as a percent of the population. All visits per person, are age-adjusted.

Table 2.33 Characteristics of Dental Visits, 1981 and 1986

	Black	White	All Races
Dental visits			
1981			
all dental visits (per person)	1.1	1.8	1.7
interval since last physician visit			
less than one year	35.5%	52.2%	49.9%
2 years or more	33.1	23.7	24.8
never visited a dentist	14.3	10.2	11.0
1986			
all dental visits (per person)	1.3	2.1	2.0
interval since last physician visit			
less than one year	41.0%	57.3%	55.1%
2 years or more	34.1	23.1	24.4
never visited a dentist	12.2	9.7	10.1

SOURCE: U.S. Department of Health and Human Services, Health United States, 1987, p. 107, table 61 (data from the National Health Interview Survey). HE 20.6223:987

NOTES: 'All Races' includes other races not shown separately.

UNITS: Dental visits in visits per person; interval since last dental visit as a percent of the population. All visits per person, are age-adjusted.

Table 2.34 Short Stay Hospitals: Discharges, Days of Care, Average Length of Stay, 1981, 1987

	Black	White	All Races
1981			
discharges	137.7	120.0	121.7
days of care	1,302.4	912.5	952.1
average length of stay	9.5	7.6	7.8
1987			
discharges	117.4	94.8	96.5
days of care	942.8	621.5	649.7
average length of stay	8.0	6.6	6.7

SOURCE: U.S. Department of Health and Human Services, Health United States, 1988, p. 111, table 66 (data from the National Health Interview Survey). HE 20.6223:988

NOTES: 'All Races' includes other races not shown separately. Data are age adjusted.

UNITS: Discharges and days of care in number per 1,000 population; average length of stay, in average number of days.

Table 2.35 Self-Assessment of Health, 1983, 1987, 1988

	Black	White	All Races
Self-assessment of health			
1983			
excellent	28.5%	42.6%	40.7%
very good	21.8	25.8	25.4
good	30.0	22.1	23.2
fair or poor	19.7	9.6	10.7
1987			
excellent	29.5%	42.1%	40.3%
very good	24.4	28.2	27.8
good	29.4	21.1	22.4
fair or poor	16.7	8.5	9.5
1988			
excellent	31.2%	40.2%	39.1%
very good	23.8	28.4	27.8
good	30.2	22.1	23.2
fair or poor	14.9	9.3	9.9

SOURCE: U.S. Department of Health and Human Services, Health United States, 1988, p. 95, table 50 (data from the National Health Interview Survey). HE 20.6223:988
U.S. Department of Health and Human Services, Vital and Health Statistics, Series 10, #173, p. 114, table 70 (data from the National Health Interview Survey). HE 20.6209/4:988

NOTES: 'All Races' includes other races not shown separately. Data are age-adjusted.

UNITS: Percent of the population

Table 2.36 Nursing Home and Personal Care Home Residency, by Age, 1977 and 1985

	residents			residency rate		
	Black	White	All Races	Black	White	All Races
1977						
persons of all ages	61	1,060	1,126	30.7	48.9	47.1
persons 65-74 years old	22	188	211	17.6	14.2	14.4
persons 75-84 years old	20	443	465	33.4	67.0	64.0
persons 85 years old and older	19	429	450	133.6	234.2	225.9
1985						
persons of all ages	82	1,227	1,318	35.0	47.7	46.2
persons 65-74 years old	23	188	212	15.4	12.3	12.5
persons 75-84 years old	31	474	509	45.3	59.1	57.7
persons 85 years old and older	29	566	597	141.5	228.7	220.3

SOURCE: U.S. Department of Health and Human Services, Health United States, 1987, p. 119, table 69. HE 20.6223:987

NOTES: 'All Races' includes other races not shown separately. 1977 data includes domiciliary care homes. A nursing home is an establishment with three or more beds that provides nursing or personal care to the aged, infirm, or chronically ill. A personal care home without nursing has no residents receiving nursing care. These homes provide administration of medications and treatments in accordance with physicians' orders, supervision of self-administered medications or three or more personal services. A domiciliary care home provides supervisory care and one or two personal services.

UNITS: Residents in thousands of persons; residency rate, residents per 1,000 population.

Table 2.37 Health Care Coverage for Persons Under 65 Years of Age, by Type of Coverage, 1980, 1982, 1986

	Black	White	All Races
1980			
private insurance	60.1%	81.9%	17.8%
Medicaid	17.9	3.9	5.9
not covered	19.0	11.4	12.5
1982			
private insurance	59.6%	80.4%	77.3%
Medicaid	17.2	3.6	5.6
not covered	21.1	13.5	14.7
1986			
private insurance	57.0%	79.1%	75.9%
Medicaid	17.4	4.0	5.9
not covered	22.6	14.0	15.3

SOURCE: U.S. Department of Health and Human Services, Health United States, 1987, p. 168, table 110 (data from the National Health Interview Survey). HE 20.6223:987

NOTES: 'All Races' includes other races not shown separately. Medicaid includes persons receiving AFDC (Aid to Families with Dependent Children) or SSI (Supplemental Security Income), or those with a current medicaid card. Not covered includes those persons not covered by private insurance, Medicaid, Medicare, and military plans. Data are age-adjusted.

UNITS: Percent of the population.

Table 2.38 Health Care Coverage for Persons Over 65 Years of Age, by Type of Coverage, 1980, 1982, 1986

	Black	White	All Races
1980			
Medicare and private insurance	26.5%	68.3%	64.4%
Medicare and Medicaid	23.3	6.6	8.1
Medicare	40.6	21.0	22.7
1982			
Medicare and private insurance	33.0%	68.9%	65.5%
Medicare and Medicaid	18.2	4.8	6.1
Medicare	38.5	21.6	23.1
1986			
Medicare and private insurance	34.2%	75.4%	71.6%
Medicare and Medicaid	19.7	4.5	5.8
Medicare	34.9	16.1	17.9

SOURCE: U.S. Department of Health and Human Services, Health United States, 1987, p. 169, table 111 (data from the National Health Interview Survey). HE 20.6223:987

NOTES: 'All Races' includes other races not shown separately. Medicaid includes persons receiving AFDC (Aid to Families with Dependent Children) or SSI (Supplemental Security Income), or those with a current medicaid card. Not covered includes those persons not covered by private insurance, Medicaid, Medicare, and military plans. Data are age-adjusted.

UNITS: Percent of the population.

Table 3.01 School Enrollment by Age, 1980, 1985, 1986

	enrollment			enrollment rate		
	Black	White	All Races	Black	White	All Races
1980						
all persons 3-34 years old	8.3	47.7	57.3	53.9	48.9	49.7
persons 3 and 4 years old	0.4	1.8	2.3	38.2	36.3	36.7
persons 5 and 6 years old	0.9	4.8	5.9	95.4	95.8	95.7
persons 7-13 years old	3.6	19.6	23.8	99.4	99.2	99.3
persons 14 and 15 years old	1.1	6.0	7.3	97.9	98.3	98.2
persons 16 and 17 years old	1.0	5.9	7.1	90.6	88.6	89.0
persons 18 and 19 years old	0.5	3.2	3.8	45.7	46.3	46.4
persons 20 and 21 years old	0.2	2.2	2.5	23.4	31.9	31.0
persons 22-24 years old	0.2	1.7	1.9	13.8	16.4	16.3
persons 25-29 years old	0.2	1.5	1.7	6.8	9.2	9.3
persons 30-34 years old	0.1	0.9	1.1	8.8	6.3	6.4
persons 35 years old and older	0.2	1.1	1.3	1.8	1.3	1.4
1985						
all persons 3-34 years old	8.4	47.5	58.0	50.9	47.8	48.3
persons 3 and 4 years old	0.5	2.3	2.8	42.7	38.6	38.9
persons 5 and 6 years old	1.0	5.4	6.7	95.7	96.4	96.1
persons 7-13 years old	3.5	18.5	22.8	99.1	99.3	99.2
persons 14 and 15 years old	1.1	6.0	7.4	97.9	98.1	98.1
persons 16 and 17 years old	1.0	5.4	6.7	91.7	91.6	91.7
persons 18 and 19 years old	0.5	3.1	3.7	44.1	52.4	51.6
persons 20 and 21 years old	0.3	2.3	2.7	27.7	36.1	35.3
persons 22-24 years old	0.2	1.7	2.1	13.7	17.0	16.9
persons 25-29 years old	0.2	1.6	1.9	7.4	9.2	9.2
persons 30-34 years old	0.1	1.0	1.2	5.1	6.2	6.1
persons 35 years old and older	0.2	1.5	1.8	1.9	1.7	1.7

continued on the next page

Table 3.01 continued

	enrollment			enrollment rate		
	Black	White	All Races	Black	White	All Races
1986						
all persons 3-34 years old	8.6	47.3	58.2	51.1	47.4	48.2
persons 3 and 4 years old	0.4	2.3	2.8	38.2	39.1	38.9
persons 5 and 6 years old	1.1	5.5	6.9	95.2	95.3	95.3
persons 7-13 years old	3.6	18.6	23.0	99.4	99.2	99.2
persons 14 and 15 years old	1.1	5.7	7.0	96.6	97.8	97.6
persons 16 and 17 years old	1.0	5.6	6.9	93.2	92.0	92.3
persons 18 and 19 years old	0.5	3.2	3.9	49.4	54.8	54.6
persons 20 and 21 years old	0.3	2.0	2.4	25.7	33.5	33.0
persons 22-24 years old	0.3	1.8	2.2	16.6	17.4	17.9
persons 25-29 years old	0.2	1.6	1.9	7.5	8.8	8.8
persons 30-34 years old	0.1	1.0	1.2	5.9	5.9	6.0
persons 35 years old and older	0.3	1.6	1.9	2.0	1.8	1.8

SOURCE: U.S. Bureau of the Census, Statistical Abstract of the United States, 1988, p. 122, table 196; 1989, p. 128, table 206 (data from *Current Population Reports*, Series P-20). C 3.134:(year)

NOTES: 'All Races' includes other races not shown separately.

UNITS: Enrollment in millions of persons enrolled; rate as a percent of the civilian non-institutionalized population, by age group.

Table 3.02 Preprimary School Enrollment of Children 3 - 5 Years Old, by Selected Characteristic of the Mother, 1980, 1985, 1986

	enrollment			enrollment rate		
	Black	White	All Races	Black	White	All Races
1980						
All children 3-5 years old enrolled in preprimary school	725	3,994	9,284	51.8	52.7	52.5
with mother in labor force	438	1,976	2,480	59.2	56.8	57.1
- mother employed	356	1,840	2,578	60.5	57.8	58.2
- employed full time	269	1,127	1,445	60.0	56.8	57.4
with mother with 0-8 years of school	72	197	287	24.1	34.5	36.9
- with mother with 4 years high school	295	1,751	2,081	54.4	50.5	51.0
- with mother with 4 or more year college	59	749	853	72.1	70.4	70.3
1985						
All children 3-5 years old enrolled in preprimary school	919	4,757	5,865	55.8	54.7	54.6
with mother in labor force	548	2,651	3,306	60.2	58.0	58.1
- mother employed	439	2,467	2,999	60.3	59.1	59.1
- employed full time	361	1,535	1,969	62.6	56.5	57.4
with mother with 0-8 years of school	65	269	369	42.4	40.9	40.9
- with mother with 4 years high school	391	2,019	2,466	56.8	52.9	53.3
- with mother with 4 or more years college	68	941	1,062	63.2	67.8	66.6

continued on the next page

Table 3.02 continued

	enrollment			enrollment rate		
	Black	White	All Races	Black	White	All Races
1986						
All children 3-5 years old enrolled in preprimary school	892	4,849	5,965	54.1	55.2	54.9
with mother in labor force	494	2,791	3,403	58.5	59.0	58.9
- mother employed	424	2,624	3,159	59.3	59.9	59.8
- employed full time	357	1,627	2,066	62.1	59.6	59.9
with mother with 0-8 years of school	80	246	354	52.3	38.7	41.5
- with mother with 4 years high school	317	2,038	2,433	49.5	53.1	52.7
- with mother with 4 or more years college	82	976	1,123	67.4	69.0	68.4

SOURCE: U.S. Bureau of the Census, Statistical Abstract of the United States, 1988, p. 123, table 198 (data from *Current Population Reports*, Series P-20). C 3.134:988

NOTES: 'All Races' includes other races not shown separately. Includes children enrolled in public and non-public nursery school and kindergarten programs. Excludes five year olds enrolled in elementary school. 'All children 3-5 years old enrolled in preprimary school' includes children whose mothers' labor force status is unknown and children with no mother present in the household.

UNITS: Enrollment in thousands of children enrolled; rate as a percent of the civilian non-institutionalized population, 3-5 years old.

Table 3.03 Estimates of the School Age Population, 1975 - 1986

	Black	White	All Races
1975			
Total	7,199	42,950	51,044
male	3,611	21,956	26,022
female	3,588	20,994	25,022
1980			
Total	6,997	39,003	47,236
male	3,523	19,982	24,139
female	3,472	19,020	23,098
1985			
Total	6,898	36,503	44,978
male	3,493	18,728	23,025
female	3,406	17,775	21,951
1986			
Total	6,959	36,534	45,143
male	3,528	18,746	23,120
female	3,431	17,787	22,024

SOURCE: U.S. Department of Education, Center for Education Statistics, Digest of Education Statistics, 1988, p. 22, table 14 (data from U.S. Bureau of the Census, *Current Population Reports*, Series P-25). ED 1.113:988

NOTES: 'All Races' includes other races not shown separately.

UNITS: Estimates of the civilian non-institutionalized population, 5-17 years old as of July 1, in thousands of persons.

Table 3.04 Enrollment in Public Elementary and Secondary Schools, by State, Fall 1984

	Black	White	All Races
UNITED STATES	16.2%	71.2	100.0%
Alabama	34.5	63.9	100.0%
Alaska	3.4	74.5	"
Arizona	3.8	62.3	"
Arkansas	25.3	73.9	"
California	10.1	52.0	"
Colorado	5.1	76.5	"
Connecticut	10.3	81.4	"
Delaware	25.8	70.7	"
District of Columbia	92.5	3.8	"
Florida	23.1	67.7	"
Georgia	35.8	63.0	"
Hawaii	1.9	23.1	"
Idaho	0.4	93.5	"
Illinois	24.8	64.7	"
Indiana	10.7	86.9	"
Iowa	1.8	96.0	"
Kansas	6.8	88.1	"
Kentucky	10.6	88.9	"
Louisiana	42.5	55.5	"
Maine	0.4	98.7	"
Maryland	37.2	58.2	"
Massachusetts	6.3	86.5	"
Michigan	16.7	79.5	"
Minnesota	2.4	93.4	"
Mississippi	50.4	49.3	"
Missouri	16.2	82.2	"
Montana	0.3	85.4	"
Nebraska	4.3	92.5	"
Nevada	9.9	78.3	"
New Hampshire	0.6	98.3	"

continued on the next page

Table 3.04 continued

	Black	White	All Races
New Jersey	18.8%	69.7%	100.0%
New Mexico	0.2	44.9	"
New York	18.7	64.4	"
North Carolina	30.0	62.2	"
North Dakota	0.5	92.4	"
Ohio	14.4	83.8	"
Oklahoma	9.9	76.4	"
Oregon	2.1	90.5	"
Pennsylvania	12.6	84.6	"
Rhode Island	5.5	88.5	"
South Carolina	40.6	58.6	"
South Dakota	0.5	92.5	"
Tennessee	20.9	78.5	"
Texas	13.9	56.6	"
Utah	0.5	93.4	"
Vermont	0.4	98.9	"
Virginia	23.8	72.4	"
Washington	3.8	85.5	"
West Virginia	4.2	95.4	"
Wisconsin	7.7	88.7	"
Wyoming	0.9	90.3	"

SOURCE: U.S. Department of Education, Center for Education Statistics, Digest of Education Statistics, 1987, p. 46, table 35. ED 1.113\987

NOTES: 'All Races' includes other races not shown separately. Both 'Black' and 'White' exclude persons of Hispanic origin.

UNITS: Enrollment as a percent of total enrollment, 100.0%.

Table 3.05 Public Elementary and Secondary School Teachers, 1976, 1981, 1986

	Black	White	All Races
1976			
elementary school teachers	9.6%	89.7%	100.0%
secondary school teachers	6.6	91.8	100.0
1981			
elementary school teachers	8.4%	90.8%	100.0%
junior high school teachers	10.3	89.4	100.0
senior high school teachers	5.3	94.0	100.0
1986			
elementary school teachers	6.2%	89.3%	100.0%
junior high school teachers	10.2	86.7	100.0
senior high school teachers	5.6	92.0	100.0
male school teachers	6.3	90.6	100.0
female school teachers	7.2	89.2	100.0

SOURCE: U.S. Bureau of the Census, Statistical Abstract of the United States, 1988, p. 129, table 210 (data from National Education Association, *Status of the American Public School Teacher*). C 3.134:988

NOTES: 'All Races' includes other races not shown separately. 'Junior high school teachers' includes those teaching in middle schools.

UNITS: Percent, as a percent of all public elementary and secondary school teachers, 100.0%.

Table 3.06 Teachers in Private Schools, 1985-86

	Black	White	All Races
1985-86			
All private schools	3.8%	92.2%	100.0%
elementary schools	4.8	91.1	"
secondary schools	1.4	95.0	"
combined schools	3.3	92.6	"
other schools	5.0	91.1	"
Catholic schools	2.5	93.5	"
other religiously affiliated schools	4.0	91.9	"
schools not religiously affiliated	5.9	90.2	"

SOURCE: U.S. Department of Education, Center for Education Statistics, Digest of Education Statistics, 1988, p. 63, table 47.
ED 1.113:988

NOTES: 'All Races' includes other races not shown separately. Elementary schools have no grade higher than 8, secondary schools have no grade lower than 7, combined schools have any other grade spans.

UNITS: Percent, as a percent of all teachers in private schools, 100.0%.

Table 3.07 Testing: Students Taking the SAT (Scholastic Aptitude Test), and the ACT (American College Testing Program), 1975 - 1986

	Black	White	All Races
1975			
SAT-Scholastic Aptitude Test	7.9%	86.0%	100.0%
ACT-American College Testing Program	7.0	77.0	100.0
1980			
SAT-Scholastic Aptitude Test	9.1%	82.1%	100.0%
ACT-American College Testing Program	8.0	83.0	100.0
1985			
SAT-Scholastic Aptitude Test	7.5%	81.0%	100.0%
ACT-American College Testing Program	8.0	82.0	100.0
1986			
SAT-Scholastic Aptitude Test	na	na	100.0%
ACT-American College Testing Program	8.0%	82.0%	100.0
1987			
SAT-Scholastic Aptitude Test	8.1%	72.9%	100.0%
ACT-American College Testing Program	8.0%	81.0%	100.0

SOURCE: U.S. Bureau of the Census, Statistical Abstract of the United States, 1989, p. 144, tables 237, 238 (data from College Entrance Examination Board, *National College-Bound Seniors*, and American College Testing Program, *High School Profile Report*). C 3.134:988

NOTES: 'All Races' includes other races not shown separately. Beginning 1985, ACT data is for seniors who graduated in the year shown and had taken the ACT in their junior or senior years.

UNITS: Percent, as a percent of all students taking the respective tests, 100.0%.

Table 3.08 SAT (Scholastic Aptitude Test) Scores, 1975 - 1987

	Black	White	All Races
1975-1976			
SAT-Scholastic Aptitude Test			
verbal score	332	451	431
math score	354	493	472
1980-1981			
SAT-Scholastic Aptitude Test			
verbal score	332	442	424
math score	362	483	466
1984-1985			
SAT-Scholastic Aptitude Test			
verbal score	346	449	431
math score	376	491	475
1986-1987			
SAT-Scholastic Aptitude Test			
verbal score	351	447	430
math score	377	489	476

SOURCE: U.S. Department of Education, Center for Education Statistics, Digest of Education Statistics, 1988, p. 108, table 89. ED 1.113:988

NOTES: 'All Races' includes other races not shown separately.

UNITS: Average scores, (minimum score, 200; maximum score 800).

Table 3.09 High School Completion Rates of Persons Aged 18 - 19 Years Old, and 20 - 24 Years Old, 1975 - 1986

	Black	White	All Races
Persons aged 18-19 years old			
1975	52.8%	77.0%	73.3%
1980	59.3	76.1	73.7
1981	59.6	74.8	72.5
1982	58.2	74.5	72.0
1983	59.1	75.6	72.7
1984	63.0	75.5	73.3
1985	62.8	76.6	74.6
1986	64.9	76.6	74.6
Persons aged 20-24 years old			
1975	70.5%	85.9%	83.9%
1980	74.3	85.1	83.8
1981	75.7	85.0	83.7
1982	76.2	85.4	84.1
1983	75.8	84.6	83.3
1984	79.3	85.7	84.6
1985	80.8	86.0	85.3
1986	81.0	85.4	84.8

SOURCE: U.S. Department of Education, Center for Education Statistics, Education Indicators, 1989, p. 160, table 1:9-1 (data from U.S. Bureau of the Census, *Current Population Reports*, Series P-20). ED 1.109:989

NOTES: 'All Races' includes other races not shown separately.

UNITS: Percent of the age group that has completed high school as of October of the year shown.

Table 3.10 High School Dropouts Among Persons 14 - 34 Years of Age, by Sex, 1975, 1980, 1986

	Black	White	All Races
1975			
All males 14-34 years old	21.9%	12.1%	13.2%
males 14 and 15 years old	2.4	1.4	1.6
males 16 and 17 years old	9.7	7.3	7.6
males 18 and 19 years old	27.7	13.7	15.5
males 20 and 21 years old	30.4	14.5	16.4
males 22 to 24 years old	25.9	12.6	14.0
males 25 to 29 years old	25.5	13.2	14.4
males 30 to 34 years old	33.1	17.4	18.9
All females 14-34 years old	24.7	13.5	15.0
females 14 and 15 years old	2.8	1.9	2.0
females 16 and 17 years old	10.7	9.6	9.6
females 18 and 19 years old	23.4	15.6	16.5
females 20 and 21 years old	27.3	15.0	16.7
females 22 to 24 years old	29.2	12.7	15.0
females 25 to 29 years old	29.9	14.7	16.5
females 30 to 34 years old	39.6	19.7	22.0
1980			
All males 14-34 years old	19.0%	12.4%	13.2%
males 14 and 15 years old	1.5	1.2	1.3
males 16 and 17 years old	7.2	9.3	8.9
males 18 and 19 years old	22.7	16.1	16.9
males 20 and 21 years old	31.3	15.6	17.8
males 22 to 24 years old	24.9	15.4	16.4
males 25 to 29 years old	22.1	12.7	13.8
males 30 to 34 years old	21.9	13.1	14.0

continued on the next page

Table 3.10 continued

	Black	White	All Races
1980 - continued			
All females 14-34 years old	18.7%	11.8%	12.8%
females 14 and 15 years old	2.5	2.1	2.2
females 16 and 17 years old	6.6	9.2	8.8
females 18 and 19 years old	19.8	13.8	14.7
females 20 and 21 years old	19.6	13.4	14.3
females 22 to 24 years old	23.3	12.6	14.0
females 25 to 29 years old	22.9	12.7	14.0
females 30 to 34 years old	24.8	13.6	15.2
1986			
All males 14-34 years old	15.5%	12.1%	12.4%
males 14 and 15 years old	3.0	2.2	2.4
males 16 and 17 years old	4.7	6.9	6.5
males 18 and 19 years old	14.6	12.8	13.1
males 20 and 21 years old	19.8	15.9	16.3
males 22 to 24 years old	19.4	15.0	15.3
males 25 to 29 years old	16.7	14.2	14.3
males 30 to 34 years old	21.7	11.9	13.0
All females 14-34 years old	15.5	10.6	11.4
females 14 and 15 years old	3.8	2.2	2.5
females 16 and 17 years old	4.7	6.0	5.7
females 18 and 19 years old	15.2	11.0	11.5
females 20 and 21 years old	16.7	12.9	13.4
females 22 to 24 years old	15.6	13.0	13.4
females 25 to 29 years old	19.4	12.4	13.5
females 30 to 34 years old	20.1	10.7	12.1

SOURCE: U.S. Department of Education, Center for Education Statistics, Digest of Education Statistics, 1988, p. 101, table 80 (data from U.S. Bureau of the Census, *Current Population Reports*, Series P-20). ED 1.113:988

NOTES: 'All Races' includes other races not shown separately. Data as of October. Dropouts are persons who are not enrolled in school and are not high school graduates. Persons who have received GED credentials are counted as graduates.

UNITS: Percent, as a percent of the civilian non-institutionalized population.

Table 3.11 College Enrollment, and High School Graduates Enrolled in and Completing One or More Years of College, by Sex, 1980, 1985, 1986

	Black	White	All Races
1980			
college enrollment			
total	718	6,546	7,475
male	292	3,303	3,700
female	426	3,243	3,778
high school graduates enrolled			
total	28.3%	32.5%	32.3%
male	27.0	34.3	33.8
female	29.2	30.9	30.9
high school graduates enrolled in college or completed one or more years of college			
total	46.2%	51.4%	51.1%
male	44.4	51.8	51.4
female	47.5	51.0	51.0
1985			
College enrollment			
total	755	6,729	7,799
male	355	3,374	3,880
female	400	3,357	3,917
high school graduates enrolled			
total	26.5%	35.0%	34.3%
male	28.2	36.6	36.0
female	25.1	33.6	33.6
high school graduates enrolled in college or completed one or more years of college			
total	43.8%	55.3%	54.3%
male	43.5	55.5	54.6
female	43.9	55.2	54.0

continued on the next page

Table 3.11 continued

	Black	White	All Races
1986			
college enrollment			
total	820	6,426	7,613
male	350	3,206	3,739
female	471	3,221	3,874
high school graduates enrolled			
total	28.8%	34.6%	34.4%
male	28.2	36.1	35.7
female	29.4	33.3	33.3
high school graduates enrolled in college or completed one or more years of college			
total	47.4%	55.3%	54.8%
male	43.7	55.0	54.2
female	50.2	55.6	55.3

SOURCE: U.S. Bureau of the Census, Statistical Abstract of the United States, 1988, p. 140, tables 233, 234 (data from *Current Population Reports*, Series P-20). C 3.134:988

NOTES: 'All Races' includes other races not shown separately.

UNITS: Enrollment in thousands of students; high school graduates enrolled as a percent of all high school graduates, as shown.

Table 3.12 Economic Outcomes of Secondary Education: Labor Force Status of High School Graduates, Dropouts, and College Students, October, 1986

	Black	White	All Races
October, 1986			
All high school graduates			
number	386	2,307	2,786
percent of all high school graduates	13.9	82.8	100.0
labor force status			
in the civilian labor force	208	1,512	1,764
labor force participation rate	53.9	65.5	63.3
- employed	136	1,288	1,462
- unemployed	72	224	302
unemployment rate	34.6%	14.8%	17.1%
High school graduates enrolled in college			
number	141	1,292	1,499
percent	9.4%	86.2%	100.0%
percent of all high school graduates	36.5%	56.0%	53.8%
labor force status			
in the civilian labor force	41	651	717
labor force participation rate	29.1	54	47.8
- employed	33	569	623
- unemployed	8	82	94
unemployment rate	na	12.6%	13.1%

continued on the next page

Table 3.12 continued

	Black	White	All Races
High school graduates not enrolled in college			
number	245	1,015	1,287
percent	19.0%	78.9%	100.0%
percent of all high school graduates	63.5%	44.0%	46.2%
labor force status			
in the civilian labor force	167	861	1,047
labor force participation rate	68.2	84.8	81.4
- employed	103	719	839
- unemployed	64	142	208
unemployment rate	38.3%	16.5%	19.9%
High school dropouts			
number	90	449	562
percent	16.0%	79.9%	100.0%
labor force status			
in the civilian labor force	50	289	359
labor force participation rate	55.6	64.4	63.9
- employed	29	213	259
- unemployed	21	76	100
unemployment rate	na	26.3%	27.9%

SOURCE: U.S. Department of Education, Center for Education Statistics, Digest of Education Statistics, 1988, pp. 324-325, tables 271, 272. ED 1.113:988

NOTES: 'All Races' includes other races not shown separately. Based on high school graduates who graduated between October, 1985 and October, 1986, now in the civilian non-institutionalized population. The labor force participation rate is the number of persons in the civilian labor force, divided by the number of persons in the civilian non-institutionalized population.

UNITS: Number of high school graduates in thousands; percent, as a percent of all high school graduates, 100.0%

Table 3.13 Enrollment in Institutions of Higher Education, by Type of Institution, 1976 - 1986

	enrollment			percent distribution		
	Black	White	All Races	Black	White	All Races
1976						
All institutions	1,033	9,076	10,986	15.4%	82.6%	100.0%
4-year institutions	604	5,999	7,107	5.5	54.6	64.7
2 year institutions	429	3,077	3,879	3.9	28.0	35.3
1980						
All institutions	1,107	9,883	12,087	16.1%	81.4%	100.0%
4-year institutions	634	6,275	7,565	5.2	51.9	62.6
2 year institutions	472	3,558	4,521	3.9	29.4	37.4
1982						
All institutions	1,101	9,997	12,388	16.6%	80.7%	100.0%
4-year institutions	612	6,306	7,648	4.9	50.9	61.7
2 year institutions	489	3,692	4,740	3.9	29.8	38.3
1984						
All institutions	1,076	9,815	12,233	17.0%	80.2%	100.0%
4-year institutions	617	6,300	7,706	5.0	51.5	63.0
2 year institutions	459	3,514	4,527	3.7	28.7	37.0
1986						
All institutions	1,081	9,915	12,501	17.9%	79.3%	100.0%
4-year institutions	615	6,340	7,826	4.9	50.7	62.6
2 year institutions	466	3,575	4,675	3.7	28.6	37.4

SOURCE: U.S. Department of Education, Center for Education Statistics, Digest of Education Statistics, 1988, p. 170, table 146.
ED 1.113:988

NOTES: 'All Races' includes other races not shown separately. Both 'Black' and 'White' exclude persons of Hispanic origin.

UNITS: Enrollment in thousands of students enrolled; percent distribution as a percent of total enrollment, 100.0%, by type of institution.

Table 3.14 Enrollment in Institutions of Higher Education, by State, Fall, 1986

	Black	White	All Races
UNITED STATES	1,080,899	9,914,483	12,500,798
Alabama	37,690	137,301	181,447
Alaska	976	22,654	27,482
Arizona	6,166	181,555	226,593
Arkansas	10,520	65,807	79,182
California	117,015	1,145,326	1,731,661
Colorado	4,283	145,961	177,387
Connecticut	7,584	140,091	158,278
Delaware	3.703	28,726	33,893
District of Columbia	22,886	41,533	77,651
Florida	44,301	362,346	477,210
Georgia	34,303	150,953	195,123
Hawaii	938	15,370	51,697
Idaho	260	42,534	45,260
Illinois	91,800	519,851	686,895
Indiana	13,570	223,687	250,178
Iowa	3,164	142,680	155,369
Kansas	6,475	126,518	143,203
Kentucky	8,803	132,581	144,548
Louisiana	39,326	119,316	171,338
Maine	540	44,285	46,232
Maryland	35,217	179,928	233,492
Massachusetts	16,787	361,916	417,513
Michigan	46,891	444,505	520,423
Minnesota	2,969	212,297	226,556
Mississippi	28,785	69,232	101,095
Missouri	18,499	216,229	246,185
Montana	143	31,671	34,691
Nebraska	2,744	93,090	100,401
Nevada	1,861	40,418	46,796
New Hampshire	667	51,521	53,876

continued on the next page

Table 3.14 continued

	Black	White	All Races
New Jersey	27,026	230,426	295,313
New Mexico	1,888	50,343	80,270
New York	110,524	754,415	1,006,000
North Carolina	57,370	253,062	322,966
North Dakota	241	34,356	37,311
Ohio	37,687	459,186	520,486
Oklahoma	10,546	141,066	170,840
Oregon	1,836	128,742	144,798
Pennsylvania	35,103	483,822	545,923
Rhode Island	2,014	63,825	69,569
South Carolina	25,924	103,801	134,116
South Dakota	190	28,322	30,935
Tennessee	27,508	162,006	197,070
Texas	66,662	543,905	776,021
Utah	728	96,143	106,217
Vermont	298	31,153	32,452
Virginia	41,545	250,004	308,318
Washington	5,899	211,111	242,443
West Virginia	2,865	71,890	76,783
Wisconsin	9,334	260,294	283,653
Wyoming	243	22,717	24,357

SOURCE: U.S. Department of Education, Center for Education Statistics, Digest of Education Statistics, 1988, p. 173, table 149.
ED 1.113\988

NOTES: 'All Races' includes other races not shown separately.

UNITS: Enrollment in thousands of students enrolled.

Table 3.15 Enrollment Rates of 18 - 24 Year Olds in Institutions of Higher Education, 1975 - 1986

	Black	White	All Races
Enrollment as a percent of 18-24 year olds			
1975	20.7%	26.9%	26.3%
1980	19.2	26.2	25.6
1981	19.9	26.7	26.2
1982	19.8	27.2	26.6
1983	19.2	27.0	26.2
1984	20.4	28.0	27.1
1985	19.8	28.7	27.8
1986	21.8	28.3	27.2
Enrollment as a percent of high school graduates			
1975	32.0%	32.4%	32.5%
1980	27.6	31.8	31.6
1981	28.0	32.5	32.5
1982	28.0	33.1	33.0
1983	27.0	32.9	32.5
1984	27.2	33.7	33.2
1985	26.1	34.4	33.7

SOURCE: U.S. Department of Education, Center for Education Statistics, Digest of Education Statistics, 1988, p. 174, table 150 (data from U.S. Bureau of the Census, *Current Population Reports*, series P-20). ED 1.113\988

U.S. Department of Education, Center for Education Statistics, 1989 Education Indicators, pp. 298-300, tables, 2:17-1, 2:18-1 (data from U.S. Bureau of the Census, *Current Population Reports*,series P-20). ED 1.109:989

NOTES: 'All Races' includes other races not shown separately.

UNITS: Percent as a percent of 18-24 year olds, and high school graduates as shown, 100.0%.

Table 3.16 Enrollment of Persons 14 - 34 Years Old in Institutions of Higher Education, by Sex, 1975 - 1986

	enrollment			percent distribution		
	Black	White	All Races	Black	White	All Races
1975						
Total	948	8,514	9,697	9.8%	87.7%	100.0%
men	442	4,771	na	5.6	49.2	na
women	506	3,743	na	4.2	38.6	na
1980						
Total	1,007	8,875	10,180	9.9%	87.2%	100.0%
men	437	4,438	na	4.3	43.6	na
women	570	4,437	na	5.6	43.6	na
1985						
Total	1,049	9,334	10,863	9.7%	85.9%	100.0%
men	458	4,663	na	4.2	42.6	na
women	591	4,701	na	5.4	43.3	na
1986						
Total	1,136	8,943	10,605	10.7%	84.3%	100.0%
men	488	4,485	na	4.6	42.3	na
women	649	4,459	na	6.1	42.0	na

SOURCE: U.S. Department of Education, Center for Education Statistics, Digest of Education Statistics, 1988, p. 175, table 151 (data from U.S. Bureau of the Census, *Current Population Reports*, series P-20). ED 1.113\988

NOTES: 'All Races' includes other races not shown separately.

UNITS: Percent as a percent of 14-34 year olds, by sex as shown, 100.0%.

Table 3.17 Enrollment in Institutions of Higher Education, by Control of the Institution and Level of Enrollment, by Sex, Fall, 1980 and 1984

	Black	White	All Races
1980			
by control of the institution			
both public and private control			
total	1,106.8	9,833.0	12,086.8
male	463.7	4,772.9	5,868.1
female	643.0	5,060.1	6,218.7
public control			
total	876.1	7,656.1	9,456.4
male	365.3	3,658.1	4,521.6
female	510.8	3,998.0	4,934.8
private control			
total	230.7	2,176.9	2,630.4
male	98.4	1,114.8	1,346.5
female	132.2	1,062.1	1,283.9
by level of enrollment			
undergraduate			
total	932.3	7,466.3	9,262.0
men	393.4	3,632.9	4,488.4
women	538.9	3,833.4	4,773.6
graduate			
total	60.0	898.7	1,096.5
men	22.8	452.9	569.0
women	37.2	445.8	527.5
first professional			
total	12.8	247.7	276.8
men	7.4	179.5	198.5
women	5.5	68.1	78.4
unclassified			
total	101.7	1,220.4	1,451.5
men	40.2	507.6	612.3
women	61.5	712.8	839.2

continued on the next page

Table 3.17 continued

	Black	White	All Races
1984			
by control of the institution			
both public and private control			
total	1,069.9	9,766.8	12,161.8
male	434.5	4,667.6	5,824.4
female	635.4	5,099.2	6,337.4
public control			
total	841.3	7,524.8	9,424.9
male	340.0	3,542.4	4,448.5
female	501.3	3,982.4	4,976.4
private control			
total	228.5	2,242.0	2,736.9
male	94.5	1,125.2	1,375.9
female	134.1	1,116.8	1,361.0
by level of enrollment			
undergraduate			
total	897.2	7,549.6	9,451.1
men	368.1	3,621.0	4,518.6
women	529.1	3,928.6	4,932.4
graduate			
total	52.8	882.3	1,100.4
men	20.0	436.9	569.5
women	32.9	445.4	530.9
first professional			
total	13.2	241.6	276.4
men	7.0	162.5	183.6
women	6.2	79.1	92.7
unclassified			
total	106.6	1,093.4	1,334.0
men	39.4	447.2	552.6
women	67.2	646.2	781.3

SOURCE: U.S. Department of Education, Center for Education Statistics, Digest of Education Statistics, 1988, p. 157, table 136. ED 1.113\988

NOTES: 'All Races' includes other races not shown separately. Both 'White' and 'Black' exclude persons of Hispanic origin.

UNITS: Enrollment in thousands of students.

Table 3.18 Traditionally Black Institutions of Higher Education: Enrollment, Fall, 1985 and Earned Degrees Conferred, 1983 - 1984

	Traditionally Black Institutions				
	public		private		
	4 year	2 year	4 year	2 year	Total
Enrollment, Fall 1985					
Total	146,111	6,050	60,292	1,323	213,776
men	65,617	2,370	26,387	624	94,998
women	80,494	3,680	33,905	699	118,778
full-time enrollment					
total	105,485	4,662	54,270	1,253	165,670
men	49,400	1,714	23,676	599	75,429
women	56,045	2,948	30,594	654	90,241
part-time enrollment					
total	40,626	1,388	6,022	70	48,106
men	16,177	656	2,711	25	19,569
women	24,449	732	2,211	45	28,537
Earned degrees conferred, 1983-84					
Associate degrees					
total	1,101	399	120	229	1,849
men	410	100	29	91	630
women	691	299	91	138	1,219
Bachelors's degrees					
total	13,789	-	7,433	7	21,229
men	6,283	-	3,054	7	9,344
women	7,506	-	4,379	-	11,885
Master's degrees					
total	3,194	-	896	-	4,090
men	1,400	-	380	-	1,780
women	1,794	-	516	-	2,310

continued on the next page

Table 3.18 continued

	Traditionally Black Institutions				
	public		private		
	4 year	2 year	4 year	2 year	Total
Earned degrees conferred, 1983-84 - continued					
Doctor's degrees					
total	22	-	96	-	118
men	11	-	63	-	74
women	11	-	33	-	44
First professional degrees					
total	239	-	674	-	913
men	166	-	399	-	565
women	73	-	275	-	248

SOURCE: U.S. Department of Education, Center for Education Statistics, Digest of Education Statistics, 1987, p. 157, table 136.
ED 1.113\987

NOTES: Includes black institutions which were established prior to 1954 for the education of black students mainly in the southern and boarder states.

UNITS: Enrollment in number of students; Earned degrees conferred, number.

Table 3.19 Undergraduates Receiving Financial Aid: Average Amount Awarded per Student, by Type and Source of Aid, 1986 - 1987

	Black	White	All Races
1986-87			
All enrolled undergraduates	551	4,270	5,592
undergraduates receiving:			
any aid			
total	$ 2,410	$ 2,061	$ 2,199
- from federal source	2,295	2,123	2,203
- from non-federal sources	1,026	1,137	1,145
grants			
total	$ 1,574	$ 1,373	$ 1,458
- from federal source	1,333	1,163	1,223
- from non-federal sources	963	1,059	1,079
loans			
total	$ 2,007	$ 2,137	$ 2,121
- from federal source	2,084	2,114	2,121
- from non-federal sources	na	1,277	1,197
work-study funds			
total	$ 1,001	$ 906	$ 913
- from federal source	916	840	856
- from non-federal sources	na	916	949

SOURCE: U.S. Department of Education, Center for Education Statistics, Digest of Education Statistics, 1988, p. 255, table 220.
ED 1.113\988

NOTES: 'All Races' includes other races not shown separately. Both 'White' and 'Black' exclude persons of Hispanic origin.

UNITS: Average 1986-1987 award in dollars per student, for students enrolled in Fall, 1986.

Table 3.20 Employed College Students, 1983 and 1985

	Black	White	All Races
1983			
Total	377.4	3,833.7	4,458.9
employed full time			
- during school year	12.6%	9.1%	9.2%
- during summer	47.8	56.2	54.7
employed part-time			
- during school year	36.7	48.0	47.2
- during summer	26.5	33.9	33.4
1985			
Total	381.9	3,863.1	4,510.7
employed full-time			
- during school year	16.1%	12.4%	12.8%
- during summer	51.4	61.0	61.9
employed part-time			
- during school year	41.2	45.7	45.4
- during summer	31.2	26.3	27.0

SOURCE: U.S. Bureau of the Census, Statistical Abstract of the United States, 1988, p. 144, table 242 (data from Simmons Market Research Bureau, *National College Study*). C 3.134:988

NOTES: 'All Races' includes other races not shown separately. Data are for school year ending in year shown; summer data, for the previous summer. Full-time is thirty or more hours per week. Part-time is less than 30 hours per week.

UNITS: Total in thousands of students; employment as a percent of all students, 100.0%.

Table 3.21 Enrollment in Schools of Medicine, 1977-78 and 1986-87

	Black	White	All Races
1977-78			
total enrollment	3,587	51,974	60,039
first year enrollment	1,085	13,732	16,136
1986-87			
total enrollment	3,892	53,136	66,125
first year enrollment	1,174	12,987	16,819

SOURCE: U.S. Department of Health and Human Services, Health United States, 1988, p. 138 table 88 (data from the National Health Interview Survey). HE 20.6223:988

NOTES: 'All Races' includes other races not shown separately.

UNITS: Enrollment in number of students.

Table 3.22 Earned Degrees Conferred, by Type of Degree, 1979, 1981, 1985

	Black	White	All Races
1979			
Bachelor's degrees	60,130	799,617	916,347
Master's degrees	19,393	249,051	299,887
Doctor's degrees	1,267	26,128	32,664
First Professional degrees	2,836	62,430	68,611
1981			
Bachelor's degrees	60,673	807,319	934,800
Master's degrees	17,133	241,216	294,183
Doctor's degrees	1,265	25,908	32,839
First Professional degrees	2,931	64,551	71,340
1985			
Bachelor's degrees	57,473	826,106	968,311
Master's degrees	13,939	223,628	280,421
Doctor's degrees	1,154	23,934	32,307
First Professional degrees	3,029	63,219	71,057

SOURCE: U.S. Department of Education, Center for Education Statistics, 1989 Education Indicators, pp. 228-229, table 2:5-1. ED 1.109:989

NOTES: 'All Races' includes other races not shown separately. Both 'White' and 'Black' exclude persons of Hispanic origin. 'First professional Degrees' include degrees awarded in chiropractic, dentistry, law, medicine, optometry, osteopathy, pharmacy, podiatry, theology, and veterinary medicine.

UNITS: Earned degrees conferred in number of degrees.

Table 3.23 Associate Degrees Conferred, by Major Field of Study and Sex of Student, 1984 - 1985

	Black	White	All Races
All Fields			
Total	35,799	355,343	429,823
men	14,192	157,278	190,417
women	21,607	198,065	239,406
agriculture and natural resources	117	5,953	6,320
men	98	4,040	4,347
women	19	1,903	1,973
architecture and environment design	46	1,028	1,182
men	17	166	211
women	29	862	971
area and ethnic studies	1	3	10
men	1	0	1
women	0	3	9
business and management	11,720	94,892	116,737
men	3,597	32,633	39,943
women	8,123	62,259	76,794
communications	335	3,306	3,864
men	222	1,960	2,319
women	113	1,346	1,545
computer and information sciences	908	9,728	11,843
men	446	5,066	6,102
women	462	4,662	5,741
education	653	5,264	7,009
men	248	1,418	2,106
women	405	3,846	4,903
engineering	148	2,260	2,843
men	119	2,009	2,524
women	29	251	319

continued on the next page

Table 3.23 continued

	Black	White	All Races
engineering technologies	3,871	47,365	56,548
men	3,398	43,565	51,806
women	473	3,800	4,742
foreign languages	29	269	350
men	21	149	183
women	8	120	167
health professions	4,578	57,719	65,864
men	560	6,530	7,758
women	4,018	51,189	58,106
home economics	1,029	7,276	9,091
men	159	2,261	2,530
women	870	5,015	6,561
law	128	1,697	1,961
men	39	210	275
women	89	1,487	1,686
letters	49	424	532
men	16	130	163
women	33	294	369
liberal studies/general	8,696	81,838	101,645
men	3,443	35,828	44,542
women	5,353	46,010	57,103
library and archival science	6	97	108
men	1	8	9
women	5	89	99
life sciences	93	662	852
men	37	296	381
women	56	366	471
mathematics	24	525	693
men	17	321	429
women	7	204	264

continued on the next page

Table 3.23 continued

	Black	White	All Races
military sciences	8	15	23
men	8	15	23
women	0	0	0
multi/interdisciplinary studies	358	6,757	7,650
men	144	3,103	3,507
women	214	3,654	4,143
parks and recreation	67	586	689
men	38	282	337
women	29	304	352
philosophy and religion	6	93	113
men	2	75	89
women	4	18	24
physical sciences	109	1,665	1,999
men	57	1,048	1,252
women	52	617	747
protective services	1,175	9,786	11,863
men	702	7,480	8,842
women	473	2,306	3,021
psychology	65	680	821
men	22	204	244
women	43	476	577
public affairs	463	2,754	3,553
men	167	1,344	1,640
women	306	1,410	1,913
social sciences	341	1,387	2,086
men	140	596	898
women	201	791	1,188
theology	31	600	689
men	21	339	390
women	10	261	299

continued on the next page

Table 3.23 continued

	Black	White	All Races
visual and performing arts	745	10,714	12,885
men	462	6,192	7,566
women	283	4,522	5,319

SOURCE: U.S. Department of Education, Center for Education Statistics, Digest of Education Statistics, 1988, pp. 217-218, table 181. ED 1.113\988

NOTES: 'All Races' includes other races not shown separately. Both 'White' and 'Black' exclude persons of Hispanic origin.

UNITS: Earned Associate degrees conferred in number of degrees.

Table 3.24 Bachelor's Degrees Conferred, by Major Field of Study and Sex of Student, 1984 - 1985

	Black	White	All Races
All Fields			
Total	57,473	826,106	968,311
men	23,018	405,085	476,148
women	34,455	421,021	492,163
agriculture and natural resources	370	16,429	18,015
men	256	11,252	12,427
women	114	5,177	5,588
architecture and environment design	328	7,647	9,217
men	215	4,888	5,946
women	113	2,759	3,271
area and ethnic studies	219	2,242	2,851
men	82	874	1,092
women	137	1,368	1,759
business and management	14,999	196,915	231,308
men	6,442	109,130	126,762
women	8,557	87,785	104,546
communications	3,135	36,156	41,547
men	1,165	14,940	17,039
women	1,970	21,216	24,508
computer and information sciences	2,143	31,321	38,589
men	1,036	20,188	24,386
women	1,107	11,133	14,203
education	5,456	77,531	87,788
men	1,569	18,119	21,146
women	3,887	59,412	66,642
engineering	2,039	60,992	75,682
men	1,479	52,167	64,660
women	560	8,825	11,022

continued on the next page

Table 3.24 continued

	Black	White	All Races
engineering technologies	1,120	15,446	18,878
men	956	14,311	17,435
women	164	1,135	1,443
foreign languages	312	8,214	9,845
men	91	2,153	2,606
women	221	6,061	7,239
health professions	3,836	55,501	63,289
men	484	8,114	9,534
women	3,352	47,387	53,755
home economics	952	13,624	15,454
men	94	841	1,002
women	858	12,783	14,452
law	85	966	1,131
men	40	364	445
women	45	602	686
letters	1,598	30,470	33,812
men	469	10,520	11,562
women	1,129	19,950	22,250
liberal studies/general	1,489	14,693	17,710
men	529	6,334	7,482
women	960	8,359	10,228
library and archival science	16	173	194
men	5	17	25
women	11	156	169
life sciences	2,045	31,807	38,115
men	806	16,805	19,905
women	1,239	15,002	18,210
mathematics	766	12,162	14,885
men	373	6,508	8,010
women	494	5,654	6,875

continued on the next page

Table 3.24 continued

	Black	White	All Races
military sciences	4	284	298
men	3	259	272
women	1	25	26
multi/interdisciplinary studies	899	13,518	15,652
men	353	6,523	7,486
women	546	6,995	8,184
parks and recreation	199	4,221	4,575
men	108	1,562	1,735
women	91	2,659	2,840
philosophy and religion	250	5,733	6,381
men	183	3,757	4,225
women	67	1,976	2,156
physical sciences	829	20,660	23,555
men	455	15,050	16,972
women	374	5,610	6,583
protective services	1,926	9,427	12,348
men	932	6,009	7,600
women	994	3,418	4,748
psychology	2,667	33,951	39,523
men	751	10,866	12,596
women	1,916	23,085	26,927
public affairs	1,953	10,692	13,649
men	492	3,654	4,559
women	1,461	7,038	9,090
social sciences	6,100	77,117	90,795
men	2,778	43,787	50,789
women	3,322	33,330	40,006
theology	195	5,269	5,874
men	156	3,836	4,278
women	39	1,433	1,596

continued on the next page

Table 3.24 continued

	Black	White	All Races
visual and performing arts	1,543	32,945	37,351
men	716	12,257	14,190
women	827	20,688	23,161

SOURCE: U.S. Department of Education, Center for Education Statistics, Digest of Education Statistics, 1988, pp. 220-221, table 183.
ED 1.113\988

NOTES: 'All Races' includes other races not shown separately. Both 'White' and 'Black' exclude persons of Hispanic origin.

UNITS: Earned Bachelor's degrees conferred in number of degrees.

Table 3.25 Master's Degrees Conferred, by Major Field of Study and Sex of Student, 1984 - 1985

	Black	White	All Races
All Fields			
Total	13,939	223,628	280,421
men	5,200	106,059	139,417
women	8,739	117,569	141,004
agriculture and natural resources	75	2,865	3,901
men	50	1,005	2,828
women	25	860	1,073
architecture and environment design	123	2,278	3,233
men	80	1,416	2,124
women	43	862	1,109
area and ethnic studies	41	508	778
men	19	249	380
women	22	259	398
business and management	2,601	54,663	66,596
men	1,574	37,256	45,884
women	1,027	17,407	20,712
communications	183	2,832	3,521
men	63	1,167	1,470
women	120	1,665	2,051
computer and information sciences	180	4,303	6,942
men	108	3,052	4,936
women	72	1,251	2,006
education	5,812	63,302	75,821
men	1,325	17,047	20,844
women	4,487	46,255	54,977
engineering	330	12,186	20,145
men	274	10,646	17,975
women	56	1,540	2,170

continued on the next page

Table 3.25 continued

	Black	White	All Races
engineering technologies	30	414	590
men	26	366	530
women	4	48	60
foreign languages	26	1,222	1,703
men	9	390	550
women	17	832	1,153
health professions	819	14,565	17,062
men	179	3,170	4,052
women	640	11,395	13,010
home economics	122	1,961	2,359
men	15	219	267
women	107	1,742	2,092
law	61	1,209	1,774
men	40	927	1,363
women	21	282	411
letters	144	4,869	5,794
men	43	1,675	2,011
women	101	3,194	3,783
liberal studies/general	38	1,020	1,174
men	12	377	447
women	36	643	727
library and archival science	172	3,398	3,846
men	24	652	749
women	148	2,746	3,097
life sciences	151	4,079	5,010
men	67	2,125	2,620
women	84	1,954	2,390
mathematics	53	1,873	2,831
men	43	1,170	1,843
women	19	703	988

continued on the next page

Table 3.25 continued

	Black	White	All Races
military sciences	4	42	50
men	3	42	49
women	1	0	1
multi/interdisciplinary studies	88	1,984	2,315
men	35	934	1,100
women	53	1,050	1,215
parks and recreation	18	487	542
men	6	289	241
women	12	278	301
philosophy and religion	27	947	1,126
men	19	541	669
women	8	406	457
physical sciences	89	4,145	5,675
men	61	3,144	4,355
women	28	1,001	1,320
protective services	159	988	1,232
men	86	697	849
women	73	291	383
psychology	426	7,218	8,379
men	146	2,600	3,042
women	280	4,618	5,337
public affairs	1,423	12,374	15,356
men	500	4,348	5,614
women	923	8,026	9,742
social sciences	422	7,333	10,223
men	234	4,326	6,298
women	188	3,007	3,925
theology	93	3,329	3,894
men	61	2,106	2,521
women	32	1,223	1,373

continued on the next page

Table 3.25 continued

	Black	White	All Races
visual and performing arts	229	7,234	8,549
men	107	3,203	3,806
women	122	4,031	4,743

SOURCE: U.S. Department of Education, Center for Education Statistics, Digest of Education Statistics, 1988, pp. 223-224, table 185. ED 1.113\988

NOTES. 'All Races' includes other races not shown separately. Both 'White' and 'Black' exclude persons of Hispanic origin.

UNITS: Earned Master's degrees conferred in number of degrees.

Table 3.26 Doctor's Degrees Conferred, by Major Field of Study and Sex of Student, 1984 - 1985

	Black	White	All Races
All Fields			
Total	1,154	23,934	32,307
men	561	15,017	21,296
women	593	8,917	11,011
agriculture and natural resources	24	790	1,216
men	21	660	1,039
women	3	130	177
architecture and environment design	5	53	89
men	4	36	66
women	1	17	23
area and ethnic studies	3	105	134
men	3	64	83
women	0	41	51
business and management	14	589	849
men	9	475	706
women	5	114	143
communications	18	164	219
men	8	95	131
women	10	69	88
computer and information sciences	3	150	240
men	3	131	216
women	0	19	24
education	521	5,615	7,032
men	184	2,645	3,366
women	337	2,970	3,666
engineering	40	1,370	3,165
men	35	1,258	2,964
women	5	112	201

continued on the next page

Table 3.26 continued

	Black	White	All Races
engineering technologies	0	7	9
men	0	6	8
women	0	1	1
foreign languages	9	305	424
men	4	123	178
women	5	182	246
health professions	33	924	1,172
men	15	405	556
women	18	519	616
home economics	8	219	276
men	0	56	78
women	8	163	198
law	3	68	89
men	2	52	72
women	1	16	17
letters	24	1,015	1,212
men	7	455	554
women	17	560	658
liberal studies/general	1	47	52
men	0	25	28
women	1	22	24
library and archival science	8	55	83
men	2	25	38
women	6	30	45
life sciences	53	2,725	3,354
men	32	1,839	2,259
women	21	886	1,095
mathematics	7	372	686
men	7	303	581
women	0	69	105

continued on the next page

Table 3.26 continued

	Black	White	All Races
military sciences	0	0	0
men	0	0	0
women	0	0	0
multi/interdisciplinary studies	6	204	272
men	4	115	170
women	2	89	102
parks and recreation	4	254	36
men	3	14	23
women	1	10	13
philosophy and religion	9	393	454
men	9	310	363
women	0	83	91
physical sciences	35	2,431	3,382
men	26	2,042	2,836
women	9	389	546
protective services	1	28	34
men	1	4	28
women	0	4	6
psychology	113	2,544	2,864
men	51	1,308	1,474
women	62	1,236	1,390
public affairs	35	283	374
men	16	130	184
women	19	153	190
social sciences	112	1,969	1,828
men	67	1,262	1,916
women	45	707	912
theology	50	903	1,090
men	41	816	987
women	9	87	103

continued on the next page

Table 3.26 continued

	Black	White	All Races
visual and performing arts	15	582	672
men	7	343	392
women	8	239	280

SOURCE: U.S. Department of Education, Center for Education Statistics, Digest of Education Statistics, 1988, pp. 226-227, table 187.
ED 1.113\988

NOTES: 'All Races' includes other races not shown separately. Both 'White' and 'Black' exclude persons of Hispanic origin.

UNITS: Earned Doctor's degrees conferred in number of degrees.

Table 3.27 Educational Attainment: Years of School Completed by Persons 25 Years Old and Older, 1980 and 1987

	Black		White		All Races
	male	female	male	female	both Sexes
1980					
percent of the population completing:					
0-4 years elementary school	10.2%	6.7%	2.8%	2.5%	3.6%
5-7 years elementary school	12.0	11.6	6.0	5.6	6.7
8 years elementary school	6.7	7.3	8.0	8.4	8.0
1-3 years high school	20.5	22.9	13.6	15.5	15.3
4 years high school	28.3	30.0	31.8	39.1	34.6
1-3 years college	14.0	13.2	16.4	15.6	15.7
4 or more years college	8.4	8.3	21.3	13.3	16.2
median school years completed	12.0	12.0	12.5	12.6	12.5
1987					
percent of the population completing:					
0-4 years elementary school	5.9%	4.3%	2.1%	2.0%	2.4%
5-7 years elementary school	8.6	7.6	4.2	4.0	4.5
8 years elementary school	5.2	5.4	5.8	6.0	5.8
1-3 years high school	17.2	19.0	10.6	11.4	11.7
4 years high school	36.5	37.5	35.6	42.6	38.7
1-3 years college	15.5	15.8	17.2	17.3	17.1
4 or more years college	11.0	10.4	24.5	16.9	19.9
median school years completed	12.4	12.4	12.8	12.6	12.7

SOURCE: U.S. Bureau of the Census, Statistical Abstract of the United States, 1989, p. 131, table 212. C 3.134:989

NOTES: 'All Races' includes other races not shown separately.

UNITS: Percent as a percent of the population 25 years old and older.

Table 3.28 Highest Educational Level and Degree Earned, by Sex, Persons 18 Years Old and Older, Spring, 1984

	Black		White		All Races	
	male	female	male	female	male	female
All persons 18 years old and older	8,274	10,201	70,276	76,871	80,834	89,398
not high school graduate	3,263	3,870	16,606	19,249	20,448	23,876
high school graduate only	2,589	3,454	23,270	29,859	26,407	33,951
some college, no degree	1,589	1,640	13,444	12,811	15,444	14,857
vocational	70	184	919	1,850	1,023	2,082
Associate degree	197	285	2,498	2,610	2,804	2,964
Bachelor's degree	416	547	8,703	7,636	9,581	8,488
Master's degree	101	185	2,923	2,430	3,110	2,685
Professional degree	35	18	1,355	279	1,432	312
Doctor's degree	14	18	558	147	585	183

SOURCE: U.S. Department of Education, Center for Education Statistics, Digest of Education Statistics, 1988, p. 19, table 11 (data from U.S. Bureau of the Census, *Current Population Reports*, series P-70, #11). ED 1.113\988

NOTES: 'All Races' includes other races not shown separately.

UNITS: Persons in thousands, by highest educational level attained.

Table 3.29 Years of College Completed by Persons 25 - 34 Years Old, 1975 - 1988

	Black	White	All Races
1975			
percent completing:			
- one or more years	25.9%	40.4%	39.4%
- two or more years	19.4	33.2	32.2
- four or more years	10.7	22.2	21.4
1980			
percent completing:			
- one or more years	33.6%	47.2%	45.8%
- two or more years	24.9	38.9	37.6
- four or more years	12.4	25.4	24.1
1985			
percent completing:			
- one or more years	35.3%	46.8%	45.8%
- two or more years	28.0	38.7	37.8
- four or more years	13.7	24.8	23.8
1988			
percent completing:			
- one or more years	34.1%	45.6%	44.8%
- two or more years	26.9	38.1	37.4
- four or more years	13.1	24.5	23.7

SOURCE: U.S. Department of Education, Center for Education Statistics, 1989 Education Indicators, pp. 213-214, table 2:1-1.
ED 1.109:989

NOTES: 'All Races' includes other races not shown separately.

UNITS: Percent as a percent of all persons 25-34 years old.

Table 3.30 Highest Level of Education Attained by 1980 High School Seniors, by Socioeconomic Status, Spring 1986

	Black	White	All Races
All 1980 high school seniors	100.0%	100.0%	100.0%
percent with:			
no high school diploma	1.2	0.8	0.9
high school diploma	69.4	60.0	61.8
license	13.9	11.5	11.9
Associate degree	5.3	6.6	6.5
Bachelor's degree	9.9	20.2	18.2
graduate/professional degree	0.2	0.9	0.7
1980 high school seniors of lower socioeconomic status	100.0%	100.0%	100.0%
percent with:			
no high school diploma	1.4	0.9	1.2
high school diploma	73.0	75.1	74.1
license	12.7	12.2	12.3
Associate degree	5.1	5.0	5.5
Bachelor's degree	7.7	6.6	6.6
graduate/professional degree	0.1	0.3	0.2
1980 high school seniors of middle socioeconomic status	100.0%	100.0%	na
percent with:			
no high school diploma	0.3	0.3	na
high school diploma	67.5	62.0	na
license	14.7	13.0	na
Associate degree	6.5	8.0	na
Bachelor's degree	10.7	16.3	na
graduate/professional degree	0.3	0.4	na

continued on the next page

Table 3.30 continued

	Black	White	All Races
1980 high school seniors of upper socioeconomic status	100.0%	100.0%	100.0%
percent with:			
no high school diploma	*	*	*
high school diploma	56.3	44.9	45.7
license	12.4	8.6	8.7
Associate degree	5.4	6.2	6.3
Bachelor's degree	25.5	38.2	37.3
graduate/professional degree	0.4	2.2	2.2

SOURCE: U.S. Department of Education, Center for Education Statistics, Digest of Education Statistics, 1988, p. 248-249, tables 214, 216. ED 1.113\988

NOTES: 'All Races' includes other races not shown separately. Data as of Spring, 1986. Both 'Black' and 'White' exclude persons of Hispanic origin. 'No high school diploma' includes seniors who dropped out after the Spring, 1980 survey; 'license' includes persons who earned a certificate for completing a program of study. Socioeconomic status was measured by a composite score based on parental education, family income, father's occupation, and household characteristics in 1980.

UNITS: Percent as a percent of all high school seniors in Spring, 1980. *Less than 0.05%.

Table 4.01 Black Elected Public Officials, by Type of Office Held, 1970 - 1988

	education	law enforcement	city & county offices	US & state legislatures	total
1970 (February)	368	213	719	179	1,479
1971 (March)	471	274	909	216	1,870
1972 (March)	676	263	1,112	224	2,275
1973 (April)	777	334	1,268	256	2,635
1974 (April)	804	340	1,607	256	3,007
1975 (April)	951	387	1,885	299	3,522
1976 (April)	1,008	387	2,284	299	4,006
1977 (July)	1,066	415	2,509	316	4,342
1978 (July)	1,154	451	2,616	316	4,544
1979 (July)	1,155	458	2,675	315	4,636
1980 (July)	1,232	491	2,871	326	4,963
1981 (July)	1,293	534	2,914	343	5,109
1982 (July)	1,309	573	3,017	342	5,241
1983 (July)	1,430	620	3,283	386	5,719
1984 (January)	1,445	657	3,367	396	5,865
1985 (January)	1,531	685	3,689	407	6,312
1986 (January)	1,498	676	3,800	410	6,384
1987 (January)	1,542	727	3,949	428	6,646
1988 (January)	1,542	738	4,089	424	6,793

SOURCE: U.S. Bureau of the Census, Statistical Abstract of the United States, 1989, p. 255, table 429 (data from Joint Center for Political Studies, *Black Elected Officials: A National Roster*). C 3.134:989

NOTES: 'U.S. and state legislatures' includes elected state administrators; 'city & county officials' includes county commissioners and councilmen, mayors, vice-mayors, aldermen, regional officials and others; 'law enforcement' includes judges, magistrates, sheriffs, justices of the peace, and others; 'education' includes members of state education agencies, college boards, school boards, and others.

UNITS: Number of Black elected public officials.

Table 4.02 Members of Congress, 1970 - 1989

	Black	White	All Races
House of Representatives			
94th Congress, 1975	15	420	435
95th Congress, 1977	16	419	"
96th Congress, 1979	16	419	"
97th Congress, 1981	17	418	"
98th Congress, 1983	21	414	"
99th Congress, 1985	22	413	"
100th Congress, 1987	23	412	"
101st Congress, 1989	25	410	"
Senate			
94th Congress, 1975	1	99	100
95th Congress, 1977	1	99	"
96th Congress, 1979	0	100	"
97th Congress, 1981	0	100	"
98th Congress, 1983	0	100	"
99th Congress, 1985	0	100	"
100th Congress, 1987	0	100	"
101st Congress, 1989	0	100	"

SOURCE: U.S. Bureau of the Census, Statistical Abstract of the United States, 1989, p. 252, table 423 (data from Congressional Quarterly, Inc.). C 3.134:989

NOTES: 'All Races' includes other races not shown separately.

UNITS: Number of members of the House and Senate respectively, as shown.

Table 4.03 Voting Age Population, Registration, and Voting, 1972 - 1986

	Black	White	All Races
Voting age population			
1972	13.5	121.2	136.2
1974	14.2	125.1	141.3
1976	14.9	129.3	146.5
1978	15.6	133.4	151.6
1980	16.4	137.7	157.1
1982	17.6	143.6	165.5
1984	18.4	146.8	170.0
1986	19.0	149.9	173.9
1988	19.7	152.8	178.1
Presidential election years			
percent reporting registration			
1972	65.5%	73.4%	72.3%
1976	58.5	68.3	66.7
1980	60.0	68.4	66.9
1984	66.3	69.6	68.3
1988	64.5	67.9	66.6
percent reporting voting			
1972	52.1%	64.5%	63.0%
1976	48.7	60.9	59.2
1980	50.5	60.9	59.2
1984	55.8	61.4	59.9
1988	51.5	59.1	57.4

continued on the next page

Table 4.03 continued

	Black	White	All Races
Congressional election years			
percent reporting registration			
1974	54.9%	63.5%	62.6%
1978	57.1	63.8	62.6
1982	59.1	65.6	64.1
1986	64.0	65.3	64.3
percent reporting voting			
1974	33.8%	46.3%	44.7%
1978	37.2	47.3	45.9
1982	43.0	49.9	48.5
1986	43.2	47.0	46.0

SOURCE: U.S. Bureau of the Census, Statistical Abstract of the United States, 1989, p. 257, table 432 (data from U.S. Bureau of the Census, *Current Population Reports*, Series P-20). C 3.134:989
U.S. Bureau of the Census, Current Population Reports: Voting and Registration in the Election of November, 1988, Series P-20, #440, pp. 48-49, table 8. C 3.186/3-2:989

NOTES: 'All Races' includes other races not shown separately.

UNITS: Voting age population in millions of persons; percent reporting registration and percent reporting voting as a percent of the voting age population.

Table 4.04 Voting Age Population, Selected Characteristics, 1986

	Black	White	All Races
Voting age population, 1986			
by age			
total 18 years and over	19,020	149,899	178,890
18-20 years old	1,601	8,793	10,740
21-24 years old	2,050	13,164	15,685
25-34 years old	5,067	35,446	41,910
35-44 years old	3,468	28,436	33,017
45-54 years old	2,430	19,686	22,873
55-64 years old	2.086	19,391	21,952
65-74 years old	1,467	15,334	17,075
75 years and over	851	9,648	10,637
by sex			
male	8,463	71,553	82,364
female	10,557	78,346	91,526
by years of school completed			
elementary			
0-4 years of school	828	2,804	3,884
5-7 years of school	1,272	5,315	6,798
8 years of school	933	7,833	8,946
high school			
1-3 years high school	3,685	17,234	21,366
4 years high school	6,986	60,053	68,500
college			
1-3 years college	3,494	28,491	33,030
4 years college	1,220	16,919	18,971
5 or more years college	603	11,249	12,345

continued on the next page

Table 4.04 continued

	Black	White	All Races
by family income			
under $5,000	2,231	4,504	6,999
$5,000-$9,999	2,853	9,944	13,272
$10,000-$14,999	2,309	13,484	16,340
$15,000-$19,999	2,031	12,581	15,043
$20,000-$24,999	1,311	12,769	14,460
$25,000-$34,999	2,021	23,056	25,742
$35,000-$49,999	1,463	21,914	24,090
$50,000 and over	776	20,023	21,515
income not reported	403	4,179	4,695

SOURCE: U.S. Bureau of the Census, Current Population Reports: Voting and Registration in the Election of November, 1986, Series P-20, #414, pp. 14-15, table 2; pp. 29-30, table 5; p. 33, table 8. C 3.186/3-2:986

NOTES: 'All Races' includes other races not shown separately.

UNITS: Voting age population in thousands of persons.

Table 4.05 Selected Characteristics of Persons Registered to Vote, 1986

	Black	White	All Races
Persons registered to vote, 1986			
by age			
total 18 years and over	64.0%	65.3%	64.3%
18-20 years old	38.9	35.3	35.4
21-24 years old	51.7	46.4	46.6
25-34 years old	60.1	56.3	55.8
35-44 years old	69.8	68.9	67.9
45-54 years old	72.5	73.3	72.1
55-64 years old	76.8	78.4	77.6
65-74 years old	74.3	80.4	79.3
75 years and over	66.2	73.9	73.0
by sex			
male	61.2%	64.6%	63.4%
female	66.2	65.9	65.0
by years of school completed			
elementary			
0-4 years of school	54.8%	32.0%	35.5%
5-7 years of school	61.1	45.4	47.6
8 years of school	60.3	59.7	59.3
high school			
1-3 years high school	57.1	52.0	52.4
4 years high school	63.1	63.6	62.9
college			
1-3 years college	68.8	71.2	70.0
4 years college	76.1	77.7	75.8
5 or more years college	87.7	82.2	80.8

continued on the next page

Table 4.05 continued

	Black	White	All Races
by households income			
under $5,000	54.8%	43.2%	46.3%
$5,000-$9,999	58.3	51.5	51.8
$10,000-$14,999	62.2	60.3	59.6
$15,000-$19,999	66.5	63.6	63.1
$20,000-$24,999	70.3	64.6	64.4
$25,000-$34,999	71.0	68.4	67.9
$35,000-$49,999	74.9	73.7	72.7
$50,000 and over	72.7	77.6	76.3
income not reported	61.3	62.0	61.2

SOURCE: U.S. Bureau of the Census, Current Population Reports: Voting and Registration in the Election of November, 1986, Series P-20, #414, pp. 14-15, table 2; pp. 29-30, table 5; p. 33, table 8. C 3.186/3-2:986

NOTES: 'All Races' includes other races not shown separately.

UNITS: Person reporting registration to vote as a percent of the voting age population, 100.0%.

Table 4.06 Selected Characteristics of Persons Voting, 1986

	Black	White	All Races
Persons voting, 1986			
by age			
total 18 years and over	43.2%	47.0%	46.0%
18-20 years old	20.6	18.4	18.6
21-24 years old	28.6	23.8	24.2
25-34 years old	36.9	35.5	35.1
35-44 years old	47.5	50.4	49.3
45-54 years old	54.3	55.8	54.8
55 64 years old	59.3	63.6	62.7
65-74 years old	57.1	66.3	65.1
75 years and over	46.9	54.9	54.0
by sex			
male	41.8%	46.9%	45.8%
female	44.4	47.1	46.1
by years of school completed			
elementary			
0-4 years of school	35.4%	18.6%	21.4%
5-7 years of school	39.1	27.2	29.1
8 years of school	39.4	40.7	40.3
high school			
1-3 years high school	35.0	34.0	33.8
4 years high school	41.8	44.9	44.1
college			
1-3 years college	47.8	51.0	49.9
4 years college	60.4	60.9	59.4
5 or more years college	74.1	68.4	67.2

continued on the next page

Table 4.06 continued

	Black	White	All Races
by households income			
under $5,000	30.1%	24.7%	26.0%
$5,000-$9,999	38.3	33.8	34.0
$10,000-$14,999	40.4	41.9	41.1
$15,000-$19,999	46.0	45.7	45.1
$20,000-$24,999	50.0	46.5	46.2
$25,000-$34,999	47.9	50.8	50.0
$35,000-$49,999	56.1	55.5	54.8
$50,000 and over	54.0	59.0	58.0
income not reported	43.7	46.2	45.6

SOURCE: U.S. Bureau of the Census, Current Population Reports: Voting and Registration in the Election of November, 1986, Series P-20, #414, pp. 14-15, table 2; pp. 29-30, table 5; p. 33, table 8. C 3.186/3-2:986

NOTES: 'All Races' includes other races not shown separately.

UNITS: Persons reporting voting as a percent of the voting age population, 100.0%.

Table 4.07 Voting Age Population, Selected Characteristics, 1988

	Black	White	All Races
Voting age population, 1988			
by age			
total 18 years and over	19,692	152,848	178,098
18-20 years old	1,543	8,824	10,742
21-24 years old	2,024	12,268	14,827
25-34 years old	5,262	35,914	42,677
35-44 years old	3,778	30,139	35,186
45-54 years old	2,548	20,903	24,277
55-64 years old	2,114	18,892	21,585
65-74 years old	1,526	15,771	17,578
75 years and over	896	10,137	11,226
by sex			
male	8,777	73,119	84,531
female	10,915	79,730	93,568
by years of school completed			
elementary			
0-4 years of school	789	2,847	3,958
5-7 years of school	1,151	5,498	6,933
8 years of school	901	7,205	8,254
high school			
1-3 years high school	3,438	17,185	21,052
4 years high school	7,846	60,565	70,033
college			
1-3 years college	3,593	29,624	34,264
4 years college	1,310	17,721	20,431
5 or more years college	664	12,204	13,473
by labor force status			
in civilian labor force	13,066	102,873	119,645
employed	11,751	98,580	113,836
unemployed	1,315	4,302	5,809

continued on the next page

Table 4.07 continued

	Black	White	All Races
by occupation			
managerial and professional	1,786	27,044	29,287
technical, sales, and administrative support	3,339	30,348	34,761
service occupations	2,571	11,533	14,627
farming, forestry, fishing	219	2,900	3,171
precision production, craft and repair	1,013	12,393	13,796
operators, fabricators, laborers	2,823	14,353	17,653
by households income			
under $5,000	1,978	3,726	5,954
$5,000-$9,999	2,409	8,177	10,929
$10,000-$14,999	2,196	12,990	15,682
$15,000-$19,999	3,021	21,184	25,009
$20,000-$24,999	1,111	10,839	12,296
$25,000-$34,999	1,696	20,634	22,995
$35,000-$49,999	1,395	22,293	24,452
$50,000 and over	727	15,555	16,990
income not reported	1,081	8,250	9,594

SOURCE: U.S. Bureau of the Census, Current Population Reports: Voting and Registration in the Election of November, 1988, Series P-20, #440, pp. 16-17, table 2; pp. 48-49, table 8; pp. 56-62, tables 10, 11; p. 65, table 13. C 3.186/3-2:989

NOTES: 'All Races' includes other races not shown separately.

UNITS: Voting age population in thousands of persons.

Table 4.08 Selected Characteristics of Persons Registered to Vote, 1988

	Black	White	All Races
Persons registered to vote, 1988			
by age			
total 18 years and over	64.5%	67.9%	66.6%
18-20 years old	42.9	45.9	44.9
21-24 years old	55.1	50.8	50.6
25-34 years old	57.9	59.1	57.8
35-44 years old	67.9	70.7	69.3
45-54 years old	74.6	75.1	74.0
55-64 years old	74.5	78.4	77.2
65-74 years old	78.9	81.6	81.0
75 years and over	70.5	75.3	74.4
by sex			
male	60.9%	66.8%	65.2%
female	67.4	69.0	67.8
by years of school completed			
elementary			
0-4 years of school	52.3%	31.4%	34.3%
5-7 years of school	59.9	42.6	44.5
8 years of school	59.4	56.3	56.2
high school			
1-3 years high school	57.7	52.4	52.8
4 years high school	62.1	65.7	64.6
college			
1-3 years college	72.1	74.9	73.5
4 years college	78.7	83.3	80.8
5 or more years college	87.8	88.5	86.6
by labor force status			
in civilian labor force	65.5%	67.3%	66.3%
employed	66.3	68.1	67.1
unemployed	57.5	49.0	50.4

continued on the next page

Table 4.08 continued

	Black	White	All Races
by occupation			
managerial and professional	81.6%	82.2%	81.2%
technical, sales, and administrative support	69.1	72.4	71.2
service occupations	60.2	57.7	57.3
farming, forestry, fishing	46.1	63.0	61.7
precision production, craft and repair	63.4	57.5	57.1
operators, fabricators, laborers	61.7	51.0	52.0
by households income			
under $5,000	59.5%	43.0%	47.6%
$5,000-$9,999	62.5	51.0	52.8
$10,000-$14,999	60.4	58.0	57.4
$15,000-$19,999	63.2	64.4	63.2
$20,000-$24,999	67.0	68.2	67.4
$25,000-$34,999	73.7	72.8	71.9
$35,000-$49,999	78.2	78.8	77.9
$50,000 and over	79.9	83.4	81.8
income not reported	50.5	63.9	61.5

SOURCE: U.S. Bureau of the Census, Current Population Reports: Voting and Registration in the Election of November, 1988, Series P-20, #440, pp. 16-17, table 2; pp. 48-49, table 8; pp. 56-62, tables 10, 11; p. 65, table 13. C 3.186/3-2:989

NOTES: 'All Races' includes other races not shown separately.

UNITS: Persons registered to vote as a percent of the voting age population, 100.0%.

Table 4.09 Selected Characteristics of Persons Voting, 1988

	Black	White	All Races
Persons voting, 1988			
by age			
total 18 years and over	51.5%	59.1%	57.4%
18-20 years old	27.8	34.5	33.2
21-24 years old	40.5	38.7	38.3
25-34 years old	41.8	50.0	48.0
35-44 years old	56.5	62.9	61.2
45-54 years old	64.3	68.0	66.6
55-64 years old	65.4	70.6	69.3
65-74 years old	69.5	73.8	73.0
75 years and over	53.3	63.6	62.2
by sex			
male	48.2%	58.3%	56.4%
female	54.2	59.8	58.3
by years of school completed			
elementary			
0-4 years of school	38.1%	22.0%	24.3%
5-7 years of school	46.2	32.4	34.0
8 years of school	48.1	45.0	44.9
high school			
1-3 years high school	43.0	41.5	41.3
4 years high school	48.4	56.2	54.7
college			
1-3 years college	59.2	66.3	64.5
4 years college	70.2	77.1	74.6
5 or more years college	84.1	84.1	82.1
by labor force status			
in civilian labor force	52.8%	58.9%	57.5%
employed	54.1	59.8	58.4
unemployed	41.5	38.3	38.6

continued on the next page

Table 4.09 continued

	Black	White	All Races
by occupation			
managerial and professional	74.2%	76.2%	75.2%
technical, sales, and administrative support	57.5	64.1	62.7
service occupations	47.4	48.1	47.2
farming, forestry, fishing	30.8	51.6	49.8
precision production, craft and repair	48.0	47.9	47.2
operators, fabricators, laborers	47.6	40.8	41.3
by households income			
under $5,000	43.8%	31.4%	34.7%
$5,000-$9,999	47.6	40.4	41.3
$10,000-$14,999	47.3	48.7	47.7
$15,000-$19,999	50.0	55.1	53.5
$20,000-$24,999	53.1	58.9	57.8
$25,000-$34,999	61.1	65.1	64.0
$35,000-$49,999	70.4	71.2	70.3
$50,000 and over	71.7	77.2	75.6
income not reported	43.0	56.6	54.2

SOURCE: U.S. Bureau of the Census, Current Population Reports: Voting and Registration in the Election of November, 1988, Series P-20, #440, pp. 16-17, table 2; pp. 48-49, table 8; pp. 56-62, tables 10, 11; p. 65, table 13. C 3.186/3-2:989

NOTES: 'All Races' includes other races not shown separately.

UNITS: Persons voting as a percent of the voting age population, 100.0%.

Table 5.01 Victimization Rates for Personal Crimes, 1975 - 1987

	Black victims	White victims	victims of All Races
1975	43	32	33
1976	44	31	33
1977	42	33	34
1978	41	33	34
1979	42	34	35
1980	41	32	33
1981	50	33	35
1982	44	33	34
1983	41	30	31
1984	41	30	31
1985	38	29	30
1986	33	28	28
1987	40	27	29

SOURCE: U.S. Bureau of the Census, Statistical Abstract of the United States, 1989, p. 171, table 287 (data from *the National Crime Survey*). C 3.134:989

U.S. Department of Justice, Bureau of Justice Statistics, Criminal Victimization in the United States, 1987, p. 16, table 3; p. 18, table 6 (data from the *National Crime Survey*). J 29.9/2:987

NOTES: 'Victims of All Races' includes victims of other races not shown separately. Personal crimes include completed and attempted rape, robbery, assault, and larceny, but exclude homicide.

UNITS: Rates per 1,000 persons, 12 years old and over.

Table 5.02 Victimization Rates for Personal Crimes, by Type of Crime, 1987

	Black	White	All Races
Crimes of violence	39.6	27.3	28.6
completed	16.3	9.8	10.5
attempted	23.3	17.5	18.1
rape	1.8	0.5	0.7
robbery	11.8	4.4	5.2
completed	8.3	2.8	3.4
- with injury	2.4	1.3	1.4
from serious assault	1.1	0.6	0.7
from minor assault	1.3	0.7	0.7
- without injury	6.0	1.5	2.0
attempted	3.4	1.6	1.8
- with injury	1.4	0.4	0.5
from serious assault	0.4*	0.2	0.2
from minor assault	1.0	0.2	0.3
- without injury	2.0	1.2	1.3
assault	26.1	22.3	22.7
aggravated	12.0	7.2	7.8
- completed with injury	3.5	2.3	2.4
- attempted with weapon	8.6	4.9	5.4
simple	14.0	15.1	14.9
- completed with injury	3.9	4.4	4.4
- attempted without weapon	10.1	10.7	10.5
Crimes of theft	62.9	68.2	67.5
completed	58.4	64.0	63.3
attempted	4.5	4.2	4.2
personal larceny with contact	4.3	2.3	2.6
purse snatching	1.4	0.8	0.9
pocket picking	2.9	1.5	1.6

continued on the next page

Table 5.02 continued

	Black	White	All Races
Crimes of theft - continued			
personal larceny without contact	58.6	66.0	64.9
completed	54.6	62.0	61.0
- less than $50.	22.1	27.6	26.9
- $50 or more	27.4	31.8	31.2
- amount not available	5.2	2.7	3.0
attempted	4.0	3.9	3.9

SOURCE: U.S. Department of Justice, Bureau of Justice Statistics, Criminal Victimization in the United States, 1987, p. 16, table 3; p. 18, table 6 (data from the *National Crime Survey*). J 29.9/2:987

NOTES: 'All Races' includes other races not shown separately. *Based on 10 or fewer sample cases.

UNITS: Rates per 1,000 persons, 12 years old and over.

Table 5.03 Victimization Rates for Personal Crimes, by Sex of the Victim, 1987

	Black		White		All Races	
	male	female	male	female	male	female
Crimes of violence	49.1	31.6	35.0	20.1	36.3	21.6
completed	17.5	15.2	12.0	7.7	12.5	8.8
attempted	31.6	16.4	23.0	12.3	23.8	12.8
rape	0.0*	3.3	0.1*	0.9	0.1*	1.3
robbery	15.2	8.9	5.7	3.2	6.6	3.9
completed	9.2	7.6	3.4	2.3	4.0	2.9
- with injury	2.9	1.9	1.6	1.0	1.8	1.1
- without injury	6.3	5.7	1.7	1.3	2.2	1.9
attempted	6.0	1.3	2.3	0.9	2.7	0.9
- with injury	2.2	0.8*	0.4	0.4	0.6	0.4
- without injury	3.8	0.5*	1.9	0.6	2.1	0.5
assault	33.9	19.5	29.2	15.9	29.5	16.4
aggravated	18.3	6.8	10.5	4.1	11.4	4.4
- completed with injury	4.9	2.3	3.5	1.2	3.7	1.3
- attempted with a weapon	13.4	4.5	7.1	2.9	7.8	3.1
simple	15.6	12.7	18.7	11.8	18.1	12.0
- completed with injury	3.4	4.3	5.1	3.8	4.8	4.0
- attempted without a weapon	12.2	8.4	13.6	8.0	13.3	8.0
Crimes of theft	70.6	56.4	72.5	64.3	72.0	63.3
completed	64.1	53.7	67.7	60.5	67.1	59.7
attempted	6.6	2.8	4.7	3.8	4.9	3.6
personal larceny with contact	4.4	4.2	1.9	2.7	2.2	2.9
personal larceny without contact	66.2	52.2	70.6	61.6	69.8	60.3
- completed	59.6	50.4	65.9	58.4	64.9	57.4
- attempted	6.6	1.8	4.7	3.2	4.9	2.9

continued on the next page

Table 5.03 continued

SOURCE: U.S. Department of Justice, Bureau of Justice Statistics, Criminal Victimization in the United States, 1987, p. 16, table 3; p. 19, table 7 (data from the *National Crime Survey*). J 29.9/2:987

NOTES: 'All Races' includes other races not shown separately. *Based on 10 or fewer sample cases.

UNITS: Rates per 1,000 persons, 12 years old and over.

Table 5.04 Victimization Rates for Personal Crimes, by Age of the Victim, 1987

	Black	White	All Races
Persons 12-15 years old			
crimes of violence	78.2	51.7	55.6
completed	34.4	23.3	24.4
attempted	43.8	25.5	31.2
crimes of theft	98.1	111.2	108.1
completed	93.9	108.0	104.8
attempted	4.2*	3.2	3.2
Persons 16-19 years old			
crimes of violence	77.3	66.4	67.5
completed	20.6	24.7	23.9
attempted	56.8	41.7	43.6
crimes of theft	98.6	124.5	121.5
completed	87.0	120.0	115.9
attempted	11.6	4.5	5.6
Persons 20-24 years old			
crimes of violence	53.0	65.1	62.5
completed	21.6	21.0	20.9
attempted	31.4	44.1	41.5
crimes of theft	87.1	113.2	108.7
completed	78.4	105.1	100.3
attempted	8.7	8.2	8.4
Persons 25-34 years old			
crimes of violence	49.7	31.7	33.5
completed	23.6	11.7	13.1
attempted	26.1	19.9	20.4
crimes of theft	67.4	80.2	78.3
completed	63.9	74.3	72.8
attempted	3.6	5.9	5.5

continued on the next page

Table 5.04 continued

	Black	White	All Races
Persons 35-49 years old			
crimes of violence	18.6	18.5	18.5
completed	12.4	5.4	5.7
attempted	6.3	13.1	12.8
crimes of theft	54.0	64.9	63.3
completed	49.9	60.7	59.2
attempted	4.1	4.2	4.1
Persons 50-64 years old			
crimes of violence	12.8	7.9	8.6
completed	9.2	2.7	3.4
attempted	3.6*	5.2	5.2
crimes of theft	36.3	37.4	36.8
completed	34.2	34.6	34.1
attempted	2.1*	2.8	2.7
Persons 65 years old and over			
crimes of violence	14.3	4.6	5.5
completed	4.7*	2.3	2.5
attempted	9.6	2.3	2.9
crimes of theft	17.9	18.7	18.6
completed	17.9	17.4	17.5
attempted	0.0*	1.3	1.2

SOURCE: U.S. Department of Justice, Bureau of Justice Statistics, Criminal Victimization in the United States, 1987, p. 17, table 4; pp. 20-21, table 9 (data from the *National Crime Survey*).
J 29.9/2:987

NOTES: 'All Races' includes other races not shown separately. *Based on 10 or fewer sample cases.

UNITS: Rates per 1,000 persons, 12 years old and over.

Table 5.05 Victimization Rates for Personal Crimes, by Age and Sex of the Victim, 1987

	Black		White		All Races	
	male	female	male	female	male	female
Crimes of violence						
persons 12-15 years old	90.8	65.2	65.7	37.1	68.4	42.1
persons 16-19 years old	101.0	54.4	89.4	42.9	90.1	44.6
persons 20-24 years old	49.2	56.3	82.1	48.5	76.4	49.1
persons 25-34 years old	62.5	38.8	37.3	25.9	39.7	27.5
persons 35-49 years old	21.1	16.6	22,9	14.2	22.6	14.7
persons 50-64 years old	22.9	5.0*	9.7	6.1	11.1	16.3
persons 65 years old and over	15.4*	13.6	4.5	4.6	5.5	5.4
Crimes of theft						
persons 12-15 years old	88.3	108.1	114.0	108.2	109.2	106.8
persons 16-19 years old	119.2	78.6	125.3	123.7	125.8	117.0
persons 20-24 years old	104.5	72.3	125.1	101.7	120.6	97.3
persons 25-34 years old	82.0	55.0	85.2	75.2	84.3	72.4
persons 35-49 years old	51.5	56.0	65.2	64.6	63.5	63.2
persons 50-64 years old	37.8	35.1	38.0	36.9	37.5	36.2
persons 65 years old and over	19.9	16.5	18.1	19.1	18.2	18.9

SOURCE: U.S. Department of Justice, Bureau of Justice Statistics, Criminal Victimization in the United States, 1987, p. 18-19, table 5; p. 22, table 10 (data from the *National Crime Survey*). J 29.9/2:987

NOTES: 'All Races' includes other races not shown separately. *Based on 10 or fewer sample cases.

UNITS: Rates per 1,000 persons, 12 years old and over.

Table 5.06 Victimization Rates for Personal Crimes, by Annual Household Income of the Victim, 1987

	Black	White	All Races
Households with incomes of:			
Less than $7,500.			
crimes of violence	57.8	53.1	53.8
completed	25.0	22.3	23.0
attempted	32.8	30.8	30.8
crimes of theft	54.5	75.8	70.0
completed	50.3	72.4	66.4
attempted	4.2	3.3	3.6
$7,500.-$9,999.			
crimes of violence	33.4	42.1	40.0
completed	18.2	16.9	17.3
attempted	15.2	25.3	22.7
crimes of theft	76.2	60.9	64.8
completed	69.3	56.8	60.3
attempted	6.9*	4.0	4.4
$10,000.-$14,999.			
crimes of violence	51.0	32.0	34.5
completed	22.5	11.1	12.9
attempted	28.5	20.9	21.7
crimes of theft	82.7	56.5	59.8
completed	70.9	53.1	55.2
attempted	11.8	3.4	4.7
$15,000.-$24,999.			
crimes of violence	24.6	25.1	25.2
completed	9.1	7.8	8.2
attempted	15.5	17.4	17.1
crimes of theft	60.1	65.7	65.2
completed	57.7	61.1	60.9
attempted	2.4*	4.6	4.4

continued on the next page

Table 5.06 continued

	Black	White	All Races
$25,000.-$29,999.			
crimes of violence	28.2	26.8	27.0
completed	8.0*	10.4	10.0
attempted	20.2	16.4	17.0
crimes of theft	55.0	70.5	69.0
completed	55.0	65.4	64.9
attempted	0.0*	4.5	4.0
$30,000.-$49,999.			
crimes of violence	23.1	20.4	20.7
completed	11.1	6.7	6.9
attempted	12.0	13.6	13.8
crimes of theft	63.4	69.1	68.9
completed	59.3	65.9	65.3
attempted	4.1*	3.7	3.6
$50,000. or more			
crimes of violence	23.6	20.5	20.5
completed	7.7*	6.0	6.0
attempted	15.9	14.5	14.5
crimes of theft	67.9	84.5	83.0
completed	64.7	78.7	77.5
attempted	3.2*	5.8	5.5

SOURCE: U.S. Department of Justice, Bureau of Justice Statistics, Criminal Victimization in the United States, 1987, pp. 26-27, tables 14-15, (data from the *National Crime Survey*). J 29.9/2:987

NOTES: 'All Races' includes other races not shown separately. *Based on 10 or fewer sample cases.

UNITS: Rates per 1,000 persons, 12 years old and over.

Table 5.07 Personal Crimes Involving Strangers, by Sex of the Victim, 1987

	Black		White		All Races	
	male	female	male	female	male	female
Crimes of violence	59.9%	52.8%	66.1%	42.3%	65.2%	44.1%
completed	59.5	54.4	64.0	37.9	62.7	41.7
attempted	60.2	51.3	67.2	45.0	66.4	45.7
rape	0*	70.3	55.4*	45.7	55.4*	54.3
robbery	77.9	87.1	85.1	69.4	83.1	74.9
with injury	71.9	83.3	82.3	65.5	79.1	69.4
without injury	80.9	88.7	86.6	72.2	85.2	78.2
assault	51.9	34.2	62.5	36.6	61.2	36.0
aggravated assault	62.6	47.1	67.2	46.2	66.3	47.2
simple assault	39.4	27.3	59.8	33.3	57.9	31.9

SOURCE: U.S. Department of Justice, Bureau of Justice Statistics, Criminal Victimization in the United States, 1987, pp. 44-45, tables 35, 36 (data from the *National Crime Survey*). J 29.9/2:987

NOTES: 'All Races' includes other races not shown separately. *Based on 10 or fewer sample cases.

UNITS: Percent as a percent of all personal crimes, 100.0%.

Table 5.08 Victimization Rates for Crimes Against Households, 1975 - 1987

	Black households	White households	All households
Burglary			
1975	129	87	92
1980	115	81	84
1985	83	60	63
1987	94	57	61
Larceny			
1975	115	127	125
1980	134	125	127
1985	120	95	97
1987	116	91	94
Motor vehicle theft			
1975	27	19	19
1980	25	16	17
1985	22	13	14
1987	21	15	16

SOURCE: U.S. Bureau of the Census, Statistical Abstract of the United States, 1989, p. 171, table 288 (data from *the National Crime Survey*). C 3.134:989

U.S. Department of Justice, Bureau of Justice Statistics, Criminal Victimization in the United States, 1987, p. 35, table 20, (data from the *National Crime Survey*). J 29.9/2:987

NOTES: 'All households' includes households of other races not shown separately.

UNITS: Rates per 1,000 households.

Table 5.09 Households Touched by Crime, 1987

	Black households	White households	All households
All households	100.0%	100.0%	100.0%
All households touched by crime	27.8%	23.9%	24.4%
violent crime	5.8	4.4	4.6
rape	0.2	0.1	0.1
robbery	2.2	0.8	1.0
assault	3.8	3.7	3.7
theft	16.8	17.2	17.1
personal	9.6	11.2	11.0
household	9.4	7.7	7.9
burglary	7.9	4.8	5.2
motor vehicle theft	2.3	1.4	1.5

SOURCE: U.S. Bureau of the Census, Statistical Abstract of the United States, 1989, p. 171, table 289 (data from *the National Crime Survey*). C 3.134:989

NOTES: 'All households' includes households of other races not shown separately. A household is considered to be touched by crime if during the year it experienced a burglary, auto theft or household theft; or if a household member was raped, robbed, or assaulted, or was a victim of a personal theft, no matter where the crime occurred. Types of crimes will not add to total since each household may report as many crime categories as they experience.

UNITS: Percent of all households, 100.0%.

Table 5.10 Victimization Rates for Household Crimes, by Type of Crime, 1987

	Black households	White households	All households
All household crimes	232.0	163.6	171.4
completed	189.7	139.0	144.5
attempted	42.3	24.7	26.8
burglary	94.4	57.0	61.3
completed	66.1	44.0	46.6
- forcible entry	39.3	18.9	21.4
- unlawful entry without force	26.8	25.1	25.2
attempted forcible entry	28.3	13.0	14.7
household larceny	116.2	91.4	94.0
completed	110.2	84.8	87.4
- less than $50.	40.1	37.7	37.7
- $50. or more	61.5	42.3	44.5
- amount not known	8.5	4.8	5.2
attempted	6.0	6.7	6.6
motor vehicle theft	21.4	15.2	16.1
completed	13.4	10.2	10.6
attempted	8.0	5.0	5.6

SOURCE: U.S. Department of Justice, Bureau of Justice Statistics, Criminal Victimization in the United States, 1987, p. 35, table 20, (data from the *National Crime Survey*). J 29.9/2:987

NOTES: 'All households' includes households of other races not shown separately.

UNITS: Rates per 1,000 households.

Table 5.11 Victimization Rates for Household Crimes, by Annual Household Income, 1987

	Black	White	All Races
Household with incomes of:			
Less than $7,500.			
burglary	105.8	80.6	86.3
larceny	108.3	97.0	98.9
motor vehicle theft	10.2	12.7	12.3
$7,500.-$9,999.			
burglary	158.4	55.8	73.6
larceny	153.2	78.4	90.1
motor vehicle theft	28.0	13.8	15.6
$10,000.-$14,999.			
burglary	104.4	65.8	70.6
larceny	111.0	86.8	89.3
motor vehicle theft	17.4	11.6	12.8
$15,000.-$24,999.			
burglary	83.2	54.3	56.9
larceny	108.3	96.8	97.3
motor vehicle theft	19.3	16.2	16.5
$25,000.-$29,999.			
burglary	85.0	52.8	55.7
larceny	138.5	99.3	102.0
motor vehicle theft	21.2*	15.7	16.3
$30,000.-$49,999.			
burglary	70.7	48.2	49.5
larceny	127.9	94.8	96.7
motor vehicle theft	37.6	16.6	18.1
$50,000. or more			
burglary	28.9*	52.1	51.6
larceny	106.7	95.3	96.4
motor vehicle theft	63.5	19.7	22.2

continued on the next page

Table 5.11 continued

SOURCE: U.S. Department of Justice, Bureau of Justice Statistics, Criminal Victimization in the United States, 1987, pp. 36-39, tables 24-27, (data from the *National Crime Survey*). J 29.9/2:987

NOTES: 'All Races' includes other races not shown separately. *Based on 10 or fewer sample cases.

UNITS: Rates per 1,000 households.

Table 5.12 Victimization Rates for Household Crimes: Type of Crime by Housing Tenure, 1987

	Black households	White households	All households
Owner households			
All household crimes	196.1	135.9	140.8
completed	164.0	117.5	121.1
attempted	32.2	18.4	19.7
burglary	66.5	46.2	47.8
completed	48.7	37.2	38.0
- forcible entry	28.1	16.7	17.7
- unlawful entry without force	20.7	20.4	20.4
attempted forcible entry	17.8	9.1	9.7
household larceny	106.7	77.9	80.3
completed	101.7	72.4	74.7
- less than $50.	39.0	33.6	33.9
- $50. or more	54.0	34.4	36.2
- amount not known	8.8	4.4	4.7
attempted	5.0	5.6	5.5
motor vehicle theft	22.9	11.7	12.7
completed	13.5	7.9	8.4
attempted	9.3	3.8	4.4
Renter households			
All household crimes	260.1	219.9	225.8
completed	209.9	182.5	186.2
attempted	50.2	37.4	39.6
burglary	116.3	78.8	85.3
completed	79.8	57.9	61.8
- forcible entry	48.1	23.4	28.0
- unlawful entry without force	31.7	34.4	33.8
attempted forcible entry	36.5	20.9	23.5

continued on the next page

Table 5.12 continued

	Black households	White households	All households
Renter households - continued			
household larceny	123.6	118.8	118.4
completed	116.8	109.9	109.9
- less than $50.	41.0	45.9	44.5
- $50. or more	67.5	58.3	59.2
- amount not known	8.3	5.7	6.1
attempted	6.8	8.9	8.5
motor vehicle theft	20.3	22.4	22.1
completed	13.3	14.8	14.5
attempted	6.9	7.6	7.7

SOURCE: U.S. Department of Justice, Bureau of Justice Statistics, Criminal Victimization in the United States, 1987, p. 40, table 29, (data from the *National Crime Survey*). J 29.9/2:987

NOTES: 'All households' includes households of other races not shown separately.

UNITS: Rates per 1,000 households.

Table 5.13 Lifetime Likelihood of Victimization by Crime, by Type of Crime and Number of Likely Victimizations

	Black	White	All Races
All violent crimes			
both sexes			
one or more victimizations	87%	82%	83%
one victimization	26	31	30
two victimization	27	26	27
three or more victimizations	34	24	25
male			
one or more victimizations	92	88	89
one victimization	21	25	24
two victimization	26	27	27
three or more victimizations	45	37	38
female			
one or more victimizations	81	71	73
one victimization	31	36	35
two victimization	26	22	23
three or more victimizations	24	13	14
All completed violent crimes			
both sexes			
one or more victimizations	53%	41%	42%
one victimization	35	31	32
two victimization	13	8	9
three or more victimizations	4	2	2

continued on the next page

Table 5.13 continued

	Black	White	All Races
rape (female victimization)			
one or more victimizations	11%	8%	8%
one victimization	10	7	8
two victimization	1	*	*
three or more victimizations	*	*	*
robbery			
one or more victimizations	51	27	30
one victimization	35	23	25
two victimization	12	4	5
three or more victimizations	4	*	1
assault			
one or more victimizations	73	74	74
one victimization	35	35	35
two victimization	25	24	24
three or more victimizations	12	16	15
Personal theft			
both sexes			
one or more victimizations	99	99	99
one victimization	5	9	4
two victimization	12	9	8
three or more victimizations	81	87	87
male			
one or more victimizations	99	99	99
one victimization	5	3	3
two victimization	10	8	8
three or more victimizations	84	88	88
female			
one or more victimizations	98	99	99
one victimization	7	4	4
two victimization	15	10	10
three or more victimizations	76	86	84

continued on the next page

Table 5.13 continued

SOURCE: U.S. Department of Justice, Bureau of Justice Statistics, Technical Report: Lifetime Likelihood of Victimization, p. 2, table 1, (data from the *National Crime Survey*). J.29.15:v66

NOTES: 'All Races' includes other races not shown separately.

UNITS: Percent of persons who will be victimized by crime, starting at 12 years of age. *less than 0.5%.

Table 5.14 Child Maltreatment Cases Reported, 1976 - 1984

	Black	White	All Races
Child			
1976	19.8%	61.1%	100.0%
1980	18.8	69.4	"
1981	21.7	67.8	"
1982	21.7	64.9	"
1983	19.7	67.5	"
1984	21.8	67.0	"
Caretaker			
1976	17.0%	65.3%	100.0%
1980	16.6	72.7	"
1981	18.6	73.0	"
1982	19.1	70.8	"
1983	17.5	73.1	"
1984	17.5	74.5	"
Perpetrator			
1976	17.7%	65.1%	100.0%
1980	17.6	72.0	"
1981	19.7	71.1	"
1982	19.7	69.0	"
1983	18.7	69.5	"
1984	19.1	69.9	"

SOURCE: U.S. Bureau of the Census, Statistical Abstract of the United States, 1989, p. 172, table 291 (data from the American Humane Association, National Study on Child Neglect and Abuse Reporting). C 3.134:989

NOTES: 'All Races' includes other races not shown separately.

UNITS: Percent, as a percent of total, 100.0%.

Table 5.15 Selected Characteristics of Murders and Nonnegligent Homicides, 1988

	Black	White	All Races
All murders and nonnegligent homicides, 1988	8,786	9,003	18,269
by age of the victim			
under 1 year old	97	136	240
1-4 years old	150	175	333
5-9 years old	58	90	152
10-14 years old	111	114	227
15-19 years old	1,011	661	1,722
20-24 years old	1,615	1,292	2,953
25-29 years old	1,793	1,461	3,321
30-34 years old	1.259	1,182	2,520
35-39 years old	881	932	1,855
40-44 years old	517	724	1,283
45-49 years old	298	452	771
50-54 years old	205	339	569
55-59 years old	164	299	472
60-64 years old	135	281	420
65-69 years old	130	239	382
70-74 years old	88	167	257
75 years old and older	155	320	484
age unknown	119	139	308
*race of the victim, by race of the offender**			
black victims	4,525	237	4,791
white victims	579	4,377	5,065
victims of all races	5,129	4,676	10,093

continued on the next page

Table 5.15 continued

SOURCE: U.S. Federal Bureau of Investigation, Crime in the United States, 1988, p. 11, (data from the Uniform Crime Reporting program). J 1.14/7:988

NOTES: 'All Races' includes other races not shown separately. *Data covers only those 10,093 murders and nonnegligent homicides in which therewas a single offender and single victim.

UNITS: Number of murders and nonnegligent homicides known to police.

Table 5.16 Law Enforcement Officers Killed, 1978 - 1987

	Black	White	All Races
1978	9%	91%	100% (93)
1979	9	88	" (106)
1980	13	86	" (104)
1981	14	85	" (91)
1982	15	84	" (92)
1983	13	84	" (98)
1984	14	85	" (72)
1985	10	88	" (78)
1986	11	89	" (66)
1987	10	90	" (73)

SOURCE: U.S. Department of Justice, Bureau of Justice Statistics, Sourcebook of Criminal Justice Statistics, 1988, p. 465, table 3.146, (data from Federal Bureau of Investigation, *Law Enforcement Officers Killed, {annual}*) J.29.9/6.988

NOTES: 'All Races' includes other races not shown separately.

UNITS: Percent distribution of law enforcement officers killed as a percent of total, 100.0% (total number of law enforcement officers killed shown in parenthesis).

Table 5.17 Arrests, by Offence Charged, 1985

	number of arrests			percent distribution		
	Black	White	All Races	Black	White	All Races
All arrests	2,721	7,338	10,239	26.6%	71.7%	100.0
Arrests for crime index crimes	713.3	1,365.6	2,118.5	33.7	64.5	"
arrests for violent crimes	202.1	221.3	429.3	47.1	51.5	"
arrests for property crimes	511.2	1,144.3	1,689.2	30.3	67.7	"
arrests for violent crimes:						
murder and nonnegligent homicide	7.6	7.8	15.6	48.4	50.1	"
forcible rape	14.7	16.5	31.6	46.5	52.2	"
robbery	73.9	44.8	119.9	61.7	37.4	"
aggravated assault	105.9	152.2	262.2	40.4	58.0	"
arrests for property crimes:						
burglary	110.1	265.1	380.6	28.9	69.7	"
larceny-theft	360.1	790.9	1,177.0	30.6	67.2	"
motor vehicle theft	37.2	75.6	114.9	32.4	65.8	"
arson	3.8	12.6	16.7	22.8	75.7	"

SOURCE: U.S. Department of Justice, Bureau of Justice Statistics, Sourcebook of Criminal Justice Statistics, 1986, p. 300, table 4.8, (data from the Uniform Crime Reporting program). J 29.9/6:986

NOTES: 'All Races' includes other races not shown separately. Crime index crimes are made up of the four violent crimes (murder and nonnegligent homicide, rape, robbery, and aggravated assault), and four property crimes (burglary, larceny-theft, motor vehicle theft, and arson) which are tracked by the FBI.

UNITS: Arrests in thousands of arrests; percent distribution as a percent of total, 100.0%

Table 5.18 Arrests, by Offence Charged, 1988

	number of arrests			percent distribution		
	Black	White	All Races	Black	White	All Races
All arrests	2,977	6,903	10,067	29.6%	68.6%	100.0%
Arrests for crime index crimes	753.0	1,315.7	2,109.9	35.7	62.4	"
arrests for violent crimes	213.6	236.3	456.9	46.8	51.7	
arrests for property crimes	539.4	1,079.4	1,653.1	32.6	65.3	"
arrests for violent crimes:						
murder and nonnegligent homicide	8.6	7.2	16.1	53.5	45.0	"
forcible rape	12.9	14.8	28.0	45.8	52.7	"
robbery	69.1	40.1	110.4	62.6	36.3	"
aggravated assault	123.1	174.2	302.3	40.7	57.6	"
arrests for property crimes:						
burglary	103.2	221.0	329.8	31.3	67.0	"
larceny-theft	372.6	758.8	1,157.2	32.2	65.6	"
motor vehicle theft	60.0	89.1	151.7	39.5	58.7	"
arson	3.6	10.6	14.4	25.0	73.5	"

SOURCE: U.S. Federal Bureau of Investigation, Crime in the United States, 1988, p. 186, table 38 (data from the Uniform Crime Reporting program). J 1.14/7:988

NOTES: 'All Races' includes other races not shown separately. Crime index crimes are made up of the four violent crimes (murder and nonnegligent homicide, rape, robbery, and aggravated assault), and four property crimes (burglary, larceny-theft, motor vehicle theft, and arson) which are tracked by the FBI.

UNITS: Arrests in thousands of arrests; percent distribution as a percent of total, 100.0%

Table 5.19 Arrests, by Offence Charged, Persons Under 18 Years of Age, 1985

	number of arrests			percent distribution		
	Black	White	All Races	Black	White	All Races
All arrests	407.8	1,317.8	1,758.8	23.2%	74.9%	100.0%
Arrests for crime index crimes	187.1	452.4	653.4	28.6	69.2	"
arrests for violent crimes	37.8	33.5	72.3	52.4	46.3	"
arrests for property crimes	149.2	418.9	581.1	25.7	72.1	"
arrests for violent crimes:						
murder and nonnegligent homicide	0.6	0.6	1.3	50.7	48.2	"
forcible rape	2.4	2.3	4.8	50.6	48.3	"
robbery	20.1	9.6	30.0	66.8	32.1	"
aggravated assault	14.7	20.9	36.2	40.7	57.8	"
arrests for property crimes:						
burglary	32.6	109.9	144.8	25.5	75.9	"
larceny-theft	103.1	273.1	385.8	27.7	07.8	"
motor vehicle theft	12.6	30.1	43.6	28.9	69.1	"
arson	0.9	5.8	6.9	13.6	84.7	"

SOURCE: U.S. Department of Justice, Bureau of Justice Statistics, Sourcebook of Criminal Justice Statistics, 1986, p. 301, table 4.8, (data from the Uniform Crime Reporting program). J 29.9/6:986

NOTES: 'All Races' includes other races not shown separately. Crime index crimes are made up of the four violent crimes (murder and nonnegligent homicide, rape, robbery, and aggravated assault), and four property crimes (burglary, larceny-theft, motor vehicle theft, and arson) which are tracked by the FBI.

UNITS: Arrests in thousands of arrests; percent distribution as a percent of total, 100.0%

Table 5.20 Arrests, by Offence Charged, Persons Under 18 Years of Age, 1988

	number of arrests			percent distribution		
	Black	White	All Races	Black	White	All Races
All arrests	420.3	1,166.3	1,624.0	25.9%	71.8%	100.0%
Arrests for crime index crimes	176.5	403.1	594.9	29.7	67.8	"
arrests for violent crimes	36.0	31.0	68.0	52.9	45.5	"
arrests for property crimes	140.5	372.2	526.9	25.9	70.6	"
arrests for violent crimes:						
murder and nonnegligent homicide	1.0	0.7	1.7	57.1	41.2	"
forcible rape	2.0	2.0	4.0	50.0	48.8	"
robbery	15.7	8.1	24.1	64.9	33.5	"
aggravated assault	17.3	20.2	38.1	45.4	53.0	"
arrests for property crimes:						
burglary	26.2	81.9	110.6	23.6	74.0	"
larceny-theft	89.8	249.7	349.6	25.7	71.4	"
motor vehicle theft	23.6	35.5	60.5	39.0	58.6	"
arson	1.0	5.1	6.2	16.1	82.0	"

SOURCE: U.S. Federal Bureau of Investigation, Crime in the United States, 1988, p. 187, table 38 (data from the Uniform Crime Reporting program). J 1.14/7:988

NOTES: 'All Races' includes other races not shown separately. Crime index crimes are made up of the four violent crimes (murder and nonnegligent homicide, rape, robbery, and aggravated assault), and four property crimes (burglary, larceny-theft, motor vehicle theft, and arson) which are tracked by the FBI.

UNITS: Arrests in thousands of arrests; percent distribution as a percent of total, 100.0%

Table 5.21 Arrests in Cities, by Offence Charged, 1985

	number of arrests			percent distribution		
	Black	White	All Races	Black	White	All Races
All arrests	2,325.6	5,443.9	7,916.9	29.4%	68.8%	100.0%
Arrests for crime index crimes	614.5	1,067.6	1,716.6	35.8	62.2	"
arrests for violent crimes	171.7	158.8	335.3	51.2	474.	"
arrests for property crimes	442.8	908.8	1,381.3	32.1	65.8	"
arrests for violent crimes:						
murder and nonnegligent homicide	6.3	4.9	11.3	55.6	42.8	"
forcible rape	12.4	10.9	23.7	52.4	46.2	"
robbery	65.5	36.6	103.2	63.5	35.5	"
aggravated assault	87.9	106.4	197.0	44.4	54.0	"
arrests for property crimes:						
burglary	91.6	186.9	282.6	32.4	66.1	"
larceny-theft	315.4	658.2	997.3	31.6	66.0	"
motor vehicle theft	32.5	54.8	89.0	36.5	61.6	"
arson	3.2	9.0	12.5	26.1	72.2	"

SOURCE: U.S. Department of Justice, Bureau of Justice Statistics, Sourcebook of Criminal Justice Statistics, 1986, p. 304, table 4.10, (data from the Uniform Crime Reporting program). J 29.9/6:986

NOTES: 'All Races' includes other races not shown separately. Crime index crimes are made up of the four violent crimes (murder and nonnegligent homicide, rape, robbery, and aggravated assault), and four property crimes (burglary, larceny-theft, motor vehicle theft, and arson) which are tracked by the FBI.

UNITS: Arrests in thousands of arrests; percent distribution as a percent of total, 100.0%

Table 5.22 Arrests in Cities, by Offence Charged, 1988

	number of arrests			percent distribution		
	Black	White	All Races	Black	White	All Races
All arrests	2,583.3	5,137.4	7,869.1	32.8%	65.3%	100.0%
Arrests for crime index crimes	666.0	1,048.3	1,749.0	38.1	59.9	"
arrests for violent crimes	189.2	176.1	370.6	51.0	47.5	"
arrests for property crimes	476.8	872.2	1,378.5	34.6	63.3	"
arrests for violent crimes:						
murder and nonnegligent homicide	7.6	4.6	12.4	61.6	37.0	"
forcible rape	11.1	10.1	21.5	51.7	46.9	"
robbery	63.6	33.9	98.5	64.5	34.4	"
aggravated assault	106.9	127.5	238.2	44.9	53.6	"
arrests for property crimes:						
burglary	88.3	157.4	249.8	35.3	63.0	"
larceny-theft	331.7	639.4	994.2	33.4	64.3	"
motor vehicle theft	53.7	67.9	123.7	43.4	54.9	"
arson	3.1	7.5	10.7	29.0	69.4	"

SOURCE: U.S. Federal Bureau of Investigation, Crime in the United States, 1988, p. 195, table 44 (data from the Uniform Crime Reporting program). J 1.14/7:988

NOTES: 'All Races' includes other races not shown separately. Crime index crimes are made up of the four violent crimes (murder and nonnegligent homicide, rape, robbery, and aggravated assault), and four property crimes (burglary, larceny-theft, motor vehicle theft, and arson) which are tracked by the FBI.

UNITS: Arrests in thousands of arrests; percent distribution as a percent of total, 100.0%

Table 5.23 Prisoners Under Jurisdiction of Federal and State Correctional Authorities, December 31, 1987

	Black	White	All Races
Total	262,958	291,606	581,020
federal institutions	14,641	32,488	48,300
state institutions	248,317	259,118	532,720

SOURCE: U.S. Department of Justice, Bureau of Justice Statistics, Sourcebook of Criminal Justice Statistics, 1988, p. 617, table 6.35. J 29.9/6:988

NOTES: 'All Races' includes other races not shown separately.

UNITS: Number of prisoners under jurisdictional authority.

Table 5.24 Criminal History of State Prison Inmates, 1986

	Black	White	All Races
Total	46.9%	49.7%	100.0%
first-time inmates	42.0	54.2	"
for non-violent crimes	33.3	63.2	"
for violent crimes	45.6	50.7	"
recidivists	48.0	48.6	"
for non-violent crimes	40.5	56.9	"
for prior violent crimes	51.6	44.9	"
for current violent crime only	48.9	47.1	"
for current and prior violent crime	56.2	40.2	"

SOURCE: U.S. Bureau of the Census, Statistical Abstract of the United States, 1989, p. 184, table 320 . C 3.134:989

NOTES: 'All Races' includes other races not shown separately.

UNITS: Percent as a percent of all state prison inmates, 100.0%.

Table 5.25 Jail Inmates, 1978 - 1987

	Black	White	All Races
1978	65,104	89,418	158,394
1983	87,508	130,118	223,552
1984	93,800	138,355	234,500
1985	102,646	151,403	256,615
1986	112,522	159,178	274,444
1987	124,267	168,648	295,873

SOURCE: U.S. Bureau of the Census, Statistical Abstract of the United States, 1989, p. 183, table 317 (data from U.S. Bureau of Justice Statistics, *Profile of Jail Inmates, 1978*, and *Jail Inmates {annual}*). C 3.134:989

U.S. Department of Justice, Bureau of Justice Statistics, Sourcebook of Criminal Justice Statistics, 1988, p. 606, table 6.26. J 29.9/6:988

NOTES: 'All Races' includes other races not shown separately. Data for 1984-1987 includes juveniles.

UNITS: Number of jail inmates.

Table 5.26 Juveniles Held in Custody, 1979 - 1987

	Black	White	All Races
1979			
total	19,595	27,707	74,113
in public custody	13,752	26,053	45,396
in private custody	5,843	21,654	28,717
1983			
total	25,842	50,182	82,272
in public custody	18,020	27,805	50,799
in private custody	7,822	22,377	31,473
1985			
total	27,473	53,968	85,514
in public custody	18,269	29,969	51,402
in private custody	9,204	23,999	34,112
1987			
total	31,080	47,577	91,646
in public custody	20,898	23,375	53,503
in private custody	10,182	24,202	38,143

SOURCE: U.S. Bureau of the Census, Statistical Abstract of the United States, 1989, p. 182, table 316. C 3.134:989
U.S. Department of Justice, Bureau of Justice Statistics, Sourcebook of Criminal Justice Statistics, 1988, p. 595, table 6.8. J 29.9/6:988

NOTES: 'All Races' includes other races not shown separately. Public and private facilities for juveniles include detention centers, shelters, reception and diagnostic centers, training schools, halfway houses, group homes, ranches, forestry camps, and farms.

UNITS: Number of juveniles held in custody.

Table 5.27 Youth in Long-Term, State Operated Juvenile Institutions, by Age and Offence, 1987

	Black	White	All Races
Total	41.1%	53.1%	100.0%
as a percent of all institutionalized youth aged:			
11-14 years old	46.7	46.4	"
15-17 years old	40.3	53.8	"
18 years old and older	40.5	54.6	"
By current offence			
All offenses	100.0%	100.0%	100.0%
violent offenses	47.0	32.9	39.3
murder	1.4	2.0	1.8
negligent manslaughter	0.7	0.6	0.6
kidnapping	0.4	0.2	0.3
rape	3.3	1.8	2.4
other sexual assaults	2.8	4.3	3.5
robbery	15.9	10.8	13.1
assault	21.4	11.9	16.3
other violent offenses	1.2	1.2	1.2
property offenses	38.6	51.1	45.6
burglary	19.4	27.2	23.8
larceny/theft	6.3	8.0	7.3
motor vehicle theft	7.1	8.2	7.8
arson	1.5	2.1	1.8
fraud	0.5	1.7	1.1
stolen property	1.7	1.1	1.4
other property offenses	2.1	2.7	2.5
drug offenses	7.4	4.2	5.6
possession	3.5	2.7	2.9
trafficking	3.8	1.3	2.5
other drug offenses	0.1	0.3	0.2

continued on the next page

Table 5.27 continued

	Black	White	All Races
By current offence - continued			
public order offenses	5.4%	8.8%	7.2%
weapons	2.2	1.6	1.9
other public order offenses	3.2	7.2	5.3
juvenile status offenses	1.6	2.7	2.2
other offenses	0.0	0.3	0.2

SOURCE: U.S. Department of Justice, Bureau of Justice Statistics, Sourcebook of Criminal Justice Statistics, 1988, pp. 598-599, tables 6.12, 6.13. J 29.9/6:988

NOTES: 'All Races' includes other races not shown separately. Data as of year-end. 'By current offence' data for persons less than 18 years old. Juvenile status offenses include non-criminal juvenile offenses such as truancy, running away, and incorrigible behavior.

UNITS: Percent, as a percent of total shown, 100.0%.

Table 5.28 Prisoners Under Sentence of Death, and Elapsed Time from Sentence to Execution, 1975 - 1988

	Black	White	All Races
Prisoners under sentence of death			
1975	262	218	488
1980	268	425	697
1981	357	499	864
1982	466	615	1,073
1983	508	694	1,214
1984	595	809	1,420
1985	664	896	1,575
1986	750	1,006	1,781
1987	821	1,138	1,984
1988	845	1,223	2,124
Average elapsed time (in months) from sentence to execution			
1977-83	58	59	58
1984	84	76	79
1985	80	65	71
1986	102	77	86
1987	96	78	86
1988	89	72	80

SOURCE: U.S. Bureau of the Census, Statistical Abstract of the United States, 1989, p. 187, table 325. C 3.134:989
U.S. Department of Justice, Bureau of Justice Statistics, Bureau of Justice Statistics Bulletin: Capital Punishment, 1988 p. 7, table 5. J 29.11:988

NOTES: 'All Races' includes other races not shown separately.

UNITS: Number of prisoners under sentence of death; Average elapsed time from sentence to execution in months.

Table 5.29 Prisoners Executed Under Civil Authority, 1930 - 1988

	Black	White	All Races
1930-1939			
All executions	816	827	1,667
for murder	687	803	1,514
for rape	115	10	125
for other offenses	14	14	28
1940-1949			
All executions	781	490	1,284
for murder	595	458	1,064
for rape	179	19	200
for other offenses	7	3	20
1950-1959			
All executions	376	336	717
for murder	280	316	601
for rape	89	13	102
for other offenses	7	7	14
1960-1964			
All executions	91	90	181
for murder	66	79	145
for rape	22	6	28
for other offenses	3	5	8
1965-1967			
All executions	2	8	10
1968-1976			
All executions	0	0	0
1977-1980			
All executions	0	3	3
1981			
All executions	0	1	1

continued on the next page

Table 5.29 continued

	Black	White	All Races
1982			
All executions	1	1	2
1983			
All executions	1	4	5
1984			
All executions	8	13	21
1985			
All executions	7	11	18
1986			
All executions	7	11	18
1987			
All executions	12	13	25
1988			
All executions	5	6	11

SOURCE: U.S. Bureau of the Census, Statistical Abstract of the United States, 1989, p. 187, table 326. C 3.134:989

U.S. Department of Justice, Bureau of Justice Statistics, Bureau of Justice Statistics Bulletin; Capital Punishment, 1988 p. 10, table 10. J 29.11:988

NOTES: 'All Races' includes other races not shown separately. Since 1965 the only executions that have taken place have been for murder. 'Other offenses' include executions for kidnapping, armed robbery, burglary, espionage, and aggravated assault.

UNITS: Number of prisoners executed under civil authority.

Table 6.01 Labor Force Participation of the Civilian Noninstitutional Population 16 Years Old and Over, by Age, 1975 - 1988

	Black	White	All Races
1975			
civilian noninstitutional population			
all persons 16 years old and over	15,751	134,790	153,153
- persons 16-19 years old	2,191	13,941	16,418
- persons 20 years old and over	13,560	120,849	136,733
- persons 65 years old and over	1,755	19,587	21,525
civilian labor force			
all persons 16 years old and over	9,263	82,831	93,775
- persons 16-19 years old	838	7,899	8,870
- persons 20 years old and over	8,426	74,932	84,904
- persons 65 years old and over	258	2,668	2,956
labor force participation rate			
all persons 16 years old and over	58.8%	61.5%	61.2%
- persons 16-19 years old	38.2	56.7	54.0
- persons 20 years old and over	62.0	62.0	62.1
- persons 65 years old and over	14.9	13.6	13.7

continued on the next page

Table 6.01 continued

	Black	White	All Races
1980			
civilian noninstitutional population			
all persons 16 years old and over	17,824	146,122	167,745
- persons 16-19 years old	2,289	13,854	16,543
- persons 20 years old and over	15,535	132,268	151,202
- persons 65 years old and over	2,030	22,050	24,350
civilian labor force			
all persons 16 years old and over	10,865	93,600	106,940
- persons 16-19 years old	891	8,312	9,378
- persons 20 years old and over	9,975	85,286	97,561
- persons 65 years old and over	257	2,759	3,054
labor force participation rate			
all persons 16 years old and over	61.0%	64.1%	63.8%
- persons 16-19 years old	38.9	60.0	56.7
- persons 20 years old and over	64.1	64.5	64.5
- persons 65 years old and over	13.0	12.5	12.5

continued on the next page

Table 6.01 continued

	Black	White	All Races
1985			
civilian noninstitutional population			
all persons 16 years old and over	19,664	153,679	178,206
- persons 16-19 years old	2,160	11,900	14,506
- persons 20 years old and over	17,504	141,780	163,700
- persons 65 years old and over	2,259	24,352	26,977
civilian labor force			
all persons 16 years old and over	12,364	99,926	115,461
- persons 16-19 years old	889	6,841	7,901
- persons 20 years old and over	11,476	93,085	107,560
- persons 65 years old and over	252	2,605	2,907
labor force participation rate			
all persons 16 years old and over	62.9%	65.0%	64.8%
- persons 16-19 years old	41.2	57.5	54.5
- persons 20 years old and over	65.6	65.7	65.7
- persons 65 years old and over	11.2	10.7	10.8

continued on the next page

Table 6.01 continued

	Black	White	All Races
1988			
civilian noninstitutional population			
all persons 16 years old and over	20,692	158,194	184,613
- persons 16-19 years old	2,179	11,838	14,527
- persons 20 years old and over	18,513	146,357	170,085
- persons 65 years old and over	2,402	25,739	28,612
civilian labor force			
all persons 16 years old and over	13,205	104,756	121,669
- persons 16-19 years old	889	6,940	8,031
- persons 20 years old and over	12,316	97,815	113,638
- persons 65 years old and over	276	2,943	3,284
labor force participation rate			
all persons 16 years old and over	63.8%	66.2%	65.9%
- persons 16-19 years old	40.8	58.6	55.3
- persons 20 years old and over	66.5	66.8	66.8
- persons 65 years old and over	11.5	11.4	11.5

SOURCE: U.S. Department of Labor, Bureau of Labor Statistics, Handbook of Labor Statistics, 1989, pp. 13-30, tables 3 5, (data from the Current Population Survey). L 2.3/5:989

NOTES: 'All Races' includes other races not shown separately.

UNITS: Civilian noninstitutional population and civilian labor force in thousands of persons; participation rate as a percent (the civilian noninstitutional population divided by the civilian labor force).

Table 6.02 Labor Force Participation of the Civilian Noninstitutional Population 16 Years Old and Over, by Sex and Age, 1975 - 1988

	Black		White		All Races	
	male	female	male	female	male	female
1975						
civilian noninstitutional population						
all persons 16 years old and over	7,060	8,691	63,981	70,810	72,291	80,860
- persons 16-19 years old	1,051	1,141	6,929	7,011	8,134	8,285
- persons 20 years old and over	6,009	7,550	57,052	63,798	64,158	72,576
- persons 65 years old and over	730	1,025	8,031	11,556	8,852	12,673
civilian labor force						
all persons 16 years old and over	5,016	4,247	50,324	32,508	56,299	37,475
- persons 16-19 years old	447	391	4,290	3,610	4,085	4,065
- persons 20 years old and over	4,569	3,857	46,034	28,898	51,494	33,410
- persons 65 years old and over	150	108	1,742	926	1,914	1,042
labor force participation rate						
all persons 16 years old and over	70.9%	48.8%	78.7%	45.9%	77.9%	46.3%
- persons 16-19 years old	42.6	34.2	61.9	51.5	59.1	49.1
- persons 20 years old and over	76.0	51.1	80.7	45.3	80.3	46.0
- persons 65 years old and over	20.7	10.7	21.7	8.0	21.6	8.2

continued on the next page

Table 6.02 continued

	Black		White		All Races	
	male	female	male	female	male	female
1980						
civilian noninstitutional population						
all persons 16 years old and over	7,944	9,880	69,634	76,489	79,398	88,348
- persons 16-19 years old	1,110	1,180	6,941	6,914	8,260	8,283
- persons 20 years old and over	6,834	8,700	62,694	69,575	71,138	80,065
- persons 65 years old and over	822	1,208	9,027	13,022	9,979	14,372
civilian labor force						
all persons 16 years old and over	5,612	5,253	54,473	39,127	61,453	45,487
- persons 16-19 years old	479	412	4,424	3,888	4,999	4,381
- persons 20 years old and over	5,134	4,841	50,049	35,239	56,455	41,106
- persons 65 years old and over	138	119	1,727	1,032	1,893	1,161
labor force participation rate						
all persons 16 years old and over	70.3%	53.1%	78.2%	51.2%	77.4%	51.5%
- persons 16-19 years old	43.2	34.9	63.7	56.2%	60.5	52.9
- persons 20 years old and over	75.1	55.6	79.8	50.6	79.4	51.3
- persons 65 years old and over	16.9	10.2	19.1	7.9	19.0	8.1

continued on the next page

Table 6.02 continued

	Black		White		All Races	
	male	female	male	female	male	female
1985						
civilian noninstitutional population						
all persons 16 years old and over	8,790	10,873	73,373	80,306	84,469	93,736
- persons 16-19 years old	1,059	1,101	5,987	5,912	7,275	7,231
- persons 20 years old and over	7,731	9,773	67,386	74,394	77,195	86,506
- persons 65 years old and over	902	1,357	10,010	14,342	11,084	15,913
civilian labor force						
all persons 16 years old and over	6,220	6,144	56,472	43,455	64,411	51,050
- persons 16-19 years old	471	417	3,576	3,265	4,134	3,767
- persons 20 years old and over	5,749	5,727	52,895	40,190	60,277	47,283
- persons 65 years old and over	125	127	1,595	1,010	1,750	1,156
labor force participation rate						
all persons 16 years old and over	70.8%	56.5%	77.0%	54.1%	76.3%	54.5%
- persons 16-19 years old	44.6	37.9	59.7	55.2	56.8	52.1
- persons 20 years old and over	74.4	58.6	78.5	54.0	78.1	54.7
- persons 65 years old and over	13.9	9.4	15.9	7.0	15.8	7.3

continued on the next page

Table 6.02 continued

	Black		White		All Races	
	male	female	male	female	male	female
1988						
civilian noninstitutional population						
all persons 16 years old and over	9,289	11,402	75,855	82,340	87,857	96,756
- persons 16-19 years old	1,074	1,105	5,968	5,869	7,304	7,224
- persons 20 years old and over	8,215	10,298	69,887	76,470	80,553	89,532
- persons 65 years old and over	970	1,432	10,688	15,052	11,859	16,753
civilian labor force						
all persons 16 years old and over	6,596	6,609	58,317	46,439	66,927	54,742
- persons 16-19 years old	469	419	3,583	3,358	4,159	3,872
- persons 20 years old and over	6,127	6,190	54,734	43,081	62,768	50,870
- persons 65 years old and over	139	137	1,787	1,156	1,960	1,324
labor force participation rate						
all persons 16 years old and over	71.0%	58.0%	76.9%	56.4%	76.2%	56.6%
- persons 16-19 years old	43.8	37.9	60.0	57.2	56.9	53.6
- persons 20 years old and over	74.6	60.1	78.3	56.3	77.9	56.8
- persons 65 years old and over	14.3	9.6	16.7	7.7	16.5	7.9

SOURCE: U.S. Department of Labor, Bureau of Labor Statistics, Handbook of Labor Statistics, 1989, pp. 13-30, tables 3-5, (data from the Current Population Survey). L 2.3/5:989

NOTES: 'All Races' includes other races not shown separately.

UNITS: Civilian noninstitutional population and civilian labor force in thousands of persons; participation rate as a percent (the civilian noninstitutional population divided by the civilian labor force).

Table 6.03 Civilian Labor Force and Civilian Labor Force Participation Rates: Projections for 1995 and 2000

	Black	White	All Races
1995			
civilian labor force			
total	15.1	111.7	131.6
men	7.4	60.5	70.4
women	7.1	51.2	61.2
labor force participation rate			
total	65.6%	67.5%	67.2%
men	71.4	75.9	75.3
women	60.9	59.7	59.8
2000			
civilian labor force			
total	16.3	116.7	138.8
men	7.9	62.3	73.1
women	8.4	54.4	65.6
labor force participation rate			
total	66.0%	68.2%	67.8%
men	70.7	75.3	74.7
women	62.1	61.5	61.5

SOURCE: U.S. Bureau of the Census, Statistical Abstract of the United States, 1988, p. 376, table 621 (data from U.S. Department of Labor, Bureau of Labor Statistics, *Monthly Labor Review*, September, 1987) C 3.134:988

NOTES: 'All Races' includes other races not shown separately.

UNITS: Civilian labor force in millions of persons; labor force participation rate as a percent (the civilian noninstitutional population divided by the civilian labor force).

Table 6.04 Employed Members of the Civilian Labor Force by Sex and Age, 1975 - 1988

	Black		White		All Races	
	male	female	male	female	male	female
1975						
all employed persons 16 years old and over	4,275	3,618	46,697	29,714	51,857	33,989
- persons 16-19 years old	276	231	3,505	2,983	3,839	3,263
- persons 20 years old and over	3,998	3,388	43,192	26,731	48,018	30,726
- persons 65 years old and over	137	104	1,656	877	1,811	989
1980						
all employed persons 16 years old and over	4,798	4,515	51,127	36,587	57,186	42,177
- persons 16-19 years old	299	248	3,708	3,314	4,085	3,625
- persons 20 years old and over	4,498	4,267	47,419	33,275	53,101	38,492
- persons 65 years old and over	126	113	1,684	1,001	1,835	1,123
1985						
all employed persons 16 years old and over	5,270	5,231	53,046	40,690	59,891	47,259
- persons 16-19 years old	278	254	2,985	2,783	3,328	3,105
- persons 20 years old and over	4,992	4,977	50,061	37,907	56,562	44,154
- persons 65 years old and over	114	121	1,552	978	1,695	1,118

continued on the next page

Table 6.04 continued

	Black		White		All Races	
	male	female	male	female	male	female
1988						
all employed persons 16 years old and over	5,824	5,834	55,550	44,262	63,273	51,696
- persons 16-19 years old	316	285	3,084	2,946	3,492	3.313
- persons 20 years old and over	5,509	1,844	52,466	41,316	59,781	48,383
- persons 65 years old and over	131	129	1,748	1,126	1,911	1,286

SOURCE: U.S. Department of Labor, Bureau of Labor Statistics, Handbook of Labor Statistics, 1989, pp. 63-68, table 15, (data from the Current Population Survey). L 2.3/5:989

NOTES: 'All Races' includes other races not shown separately. Data covers members of the civilian labor force.

UNITS: Employed members of the civilian labor force in thousands of persons, by age group as shown.

Table 6.05 Employment Status of the Civilian Labor Force, by Sex and Marital Status, 1975 - 1988

	Black		White		All Races	
	male	female	male	female	male	female
1975						
Single persons						
civilian labor force	1,332	1,111	10,691	7,810	12,287	9,125
employed	960	833	9,119	6,930	10,313	7,943
unemployed						
number	372	278	1,572	879	1,973	1,181
percent	15.5%	11.4%	14.7%	11.3%	16.1%	12.9%
Married persons*						
civilian labor force	3,007	1,863	36,673	19,192	40,312	21,484
employed	2,744	1,658	34,912	17,728	38,249	19,788
unemployed						
number	264	205	1,761	1,463	2,063	1,696
percent	8.7%	11.0%	4.8%	7.6%	5.1%	7.9%
Widowed, divorced, separated persons						
civilian labor force	671	1,272	2,959	5,507	3,700	6,866
employed	571	1,127	2,666	5,055	3,294	6,258
unemployed						
number	105	145	293	452	406	609
percent	15.5%	11.4%	9.9%	8.2%	11.0%	8.9%
1980						
Single persons						
civilian labor force	1,895	1,652	13,340	9,924	15,636	11,865
employed	1,407	1,257	11,757	9,055	13,515	10,567
unemployed						
number	488	395	1,582	870	2,120	1,298
percent	25.8%	24.0%	11.9%	8.8%	13.6%	10.9%

continued on the next page

Table 6.05 continued

	Black		White		All Races	
	male	female	male	female	male	female
1980 - continued						
Married persons*						
civilian labor force	2,900	2,050	39,650	22,260	40,713	24,980
employed	2,683	1,875	35,504	21,035	39,004	23,532
unemployed						
number	217	175	1,445	1,226	1,709	1,448
percent	7.4%	8.4%	3.9	5.5%	4.2%	5.8%
Widowed, divorced, separated persons						
civilian labor force	817	1,551	4,183	6,943	5,104	8,643
employed	708	1,383	3,866	6,499	4,667	8,017
unemployed						
number	110	167	317	444	437	626
percent	13.3%	10.7%	7.6%	6.4%	8.6%	7.2%
1985						
Single persons						
civilian labor force	2,272	2,094	14,426	10,705	17,208	13,163
employed	1,702	1,603	12,875	9,828	15,022	11,758
unemployed						
number	570	491	1,550	877	2,186	1,404
percent	25.1%	23.4%	10.7%	8.2%	12.7%	10.7%
Married persons*						
civilian labor force	3,008	2,261	36,934	24,777	41,014	27,894
employed	2,766	2,064	35,472	23,468	39,248	26,336
unemployed						
number	242	197	1,462	1,308	1,767	1,558
percent	8.0%	8.7%	4.0%	5.3%	4.3%	5.6%

continued on the next page

Table 6.05 continued

	Black		White		All Races	
	male	female	male	female	male	female
1985 - continued						
Widowed, divorced, separated persons						
civilian labor force	940	1,790	5,112	7,973	6,190	9,993
employed	801	1,564	4,698	7,393	5,621	9,165
unemployed						
number	139	226	414	580	568	828
percent	14.8%	12.6%	8.1%	7.3%	9.2%	8.3%
1988						
Single persons						
civilian labor force	2,445	2,337	15,279	11,428	18,345	14,194
employed	1,971	1,909	13,982	10,674	16,521	12,979
unemployed						
number	474	428	1,297	754	1,824	1,215
percent	19.4%	18.3%	8.5%	6.6%	9.9%	8.6%
Married persons*						
civilian labor force	3,180	2,400	37,429	26,499	41,832	29,921
employed	2,995	2,238	36,304	25,540	40,472	28,756
unemployed						
number	185	162	1,125	959	1,360	1,166
percent	5.8%	6.7%	3.0%	3.6%	3.3%	3.9%
Widowed, divorced, separated persons						
civilian labor force	972	1,873	5,608	8,512	6,751	10,627
employed	860	1,687	5,265	8,047	6,280	9,962
unemployed						
number	112	186	344	464	471	665
percent	11.5%	9.9%	6.1%	5.5%	7.0%	6.3%

continued on the next page

Table 6.05 continued

SOURCE: U.S. Department of Labor, Bureau of Labor Statistics, Handbook of Labor Statistics, 1989, pp. 31-37, table 6, (data from Current Population Survey). L 2.3/5:989

NOTES: 'All Races' includes other races not shown separately. *Married persons with spouse present.

UNITS: Civilian labor force in thousands of persons; number of unemployed in thousands, percent unemployed as a percent of the labor force.

Table 6.06 Persons Not in the Labor Force, by Reason, 1975 - 1988

	Black	White	All Races
1975			
Total not in labor force	6,487	51,959	59,377
do not want a job now	5,389	47,930	54,102
current activity			
going to school	1,012	5,193	6,339
ill, disabled	879	3,900	4,834
keeping house	2,462	28,794	31,666
retired	597	7,325	7,970
other activity	440	2,718	3,239
want a job now	1,099	4,027	5,271
reason not looking:			
school attendance	303	1,116	1,462
ill health, disability	167	492	680
home responsibilities	232	886	1,125
think cannot get a job	282	781	1,093
other reasons*	115	752	909
1980			
Total not in labor force	6,959	52,523	60,806
do not want a job now	5,679	48,305	55,131
current activity:			
going to school	1,046	4,997	6,350
ill, disabled	805	3,575	4,460
keeping house	2,297	26,475	29,278
retired	902	9,952	10,963
other activity	630	3,305	4,080
want a job now	1,282	4,218	5,675
reason not looking:			
school attendance	350	1,087	1,511
ill health, disability	204	537	755
home responsibilities	274	991	1,267
think cannot get a job	275	673	993
other reasons*	178	930	1,148

continued on the next page

Table 6.06 continued

	Black	White	All Races
1985			
Total not in labor force	7,299	53,753	62,744
do not want a job now	5,926	49,399	56,812
current activity:			
going to school	1,001	4,909	6,288
ill, disabled	687	3,150	3,914
keeping house	2,255	24,238	27,136
retired	1,253	13,389	14,857
other activity	730	3,713	4,617
want a job now	1,373	4,357	5,933
reason not looking:			
school attendance	366	1,028	1,455
ill health, disability	215	576	803
home responsibilities	277	999	1,317
think cannot get a job	348	810	1,204
other reasons*	167	944	1,154
1988			
Total not in labor force	7,487	53,439	62,944
do not want a job now	6,215	49,576	57,571
current activity:			
going to school	1,066	4,870	6,383
ill, disabled	877	3,516	4,485
keeping house	2,080	22,287	25,139
retired	1,447	15,228	16,930
other activity	745	3,675	4,634
want a job now	1,272	3,863	5,373
reason not looking:			
school attendance	347	928	1,353
ill health, disability	201	585	805
home responsibilities	291	833	1,168
think cannot get a job	261	639	954
other reasons*	173	878	1,093

continued on the next page

Table 6.06 continued

SOURCE: U.S. Department of Labor, Bureau of Labor Statistics, Handbook of Labor Statistics, 1989, pp. 57-60, table 13, (data from the Current Population Survey). L 2.3/5:989

NOTES: 'All Races' includes other races not shown separately. *Includes a small number of men not looking for work due to 'home responsibilities'.

UNITS: Persons not in the labor force in thousands of persons.

Table 6.07 Employed Black Persons as Percent of All Employed Persons in the Civilian Labor Force, by Selected Occupation, 1988

1988	
All occupations	10.1%
Managerial and professional specialty	6.1
executive, administrative and managerial	5.6
professional specialty	6.7
architects	4.4
engineers	3.8
mathematical and computer scientists	7.4
natural scientists	2.5
physicians	3.3
dentists	1.9
health assessment and treatment occupations	7.8
college and university teachers	4.0
teachers, except college and university	8.8
lawyers and judges	2.3
writers, artists, entertainers, and athletes	4.3
Technicians, sales, and administrative support	9.1
technical and related support	9.4
health technologists	14.2
engineering and related technologists and technicians	6.1
science technicians	8.7
sales occupations	6.1
administrative support, including clerical	11.3
supervisors	13.5
computer equipment operators	14.4
secretaries, stenographers, typists	8.5
Service occupations	17.6
private household	22.5

continued on the next page

Table 6.07 continued

Service occupations - continued	
protective service	16.7
supervisors	15.3
fire fighting and fire prevention	8.3
police and detectives	15.8
guards	20.1
Service occupations (except private household and protective service)	17.2
food preparation and service occupations	12.4
health service occupations	28.2
cleaning and building service occupations	23.0
personal service occupations	12.0
Precision production, craft and repair	7.5
mechanics and repairers	7.1
construction trades	7.1
precision production occupations	8.6
Operators, fabricators, and laborers	15.0
machine operators, assemblers, and inspectors	14.8
transportation and material moving occupations	14.9
handlers, equipment cleaners, helpers, and laborers	15.5
Farming, forestry, and fishing	6.6
farm operators and managers	1.1

SOURCE: U.S. Department of Labor, Bureau of Labor Statistics, Handbook of Labor Statistics, 1989, pp. 90-95, table 18, (data from the Current Population Survey). L 2.3/5:989

NOTES: Only selected subcategories of occupational groups are displayed.

UNITS: Employed Black persons as a percent of all employed persons, by occupation.

Table 6.08 Employed Black Persons as Percent of All Employed Persons in the Civilian Labor Force, by Industry Group, 1988

1988

All industries	10.1%
agriculture	4.9
mining	3.9
construction	6.8
manufacturing	10.2
transportation, communications, and other public utilities	14.3
wholesale and retail trade	7.8
wholesale trade	5.7
retail trade	8.3
finance, insurance and real estate	8.0
services	11.8
public administration	14.4

SOURCE: U.S. Department of Labor, Bureau of Labor Statistics, Handbook of Labor Statistics, 1989, pp. 104-107, table 19, (data from the Current Population Survey). L 2.3/5:989

NOTES: Only selected subcategories of industry groups are displayed.

UNITS: Employed Black persons as a percent of all employed persons, by industry group.

Table 6.09 Full-Time and Part-Time Status of Employed Persons in Nonagricultural Industries, by Sex, 1975 - 1988

	Black	White	All Races
1975			
All employed persons in nonagricultural industries	7,149	68,815	77,381
full-time	5,750	56,225	63,145
part-time	1,399	12,590	14,236
part time for economic reasons	562	2,919	3,542
1980			
All employed persons in nonagricultural industries	8,502	79,614	90,209
full-time	6,998	64,835	73,590
part-time	1,504	14,780	16,619
part time for economic reasons	601	3,375	4,064
1985			
All employed persons in nonagricultural industries	9,711	85,857	98,303
full-time	7,951	69,713	79,931
part-time	1,760	16,144	18,372
part time for economic reasons	875	4,322	5,334

continued on the next page

Table 6.09 continued

	Black	White	All Races
1988			
All employed persons in nonagricultural industries	10,869	91,929	106,101
full-time	9,022	74,881	86,627
part-time	1,847	17,048	19,474
part time for economic reasons	786	4,026	4,965

SOURCE: U.S. Department of Labor, Bureau of Labor Statistics, Handbook of Labor Statistics, 1989, pp. 121-124, table 23, (data from the Current Population Survey). L 2.3/5:989

NOTES: 'All Races' includes other races not shown separately. Economic reasons for persons who are employed part-time are: slack work; material shortages; repairs to plant or equipment; start or termination of a job during the week; and inability to find full time work.

UNITS: Employed members of the civilian labor force in thousands of persons, by status, as shown.

Table 6.10 Unemployment Rates for the Civilian Labor Force, by Age, 1975 - 1988

	Black	White	All Races
1975			
unemployment rate			
all ages	14.8%	7.8%	8.5%
- persons 16-19 years old	39.5	17.9	19.9
- persons 20 years old and over	12.3	6.7	7.3
- persons 65 years old and over	6.6	5.1	5.2
1980			
unemployment rate			
all ages	14.3%	6.3%	7.1%
- persons 16-19 years old	38.5	15.5	17.8
- persons 20 years old and over	12.1	5.4	6.1
- persons 65 years old and over	6.9	2.7	3.1
1985			
unemployment rate			
all ages	15.1%	6.2%	7.2%
- persons 16-19 years old	40.2	15.7	18.6
- persons 20 years old and over	13.1	5.5	6.4
- persons 65 years old and over	7.0	2.9	3.2

continued on the next page

Table 6.10 continued

	Black	White	All Races
1988			
unemployment rate			
all ages	11.7%	4.7%	5.5%
- persons 16-19 years old	32.4	13.1	15.3
- persons 20 years old and over	10.2	4.1	4.8
- persons 65 years old and over	5.5	2.4	2.7

SOURCE: U.S. Department of Labor, Bureau of Labor Statistics, Handbook of Labor Statistics, 1989, pp. 136-141, table 28, (data from the Current Population Survey). L 2.3/5:989

NOTES: 'All Races' includes other races not shown separately. Data covers members of the civilian labor force.

UNITS: Unemployment rate, by age group as shown.

Table 6.11 Unemployment Rates for the Civilian Labor Force, by Sex and Age, 1975 - 1988

	Black		White		All Races	
	male	female	male	female	male	female
1975						
unemployment rate						
all ages	14.8%	14.8%	7.2%	8.6%	7.9%	9.3%
- persons 16-19 years old	38.1	41.0	18.3	17.4	20.1	19.7
- persons 20 years old and over	12.5	12.2	6.2	7.5	6.8	8.0
- persons 65 years old and over	8.7	3.6	5.0	5.3	5.4	5.0
1980						
unemployment rate						
all ages	14.5%	14.0%	6.1%	6.5%	6.9%	7.4%
- persons 16-19 years old	37.5	39.8	16.2	14.8	18.3	17.2
- persons 20 years old and over	12.4	11.9	5.3	5.6	5.9	6.4
- persons 65 years old and over	8.7	4.9	2.5	3.0	3.1	3.1
1985						
unemployment rate						
all ages	15.3	14.9%	6.1%	6.4%	7.0%	7.4%
- persons 16-19 years old	41.0	39.2	16.5	14.8	19.5	17.6
- persons 20 years old and over	13.2	13.1	5.4	5.7	6.2	6.6
- persons 65 years old and over	8.9	5.2	2.7	3.1	3.1	3.3

continued on the next page

Table 6.11 continued

	Black		White		All Races	
	male	female	male	female	male	female
1988						
unemployment rate						
all ages	11.7%	11.7%	4.7%	4.7%	5.5%	5.6%
- persons 16-19 years old	32.7	32.0	13.9	12.3	16.0	14.4
- persons 20 years old and over	10.1	10.4	4.1	4.1	4.8	4.9
- persons 65 years old and over	5.6	5.4	2.2	2.6	2.5	2.9

SOURCE: U.S. Department of Labor, Bureau of Labor Statistics, Handbook of Labor Statistics, 1989, pp. 136-141, table 28, (data from the Current Population Survey). L 2.3/5:989

NOTES: 'All Races' includes other races not shown separately. Data covers members of the civilian labor force.

UNITS: Unemployment rate, by age group as shown.

Table 6.12 Unemployment by Reason for Unemployment, 1975 - 1988

	Black	White	All Races
1975			
Total	1,369	6,421	7,929
job losers	na	3,593	4,386
job leavers	na	706	827
reentrants to the labor force	353	1,508	1,892
new entrants to the labor force	187	615	823
1980			
Total	1,553	5,884	7,637
job losers	na	3,100	3,947
job leavers	na	733	891
reentrants to the labor force	424	1,447	1,927
new entrants to the labor force	239	603	872
1985			
Total	1,864	6,191	8,312
job losers	890	3,146	4,139
job leavers	110	727	877
reentrants to the labor force	546	1,635	2,256
new entrants to the labor force	317	682	1,039
1988			
Total	1,547	4,944	6,701
job losers	674	2,338	3,092
job leavers	180	776	983
reentrants to the labor force	445	1,298	1,809
new entrants to the labor force	249	532	816

SOURCE: U.S. Department of Labor, Bureau of Labor Statistics, Handbook of Labor Statistics, 1989, pp. 151-153, table 37, (data from the Current Population Survey). L 2.3/5:989

NOTES: 'All Races' includes other races not shown separately. Data covers members of the civilian labor force.

UNITS: Unemployed members of the civilian labor force in thousands of persons, by reason for unemployment as shown.

Table 6.13 Duration of Unemployment, by Region of Residence, 1985 and 1988

	Black	White	All Races
1985			
Northeast			
less than 5 weeks	34.1%	40.4%	39.3%
5-14 weeks	32.0	30.5	30.8
15 weeks and over	33.8	29.0	29.9
27 weeks and over	18.4	15.3	15.9
52 weeks and over	12.5	9.2	9.8
Midwest			
less than 5 weeks	33.6%	38.7%	37.6%
5-14 weeks	27.3	29.2	28.7
15 weeks and over	39.0	32.1	33.7
27 weeks and over	25.2	18.9	20.3
52 weeks and over	17.6	12.4	13.6
South			
less than 5 weeks	41.8%	47.8%	45.7%
5-14 weeks	31.0	29.9	30.2
15 weeks and over	27.2	22.3	24.0
27 weeks and over	15.3	12.0	13.1
52 weeks and over	9.0	6.9	7.6
West			
less than 5 weeks	39.5%	45.5%	44.8%
5-14 weeks	30.4	31.6	31.5
15 weeks and over	30.1	22.9	23.7
27 weeks and over	14.5	11.4	11.9
52 weeks and over	9.2	6.0	6.4
1988			
Northeast			
less than 5 weeks	40.1%	47.2%	45.7%
5-14 weeks	29.6	31.2	30.9
15 weeks and over	30.3	21.5	23.5
27 weeks and over	14.9	9.2	10.4
52 weeks and over	8.2	5.3	5.9

continued on the next page

Table 6.13 continued

	Black	White	All Races
1988 - continued			
Midwest			
less than 5 weeks	39.5%	43.5%	42.7%
5-14 weeks	32.3	29.4	29.9
15 weeks and over	28.2	27.1	27.4
27 weeks and over	15.7	13.9	14.3
52 weeks and over	11.3	8.4	9.0
South			
less than 5 weeks	43.6%	48.8%	47.1%
5-14 weeks	30.5	29.5	29.8
15 weeks and over	25.9	21.6	23.1
27 weeks and over	14.4	11.0	12.1
52 weeks and over	9.6	6.8	7.7
West			
less than 5 weeks	47.5%	48.9%	48.5%
5-14 weeks	29.9	29.3	29.5
15 weeks and over	22.6	21.8	22.0
27 weeks and over	12.8	10.0	10.4
52 weeks and over	9.1	5.3	5.9

SOURCE: U.S. Department of Labor, Bureau of Labor Statistics, Geographic Profile of Employment and Unemployment, 1985, pp. 31-32, table 11; 1988, pp. 31-32, table 11. L 2.3/12:(year)

NOTES: 'All Races' includes other races not shown separately.

UNITS: Duration of unemployment by region as a percent of total unemployment in each region, 100.0%.

Table 6.14 Labor Force Status of the Civilian Noninstitutional Population 16 - 24 Years of Age Enrolled in School, 1980, 1985, 1987

	Black	White	All Races
1980			
Enrolled in high school	1,282	6,603	8,083
in civilian labor force	291	3,123	3,475
employed	172	2,601	2,815
unemployed	119	552	660
Enrolled in college full-time	643	5,527	6,360
in civilian labor force	217	2,560	2,834
employed	152	2,333	2,537
unemployed	64	227	297
Enrolled in college part-time	107	1,115	1,269
in civilian labor force	84	1,011	1,147
employed	78	960	1,076
unemployed	6	51	61
1985			
Enrolled in high school	1,231	5,897	7,363
in civilian labor force	318	2,535	2,897
employed	180	2,077	2,294
unemployed	138	458	603
Enrolled in college full-time	612	5,682	6,552
in civilian labor force	229	2,890	3,193
employed	150	2,680	2,892
unemployed	79	210	301
Enrolled in college part-time	136	1,039	1,230
in civilian labor force	115	956	1,125
employed	97	910	1,057
unemployed	18	46	68

continued on the next page

Table 6.14 continued

	Black	White	All Races
1987			
Enrolled in high school	1,281	6,222	7,811
in civilian labor force	366	2,879	3,329
employed	224	2,413	2,691
unemployed	142	466	638
Enrolled in college full-time	685	5,459	6,474
in civilian labor force	284	2,703	3,135
employed	228	2,512	2,871
unemployed	56	191	263
Enrolled in college part-time	143	1,158	1,372
in civilian labor force	126	1,083	1,274
employed	114	1,046	1,224
unemployed	11	38	50

SOURCE: U.S. Department of Labor, Bureau of Labor Statistics, Handbook of Labor Statistics, 1989, pp. 257-262, table 62, (data from the Current Population Survey). L 2.3/5:989

NOTES: 'All Races' includes other races not shown separately.

UNITS: Civilian noninstitutional population, civilian labor force, employed and unemployed, in thousands of persons.

Table 6.15 Labor Force Status of the Civilian Noninstitutional Population 16 - 24 Years of Age Not Enrolled in School, by Educational Attainment, 1980, 1985, 1987

	Black	White	All Races
1980			
All 16-24 years old not enrolled in school	2,865	18,103	21,389
in civilian labor force	2,054	15,120	17,463
employed	1,453	13,319	15,020
unemployed	601	1,801	2,443
16-24 year olds with less than 4 years of high school	955	4,181	5,254
in civilian labor force	544	2,946	3,549
employed	305	2,310	2,651
unemployed	239	636	898
16-24 year olds with 4 years of high school only	1,438	9,998	11,622
in civilian labor force	1,106	8,563	9,795
employed	817	7,638	8,567
unemployed	289	924	1,228
16-24 year olds with 1-3 years of college	370	2,593	3,044
in civilian labor force	305	2,350	2,721
employed	238	2,181	2,483
unemployed	68	169	238
16-24 year olds with 4 years of college or more	104	1,329	1,417
in civilian labor force	100	1,262	1,402
employed	93	1,191	1,319
unemployed	7	72	83

continued on the next page

Table 6.15 continued

	Black	White	All Races
1985			
All 16-24 years old not			
enrolled in school	2,821	15,963	19,237
in civilian labor force	2,034	13,593	15,956
employed	1,430	12,072	13,782
unemployed	604	1,521	2,174
16-24 year olds with less than 4			
years of high school	725	3,474	4,323
in civilian labor force	386	2,470	2,920
employed	226	1,888	2,165
unemployed	160	582	755
16-24 year olds with 4 years of			
high school only	1,602	8,578	10,381
in civilian labor force	1,225	7,461	8,825
employed	865	6,732	7,707
unemployed	360	729	1,118
16-24 year olds with 1-3 years			
of college	393	2,494	2,946
in civilian labor force	338	2,284	2,680
employed	269	2,141	2,464
unemployed	69	143	216
16-24 year olds with 4 years of			
college or more	101	1,417	1,584
in civilian labor force	88	1,379	1,529
employed	72	1,313	1,446
unemployed	16	66	83
1987			
All 16-24 years old not			
enrolled in school	2,625	14,743	17,793
in civilian labor force	1,914	12,395	14,652
employed	1,474	11,290	13,060
unemployed	441	1,105	1,592

continued on the next page

Table 6.15 continued

	Black	White	All Races
1987 - continued			
16-24 year olds with less than 4 years of high school	673	3,412	4,203
in civilian labor force	361	2,310	2,745
employed	232	1,911	2,197
unemployed	128	399	547
16-24 year olds with 4 years of high school only	1,434	7,732	9,352
in civilian labor force	1,122	6,697	7,975
employed	868	6,141	7,148
unemployed	255	555	827
16-24 year olds with 1-3 years of college	416	2,249	2,745
in civilian labor force	339	2,072	2,483
employed	289	1,976	2,329
unemployed	50	96	154
16-24 year olds with 4 years of college or more	102	1,350	1,492
in civilian labor force	92	1,317	1,449
employed	84	1,262	1,386
unemployed	8	55	64

SOURCE: U.S. Department of Labor, Bureau of Labor Statistics, Handbook of Labor Statistics, 1989, pp. 263-272, table 63, (data from the Current Population Survey). L 2.3/5:989

NOTES: 'All Races' includes other races not shown separately.

UNITS: Civilian noninstitutional population, civilian labor force, employed and unemployed, in thousands of persons.

Table 6.16 Percent Distribution of the Civilian Labor Force 25 - 64 Years of Age, by Educational Attainment, 1975 - 1988

	Black	White	All Races
1975			
Total	100.0%	100.0%	100.0%
less than 4 years of high school	41.9	25.7	27.5
4 years of high school only	33.1	40.6	39.7
1-3 years of college	12.4	14.7	14.4
4 or more years of college	12.6	19.0	18.3
1980			
Total	100.0%	100.0%	100.0%
less than 4 years of high school	34.7	19.1	20.6
4 years of high school only	38.1	40.2	39.8
1-3 years of college	16.3	17.7	17.6
4 or more years of college	11.0	22.9	22.0
1985			
Total	100.0%	100.0%	100.0%
less than 4 years of high school	26.2	14.7	15.9
4 years of high school only	39.5	40.7	40.2
1-3 years of college	19.2	19.1	19.0
4 or more years of college	15.0	25.6	24.9
1988			
Total	100.0%	100.0%	100.0%
less than 4 years of high school	22.6	13.8	14.7
4 years of high school only	43.0	40.1	39.9
1-3 years of college	19.2	19.7	19.7
4 or more years of college	15.2	26.4	25.7

SOURCE: U.S. Department of Labor, Bureau of Labor Statistics, Handbook of Labor Statistics, 1989, pp. 280-281, table 65, (data from the Current Population Survey). L 2.3/5:989

NOTES: 'All Races' includes other races not shown separately.

UNITS: Percent distribution as a percent of total, 100.0%.

Table 6.17 Unemployment Rates of the Civilian Labor Force 25 - 64 Years of Age, by Educational Attainment, 1975 - 1988

	Black	White	All Races
1975			
Total	10.9%	6.5%	6.9%
less than 4 years of high school	13.5	10.1	10.7
4 years of high school only	10.7	6.5	6.9
1-3 years of college	9.8	5.1	5.5
4 or more years of college	3.9	2.4	2.5
1980			
Total	9.6%	4.4%	5.0%
less than 4 years of high school	11.7	7.8	8.4
4 years of high school only	9.5	4.6	5.1
1-3 years of college	9.0	3.9	4.3
4 or more years of college	4.0	1.8	1.9
1985			
Total	12.0%	5.3%	6.1%
less than 4 years of high school	15.3	10.6	11.4
4 years of high school only	13.0	6.1	6.9
1-3 years of college	10.6	3.9	4.7
4 or more years of college	5.4	2.1	2.4
1988			
Total	10.0%	4.0%	4.7%
less than 4 years of high school	14.6	8.3	9.4
4 years of high school only	11.2	4.6	5.4
1-3 years of college	7.5	3.2	3.7
4 or more years of college	3.3	1.5	1.7

SOURCE: U.S. Department of Labor, Bureau of Labor Statistics, Handbook of Labor Statistics, 1989, pp. 284-285, table 67, (data from the Current Population Survey). L 2.3/5:989

NOTES: 'All Races' includes other races not shown separately.

UNITS: Unemployment rates (percent of the civilian labor force that is unemployed) expressed as a percent of the total civilian labor force, by educational attainment.

Table 6.18 Self-Employed Workers, 1975 - 1987

	Black	White	All Races
1975	293	7,012	7,427
1980	342	8,116	8,642
1983	345	8,581	9,140
1984	365	8,763	9,338
1985	379	8,659	9,269
1986	380	8,706	9,328
1987	403	8,956	9,624

SOURCE: U.S. Bureau of the Census, Statistical Abstract of the United States, 1989, p. 380, table 627 (data from U.S. Department of Labor, Bureau of Labor Statistics, *Employment and Earnings*).
C 3.134:989

NOTES: 'All Races' includes other races not shown separately.

UNITS: Self-employed workers in thousands of persons.

Table 6.19 Labor Force Participation Rates for Wives in Married Couple Families, by Age of Own Youngest Child, 1975 - 1988

	Black	White	All Races
1975			
All wives in married couple families	54.3	43.7	44.5
wives with no children under 18	47.7	43.5	44.0
wives with children under 18	58.8	43.9	44.9
with children under 6	56.4	35.0	36.8
with children under 3	52.2	30.9	32.6
- 1 year or under	50.0	29.2	30.8
- 2 years old	56.4	35.1	37.1
with children 3-5	61.7	40.3	42.2
- 3 years old	62.7	39.0	41.2
- 4 years old	64.9	38.7	41.2
- 5 years old	56.3	43.8	44.4
with children 6-13 years	64.9	50.8	51.8
with children 14-17 years	51.0	53.6	53.8
1980			
All wives in married couple families	59.3	49.3	50.2
wives with no children under 18	51.2	45.5	46.0
wives with children under 18	65.6	53.2	54.3
with children under 6	63.4	43.5	45.3
with children under 3	57.7	40.0	41.5
- 1 year or under	52.9	37.7	39.0
- 2 years old	71.0	46.1	48.1
with children 3-5	72.3	49.4	51.7
- 3 years old	73.4	48.4	51.5
- 4 years old	66.4	49.8	51.4
- 5 years old	77.8	50.4	52.4
with children 6-13 years	71.8	61.4	62.6
with children 14-17 years	58.4	60.6	60.5

continued on the next page

Table 6.19 continued

	Black	White	All Races
1985			
All wives in married couple families	64.2	53.4	54.3
wives with no children under 18	56.1	47.5	48.2
wives with children under 18	71.5	60.0	61.0
with children under 6	69.3	52.3	53.7
with children under 3	65.7	49.8	50.7
- 1 year or under	63.7	48.6	49.4
- 2 years old	69.9	52.7	54.0
with children 3-5	73.8	56.6	58.6
- 3 years old	72.3	52.7	55.1
- 4 years old	70.6	58.4	59.7
- 5 years old	79.1	59.9	62.1
with children 6-13 years	73.5	67.7	68.1
with children 14-17 years	74.1	66.3	67.0
1988			
All wives in married couple families	66.1	55.8	56.7
wives with no children under 18	54.4	48.5	49.1
wives with children under 18	75.8	64.3	65.2
with children under 6	71.7	56.3	57.4
with children under 3	73.0	53.3	54.8
- 1 year or under	71.5	50.5	51.9
- 2 years old	76.2	60.2	61.7
with children 3-5	69.8	60.9	61.4
- 3 years old	76.1	58.1	59.3
- 4 years old	70.3	61.0	61.4
- 5 years old	62.5	64.0	63.6
with children 6-13 years	81.4	71.5	72.3
with children 14-17 years	74.6	72.5	72.9

SOURCE: U.S. Bureau of the Census, Statistical Abstract of the United States, 1989, p. 386, table 640 (data from the Current Population Survey). C 3.134:989

NOTES: 'All Races' includes other races not shown separately.

UNITS: Participation rates in percent.

Table 6.20 Workers Paid Hourly Rates With Earnings at or Below the Minimum Wage, 1987

	Black	White	All Races
Number of workers			
All workers paid hourly rates	7,667	50,180	59,552
at or below $3.35 per hour	670	3,909	4,697
at $3.35 per hour	547	2,598	3,229
below $3.35 per hour	123	1,311	1,468
Percent distribution			
All workers paid hourly rates	12.9%	84.3%	100.0%
at or below $3.35 per hour	14.3%	83.2	100.0
at $3.35 per hour	16.9	80.5	100.0
below $3.35 per hour	8.4	89.3	100.0
Percent of all workers paid hourly rates			
All at or below $3.35 per hour	8.7%	7.8%	7.9%
at $3.35 per hour	7.1	5.2	5.4
below $3.35 per hour	1.6	2.6	2.5

SOURCE: U.S. Bureau of the Census, Statistical Abstract of the United States, 1989, p. 411, table 675 (data from the U.S. Bureau of Labor Statistics). C 3.134:989

NOTES: 'All Races' includes other races not shown separately.

UNITS: Number of workers in thousands; percent distribution and percent in percent, as a percent of total, 100.0%.

Table 6.21 Union Membership, by Sex, 1988

	Black	White	All Races
Men			
total employed	5,502	46,783	53,912
members of unions			
number	1,438	9,294	11,019
as a percent of total employed	26.1%	19.9%	20.4%
represented by unions			
total	1,601	10,210	12,132
as a percent of total employed	29.1%	21.8%	22.5%
Women			
total employed	5,674	40,393	47,495
members of unions			
number	1,121	4,638	5,982
as a percent of total employed	19.8%	11.5%	12.6%
represented by unions			
total	1,297	5,549	7,109
as a percent of total employed	22.9%	13.7%	15.0%

SOURCE: U.S. Department of Labor, Bureau of Labor Statistics, *Employment and Earnings*, January 1989, p. 225, table 59, (data from the Current Population Survey). L 2.41/2:989

NOTES: 'All Races' includes other races not shown separately. 'Members of unions' includes members of a labor union or an employee association similar to a union. 'Represented by unions' includes members of a labor union or an employee association similar to a union as well as workers who report no union affiliation but whose jobs are covered by a union or an employee association contract.

UNITS: Total employed, members of unions and represented by unions in thousands of persons 16 years old and older; percent as shown.

Table 7.01 Money Income of Households in Current and Constant Dollars, 1975 - 1987

	Black	White	All Races
Current dollars			
1975	$ 7,408	$12,340	$11,800
1980	10,764	18,684	17,710
1981	11,309	20,153	19,074
1982	11,968	21,117	20,171
1983	12,473	22,035	21,018
1984	13,471	23,647	22,415
1985	14,819	24,908	23,618
1986	15,080	26,175	24,897
1987	15,475	27,427	25,986
Constant dollars			
1975	$15,643	$26,058	$24,917
1980	14,846	25,770	24,426
1981	14,132	25,184	23,835
1982	14,092	24,865	23,750
1983	14,229	25,136	23,976
1984	14,740	25,874	24,526
1985	15,656	26,315	24,952
1986	15,631	27,131	25,807
1987	15,475	27,427	25,986

SOURCE: U.S. Bureau of the Census, Statistical Abstract of the United States, 1989, p. 440, table 712, (data from *the Current Population Survey*). C 3.134:989

NOTES: 'All Races' includes other races not shown separately.

UNITS: Median money income in current and constant dollars, as shown.

Table 7.02 Money Income of Households by Selected Household Characteristic, 1980, 1985, 1987

	Black	White	All Races
1980			
Number of households	8,847	71,872	82,368
percent of households with current dollar incomes of:			
under $2,500	7.3	2.5%	3.0
$2,500-$4,499	17.0	7.7	8.7
$5,000-$7,499	13.0	7.7	8.3
$7,500-$9,999	10.0	7.2	7.5
$10,000-$12,499	9.0	7.8	7.9
$12,500-$14,999	7.3	6.9	7.0
$15,000-$19,999	11.8	13.5	13.3
$20,000-$24,999	8.9	12.6	12.2
$25,000-$34,999	9.6	17.4	16.5
$35,000-$49,999	4.9	10.9	10.3
$50,000 and over	1.3	5.8	5.3
mean income	$13,970	$21,913	$21,063
Mean income by:			
occupation of the householder			
white collar workers	$20,500	$29,985	$29,400
blue collar workers	19,558	23,229	22,835
farm workers	11,437	16,993	16,649
service workers	13,504	17,490	16,687
work experience of the householder			
worked at full time jobs	$18,991	$26,390	$25,720
worked 50-52 weeks	20,738	28,414	27,782
type of household			
family households	$16,010	$25,074	$24,118
married couple families	20,654	26,528	26,128
non-family households	8,879	13,218	12,711
single person households	4,026	15,289	14,730

continued on the next page

Table 7.02 continued

	Black	White	All Races
1985			
Number of households	9,797	76,576	88,458
percent of households with current dollar incomes of:			
under $2,500	5.0%	2.1%	2.4%
$2,500-$4,499	12.6	4.4	5.2
$5,000-$7,499	10.6	6.4	6.8
$7,500-$9,999	8.2	5.3	5.6
$10,000-$12,499	7.9	5.8	6.0
$12,500-$14,999	6.2	5.4	5.4
$15,000-$19,999	12.4	10.8	10.9
$20,000-$24,999	8.4	10.1	10.0
$25,000-$34,999	12.9	17.5	17.0
$35,000-$49,999	9.9	16.5	15.8
$50,000 and over	5.8	15.8	14.8
mean income	$19,335	$30,259	$29,066
Mean income by:			
occupation of the householder			
managerial, professional specialty	$36,191	$47,731	$47,042
technical, sales, administrative support	23,570	34,467	33,437
service workers	17,324	23,651	22,169
farming, forestry, fishing	12,001	20,183	19,756
precision production, craft, repair	27,996	32,388	32,110
operators, fabricators, laborers	23,037	28,015	27,314
work experience of the householder			
worked at full time jobs	$26,198	$36,779	$35,756
worked 50-52 weeks	28,394	39,304	38,307
type of household			
family households	$21,673	$34,605	$33,182
married couple families	28,258	36,991	36,350
non-family households	13,708	19,187	18,559
single person households	11,995	16,550	15,997

continued on the next page

Table 7.02 continued

	Black	White	All Races
1987			
Number of households	10,186	78,469	91,066
percent of households with current dollar incomes of:			
under $2,500	5.7%	1.8%	2.3%
$2,500-$4,499	12.2	3.6	4.6
$5,000-$7,499	10.4	5.8	6.3
$7,500-$9,999	7.3	4.9	5.2
$10,000-$12,499	7.5	5.4	5.6
$12,500-$14,999	5.8	4.9	5.0
$15,000-$19,999	11.0	10.0	10.0
$20,000-$24,999	9.7	9.2	9.2
$25,000-$34,999	12.2	16.7	16.1
$35,000-$49,999	10.8	18.1	17.2
$50,000 and over	7.5	19.7	18.5
mean income	$20,743	$33,526	$32,144
Mean income by:			
occupation of the householder			
managerial, professional specialty	$40,714	$53,036	$52,465
technical, sales, administrative support	26,303	38,564	37,456
service workers	18,188	24,542	23,039
farming, forestry, fishing	14,902	25,228	24,707
precision production, craft, repair	30,533	35,429	35,120
operators, fabricators, laborers	25,681	30,343	29,664
work experience of the householder			
worked at full time jobs	$28,682	$41,051	$38,017
worked 50-52 weeks	31,680	43,584	39,915
type of household			
family households	$23,468	$38,484	$35,395
married couple families	31,489	41,188	38,679
non-family households	13,817	21,134	23,560
single person households	12,355	18,048	20,277

continued on the next page

Table 7.02 continued

SOURCE: U.S. Bureau of the Census, Current Population Reports: Money Income of Households in the United States; March 1980, Series P-60, #132, p. 11, table 2; pp. 13-18, table 4; pp. 35-36, table 12; pp. 81-89, table 26. C3.186:P-60/132

U.S. Bureau of the Census, Current Population Reports: Money Income of Households in the United States; March 1985, Series P-60, #156, p. 7, table 2; pp. 9-14, table 4; pp. 19-20, table 6. C3.186:P-60/156

U.S. Bureau of the Census, Current Population Reports: Money Income of Households Families and Persons in the United States; March 1987, Series P-60, #162, pp. 9-11, tables 1, 2; pp.14-21, table 4; pp. 24-25, table 6. C3.186/2:989

NOTES: 'All Races' includes other races not shown separately. Number of households as of March of the following year. 'Occupation of the householder' represents the longest job held by the householder.

UNITS: Number of households in thousands; percent as a percent of total, as shown; mean income in current dollars.

Table 7.03 Money Income of Families in Current and Constant Dollars, 1975 - 1987

	Black	White	All Races
Current dollars			
1975	$ 8,779	$14,268	$13,719
1980	12,674	21,904	21,023
1981	13,266	23,517	22,388
1982	13,598	24,603	23,433
1983	14,561	25,837	24,674
1984	15,432	27,686	26,433
1985	16,786	29,152	27,735
1986	17,604	30,809	29,458
1987	18,098	32,274	30,853
Constant dollars			
1975	$18,538	$30,129	$28,970
1980	17,481	30,211	28,996
1981	16,578	29,388	27,977
1982	16,011	28,969	27,591
1983	16,610	29,474	28,147
1984	16,884	30,294	28,923
1985	17,734	30,799	29,302
1986	18,247	31,935	30,534
1987	18,098	32,274	30,853

SOURCE: U.S. Bureau of the Census, Statistical Abstract of the United States, 1989, p. 445, table 721, (data from *the Current Population Survey*). C 3.134:989

NOTES: 'All Races' includes other races not shown separately.

UNITS: Median money income in current and constant dollars, as shown.

Table 7.04 Money Income of Families, by Selected Family Characteristic, 1980

	Black	White	All Races
Families			
Number of families	6,317	52,710	60,309
percent of families with incomes:			
under $2,500	5.3%	1.6%	2.1%
$2,500-$4,499	11.3	3.3	4.1
$5,000-$7,499	13.4	5.3	6.2
$7,500-$9,999	10.4	6.0	6.5
$10,000-$12,499	9.1	7.1	7.3
$12,500-$14,999	7.7	6.8	6.9
$15,000-$19,999	12.8	14.1	14.0
$20,000-$24,999	10.2	14.2	13.7
$25,000-$34,999	11.8	20.8	19.8
$35,000-$49,999	6.3	13.6	12.8
$50,000 and over	1.7	7.2	6.7
median income	$12,674	$21,904	$21,023
mean income	$15,806	$24,939	$23,974
Mean family income by:			
occupation of the householder			
white collar workers	$22,276	$33,234	$32,583
blue collar workers	21,065	24,188	23,875
farm workers	na	17,473	17,197
service workers	15,110	20,100	19,053
work experience of the householder			
worked at full time jobs	$20,557	$28,239	$27,581
worked 50-52 weeks	22,258	30,143	29,538

continued on the next page

Table 7.04 continued

	Black	White	All Races
Mean family income - continued			
type of family			
married couple families	$20,654	$26,528	$26,128
wife in paid labor force	24,343	29,734	29,291
wife not in paid labor force	15,211	23,403	22,938
male householder, no wife present	16,067	21,680	20,820
female householder, no husband present	9,534	14,388	12,953
type of income			
wages and salaries	$15,971	$22,761	$22,047
non-farm self-employment	8,316	11,291	11,245
farm self employment	na	6,953	6,851
property income	520	2,022	1,937
- interest income	312	1,325	1,271
transfer payments and all other income	4,222	5,514	5,336
- social security or railroad retirement income	4,041	5,509	5,342
-public assistance and supplemental income	2,890	2,665	2,778

SOURCE: U.S. Bureau of the Census, Current Population Reports: Money Income of Households in the United States; March 1980, Series P-60, #132, pp. 39-42, table 14; pp. 45-47, table 16; pp. 61-63, tables 20, 21; pp. 81-89, table 26; pp. 114-116, table 36. C3.186:P-60/132

NOTES: 'All Races' includes other races not shown separately. Number of families as of March of the following year. 'Occupation of the householder' represents the longest job held by the householder. 'Property income' includes interest, dividends, net rental income, income from trusts and estates, and net royalty income.

UNITS: Number of families and families with income, in thousands of families; percent as a percent as shown; mean income in current dollars.

Table 7.05 Money Income of Families, by Selected Family Characteristic, 1985

	Black	White	All Races
Families			
Number of families	6,921	54,991	63,558
percent of families with incomes:			
under $2,500	4.2%	1.6%	1.9%
$2,500-$4,499	9.3	2.1	2.9
$5,000-$7,499	9.4	3.6	4.2
$7,500-$9,999	7.7	3.9	4.3
$10,000-$12,499	7.9	4.8	5.2
$12,500-$14,999	6.4	4.9	5.0
$15,000-$19,999	13.0	10.3	10.5
$20,000-$24,999	9.0	10.4	10.3
$25,000-$34,999	14.3	19.2	18.6
$35,000-$49,999	11.8	19.7	18.8
$50,000 and over	7.0	19.6	18.3
median income	$16,786	$29,152	$27,735
mean income	$21,359	$34,375	$32,944
Mean family income by:			
occupation of the householder			
managerial, professional specialty	$38,870	$52,649	$51,820
technical, sales, administrative support	24,732	38,798	37,436
service occupations	19,485	26,604	24,846
farming, forestry, fishing	16,185	21,305	21,285
precision production, craft, repair	30,315	33,691	33,507
operators, fabricators, laborers	24,223	29,449	28,725
work experience of the householder			
worked at full time jobs	$28,022	$39,510	$38,437
worked 50-52 weeks	30,281	41,992	40,968

continued on the next page

Table 7.05 continued

	Black	White	All Races
Mean family income - continued			
type of family			
married couple families	$28,163	$36,911	$36,267
wife in paid labor force	33,120	41,818	41,058
wife not in paid labor force	19,306	31,934	30,650
male householder, no wife present	18,205	29,041	27,525
female householder, no husband present	13,050	19,468	17,647
type of income			
wages and salaries	$21,651	$31,277	$30,258
non-farm self-employment	10,165	14,565	14,420
farm self employment	na	4,593	4,557
property income	1,042	3,486	3,327
- interest income	722	2,440	2,328
transfer payments and all other income	5,491	7,776	7,469
- social security or railroad retirement income	5,801	7,684	7,488
-public assistance and supplemental income	3,475	3,416	3,498

SOURCE: U.S. Bureau of the Census, Current Population Reports: Money Income of Households Families and Persons in the United States; March 1985, Series P-60, #156, pp. 26-29, tables 9, 10; pp. 40-46, tables 13, 14; pp. 56 64, table 17; pp. 86-88, table 25. C3.186:P-60/156

NOTES: 'All Races' includes other races not shown separately. Number of families as of March of the following year. 'Occupation of the householder' represents the longest job held by the householder. 'Property income' includes interest, dividends, net rental income, income from trusts and estates, and net royalty income.

UNITS: Number of families and families with income, in thousands of families; percent as a percent as shown; mean income in current dollars.

Table 7.06 Money Income of Families, by Selected Family Characteristic, 1987

	Black	White	All Races
Families			
Number of families	7,177	56,044	65,133
percent of families with incomes:			
under $2,500	5.0%	1.3%	1.8%
$2,500-$4,499	8.5	1.9	2.6
$5,000-$7,499	8.7	2.9	3.6
$7,500-$9,999	7.8	3.2	3.7
$10,000-$12,499	7.1	4.2	4.6
$12,500-$14,999	5.4	4.4	4.5
$15,000-$19,999	11.8	9.3	9.5
$20,000-$24,999	10.0	9.1	9.2
$25,000-$34,999	13.6	18.1	17.5
$35,000-$49,999	12.8	21.2	20.2
$50,000 and over	9.5	24.4	22.9
median income	$18,098	$32,274	$30,853
mean income	$23,252	$38,203	$36,568
Mean family income by:			
occupation of the householder			
managerial, professional specialty	$28,657	$58,487	$57,729
technical, sales, administrative support	27,400	43,159	41,724
service occupations	19,967	27,749	25,776
farming, forestry, fishing	18,420	26,452	26,200
precision production, craft, repair	33,078	37,138	36,910
operators, fabricators, laborers	27,834	32,068	31,472
work experience of the householder			
worked last year	$28,657	$42,625	$41,318
worked at full time jobs	30,595	44,136	42,915
worked 50-52 weeks	34,050	46,713	45,705

continued on the next page

Table 7.06 continued

	Black	White	All Races
Mean family income continued			
type of family			
married couple families	$31,426	$41,118	$40,481
wife in paid labor force	36,912	46,423	45,700
wife not in paid labor force	20,286	34,551	33,787
male householder, no wife present	21,183	31,112	29,521
female householder, no husband present	13,744	21,529	19,260
type of income			
wages and salaries	$24,074	$34,702	$33,641
non-farm self-employment	8,185	17,048	16,761
farm self employment	na	9,793	9,922
property income	876	3,467	3,301
- interest income	550	2,257	2,145
transfer payments and all other income	5,845	8,757	8,345
- social security or railroad retirement income	6,049	8,192	7,943
-public assistance and supplemental income	3,643	3,588	3,690

SOURCE: U.S. Bureau of the Census, Current Population Reports; Money Income of Households Families and Persons in the United States; March 1987, Series P-60, #162, pp. 31-35, tables 9, 10; pp. 47-52, table 14; pp. 61-71, table 17; pp. 91-93, table 25. C3.186/2:989

NOTES: 'All Races' includes other races not shown separately. Number of families as of March of the following year. 'Occupation of the householder' represents the longest job held by the householder. 'Property income' includes interest, dividends, net rental income, income from trusts and estates, and net royalty income.

UNITS: Number of families and families with income, in thousands of families; percent as a percent as shown; mean income in current dollars.

Table 7.07 Median Weekly Earnings of Families, by Type of Family and Number of Earners, 1980, 1985, 1988

	Black	White	All Races
1980			
All families with earners	$299	$411	$400
married couple families	366	438	433
with one earner	210	311	303
with two or more earners	472	542	535
families maintained by women	192	233	222
families maintained by men	307	374	360
1985			
All families with earners	$378	$543	$522
married couple families	487	589	582
with one earner	257	395	385
with two or more earners	622	723	715
families maintained by women	259	311	297
families maintained by men	360	475	450
1988			
All families with earners	$435	$616	$596
married couple families	576	677	668
with one earner	281	432	418
with two or more earners	713	818	811
families maintained by women	291	351	334
families maintained by men	419	496	486

SOURCE: U.S. Department of Labor, Bureau of Labor Statistics, Handbook of Labor Statistics, 1989, p. 200, table 44 (data from the Current Population Survey). L 2.3/5:989

NOTES: 'All Races' includes other races not shown separately. Data excludes families in which there is no wage or salary earner, or in which the husband, wife, or other person maintaining the family is either self-employed or in the armed forces.

UNITS: Median weekly earnings in dollars.

Table 7.08 Money Income of Persons 15 Years Old and Older, by Selected Characteristic, 1980

	Black		White		All Races	
	male	female	male	female	male	female
Number of persons	8,448	10,317	72,449	78,766	82,949	91,133
persons with incomes:						
under $2,000	1,083	1,696	5,800	17,918	7,125	20,036
$2,000-$2,999	553	1,150	2,393	6,504	3,014	7,766
$3,000-$3,999	549	1,095	2,663	6,019	3,309	7,228
$4,000-$4,999	447	616	2,796	5,120	3,347	5,853
$5,000-$5,999	382	572	2,629	4,205	3,086	4,860
$6,000 $6,999	328	492	2,570	3,738	3,001	4,350
$7,000-$8,499	523	654	4,087	5,220	4,739	6,013
$8,500-$9,999	425	390	3,259	3,931	3,770	4,421
$10,000-$12,499	830	810	6,879	6,411	7,870	7,373
$12,500-$14,999	529	361	4,928	3,691	5,572	4,147
$15,000-$17,499	517	329	5,636	2,912	6,274	3,321
$17,500-$19,999	308	174	4,495	1,663	4,891	1,877
$20,000-$24,999	487	175	8,241	1,854	8,915	2,072
$25,000-$29,999	246	46	5,160	657	5,533	720
$30,000-$34,999	99	23	2,853	333	2,988	359
$35,000-$49,999	51	11	3,164	261	3,274	286
$50,000-$74,999	25	3	1,312	92	1,375	95
$75,000 and over	5	-	555	45	575	47
median income	$ 8,009	$ 4,580	$13,328	$ 4,947	$12,530	$ 4,920
mean income	$ 9,843	$ 6,327	$15,967	$ 6,817	$15,340	$ 6,772
Mean income by:						
occupation						
white collar workers	$14,245	$ 9,833	$22,043	$ 9,090	$21,596	$ 9,174
blue collar workers	11,185	7,199	14,054	7,345	13,725	7,300
farm workers	7,495	4,951	9,984	4,363	9,504	4,494
service workers	4,539	na	8,242	2,888	7,885	2.852
work experience						
worked at full time jobs	$12,127	$ 9,193	$18,168	$ 9,846	$17,613	$ 9,762
worked 50-52 weeks	14,709	11,230	21,023	12,156	20,521	12,038

continued on the next page

Table 7.08 continued

	Black		White		All Races	
	male	female	male	female	male	female
Mean income by:						
educational attainment						
less than 8 years of school	$ 6,262	$ 3,692	$ 8,749	$ 4,076	$ 8,201	$ 3,989
high school graduates	13,154	7,757	17,586	7,077	17,181	7,138
1-3 years of college	14,566	9,338	19,919	8,747	19,358	8,814
4 or more years of college	18,192	14,097	27,651	11,765	27,216	11,901
type of income						
wages and salaries	$ 10,545	$ 7,506	$16,191	$ 7,704	$15,611	$ 7,695
non-farm self-employment	9,496	3,355	12,670	3,834	12,613	3,808
farm self employment	na	na	6,464	3,311	6,357	3,305
property income	427	322	1,085	1,119	1,051	1,077
- interest income	218	212	701	758	680	730
transfer payments and all other income	3,414	2,787	4,684	3,195	4,553	3,131
- social security or railroad retirement	3,187	2,531	4,071	3,074	3,982	3,018
-public assistance and supplemental	1,822	2,423	1,681	2,170	1,784	2,270

SOURCE: U.S. Bureau of the Census, Current Population Reports: Money Income of Households in the United States; March 1980, Series P-60, #132, pp. 130-131, table 46; p. 200, table 56; pp. 171-178, table 51; pp. 181-184, table 53; p. 212, table 59. C3.186:P-60/132

NOTES: 'All Races' includes other races not shown separately. Number of persons as of March of the following year. Data is based on persons living in households. Persons with incomes under $2,000 includes those with a loss. Occupation represents the longest job held by the person during the year. Educational attainment covers persons 25 years old and older; income covers persons 15 years old and older. 'Property income' includes interest, dividends, net rental income, income from trusts and estates, and net royalty income.

UNITS: Number of persons and persons by income in thousands of persons; median and mean income in dollars.

Table 7.09 Money Income of Persons 15 Years Old and Older, by Selected Characteristic, 1985

	Black		White		All Races	
	male	female	male	female	male	female
Number of persons	9,309	11,263	76,617	82,345	88,474	96,354
persons with incomes:						
under $2,000	909	1,301	5,180	14,024	6,304	15,848
$2,000-$2,999	400	871	1,808	4,420	2,297	5,425
$3,000-$3,999	407	993	2,190	4,856	2,671	5,958
$4,000-$4,999	479	946	2,095	4,635	2,642	5,693
$5,000-$5,999	351	540	2,169	4,201	2,595	4,848
$6,000-$6,999	353	556	2,278	3,992	2,708	4,648
$7,000-$8,499	584	707	3,402	5,006	4,132	5,855
$8,500-$9,999	365	416	2,896	3,779	3,353	4,288
$10,000-$12,499	737	788	5,895	6,579	6,859	7,576
$12,500-$14,999	598	530	4,527	4,672	5,245	5,339
$15,000-$17,499	673	531	4,940	4,359	5,739	5,012
$17,500-$19,999	453	363	3,869	2,980	4,423	3,432
$20,000-$24,999	672	483	7,521	4,839	8,410	5,513
$25,000-$29,999	454	336	6,374	2,759	7,018	3,194
$30,000-$34,999	301	135	5,324	1,437	5,767	1,633
$35,000-$49,999	289	99	7,730	1,450	8,211	1,585
$50,000-$74,999	80	14	3,421	484	3,588	509
$75,000 and over	32	4	1,603	169	1,669	177
median income	$10,768	$ 6,277	$17,111	$ 7,357	$16,311	$ 7,217
mean income	$13,376	$ 9,001	$21,523	$10,317	$20,652	$10,173
Mean income by:						
occupation						
managerial, professional specialty	$25,575	$18,273	$34,711	$17,763	$34,201	$17,857
technical, sales, administrative support	16,026	11,645	24,050	10,988	23,293	11,076
service occupations	10,270	6,800	13,161	5,935	12,549	6,104
farming, forestry, fishing	4,800	na	8,241	3,865	8,024	3,762

continued on the next page

Table 7.09 continued

	Black		White		All Races	
	male	female	male	female	male	female
Mean income by:						
occupation - continued						
precision production, craft, repair	$16,314	$11,217	$20,593	$12,998	$20,277	$12,595
operators, fabricators, laborers	13,808	9,649	16,378	9,528	15,971	$9,548
work experience						
worked at full time jobs	$16,618	$12,988	$24,531	$14,556	$23,767	$14,364
worked 50-52 weeks	19,940	15,448	28,140	17,249	27,414	17,028
educational attainment						
less than 8 years of school	$ 7,962	$ 4,684	$10,593	$ 5,809	$10,016	$ 5,582
high school graduates	15,392	10,155	21,584	10,121	20,916	10,120
1-3 years of college	18,658	12,687	25,768	12,763	24,987	12,754
4 or more years of college	27,210	19,587	38,460	18,367	37,570	18,410
type of income						
wages and salaries	$14,446	$10,668	$21,848	$11,295	$21,056	$11,239
non-farm self-employment	10,222	5,565	16,083	5,885	15,834	5,867
farm self employment	na	na	4,234	1,654	4,184	1,695
property income	709	708	1,866	2,021	1,794	1,937
- interest income	505	483	1,305	1,454	1,254	1,395
transfer payments and all other income	4,777	3,641	6,812	4,428	6,572	4,318
- social security or railroad retirement	4,757	3,620	5,803	4,330	5,701	4,261
-public assistance and supplemental income	2,383	2,922	2,526	2,881	2,560	2,919

continued on the next page

Table 7.09 continued

SOURCE: U.S. Bureau of the Census, Current Population Reports: Money Income of Households in the United States; March 1985, Series P-60, #156, pp. 107-109, table 31; pp. 135-138, table 35; pp. 141-143, table 37; pp. 160-163, tables 40, 41. C3.186:P-60/156

NOTES: 'All Races' includes other races not shown separately. Number of persons as of March of the following year. Data is based on persons living in households. Persons with incomes under $2,000 include those with a loss. Occupation represents the longest job held by the person during the year. Educational attainment covers persons 25 years old and older; income covers persons 15 years old and older. 'Property income' includes interest, dividends, net rental income, income from trusts and estates, and net royalty income.

UNITS: Number of persons and persons by income in thousands of persons; median and mean income in dollars.

Table 7.10 Money Income of Persons 15 Years Old and Older, by Selected Characteristic, 1987

	Black		White		All Races	
	male	female	male	female	male	female
Number of persons	9,603	11,618	77,823	83,518	90,284	98,168
persons with incomes:						
under $2,000	878	1,310	4,742	12,886	5,859	14,759
$2,000-$2,999	340	740	1,824	4,043	2,279	4,901
$3,000-$3,999	390	839	1,735	4,448	2,218	5,429
$4,000-$4,999	542	1,085	2,043	4,405	2,669	5,626
$5,000-$5,999	395	630	2,050	4,071	2,554	4,807
$6,000-$6,999	348	545	2,021	3,983	2,440	4,620
$7,000-$8,499	528	704	3,238	5,271	3,873	6,127
$8,500-$9,999	396	406	2,697	3,714	3,199	4,228
$10,000-$12,499	803	799	5,700	6,773	6,699	7,789
$12,500-$14,999	533	576	4,379	4,797	5,009	5,524
$15,000-$17,499	574	664	4,850	4,814	5,578	5,615
$17,500-$19,999	385	376	3,814	3,376	4,309	3,855
$20,000-$24,999	741	625	7,723	5,523	8,714	6,321
$25,000-$29,999	526	352	6,567	3,312	7,266	3,768
$30,000-$34,999	407	222	5,550	2,010	6,124	2,331
$35,000-$49,999	407	165	9,243	2,326	9,941	2,602
$50,000-$74,999	110	32	4,397	653	4,669	708
$75,000 and over	37	5	2,115	255	2,225	268
median income	$11,101	$ 6,796	$18,854	$17,775	$26,772	$ 8,101
mean income	$14,391	$ 9,919	$23,643	$20216	$31,304	$11,435
Mean income by:						
occupation						
managerial, professional specialty	763	1,071	15,274	12,718	16,635	13,813
technical, sales, administrative support	941	2,426	11,646	22,347	13,091	25,442
service occupations	1,210	1,846	4,872	8,278	6,377	10,420
farming, forestry, fishing	236	19	2,803	550	3,086	584

continued on the next page

Table 7.10 continued

	Black		White		All Races	
	male	female	male	female	male	female
Mean income by:						
occupation - continued						
precision production, craft, repair	950	148	12,066	1,151	13,252	1,371
operators, fabricators, laborers	2,115	934	11,894	4,123	14,348	5,268
work experience						
worked at full time jobs	$18,012	$14,282	$27,010	$16,436	$26,197	$16,221
worked 50-52 weeks	21,302	17,052	30,631	19,024	29,866	18,839
educational attainment						
less than 8 years of school	$ 9,018	$ 5,075	$11,759	$ 6,246	$11,195	$ 5,970
high school graduates	15,613	11,199	23,340	11,092	22,515	11,083
1-3 years of college	20,708	14,480	28,209	14,397	27,401	14,443
4 or more years of college	24,792	18,925	37,229	18,367	36,262	18,321
type of income						
wages and salaries	6,391	6,542	55,988	48,016	64,355	56,233
non-farm self-employment	266	161	6,948	3,603	7,440	3,891
farm self employment	12	2	1,455	261	1,481	265
property income	2,353	2,754	47,940	51,409	51,752	55,666
- interest income	2,233	2,628	46,552	50,032	50,191	54,118
transfer payments and all other income	2,961	4,995	24,771	30,012	28,535	35,776
- social security or railroad retirement	1,385	1,959	12,803	17,755	14,448	20,002
-public assistance and supplemental	601	2,189	356	3,423	2,077	5,843

continued on the next page

Table 7.10 continued

SOURCE: U.S. Bureau of the Census, Current Population Reports: Money Income of Households Families and Persons in the United States; March 1987, Series P-60, #162, pp. 104-105, table 27; pp. 113-115, table 31; pp. 137-144, table 35; pp. 147-150, table 37; pp. 166-168, tables 40, 41. C3.186/2:989

NOTES: 'All Races' includes other races not shown separately. Number of persons as of March of the following year. Data is based on persons living in households. Persons with incomes under $2,000 includes those with a loss. Occupation represents the longest job held by the person during the year. Educational attainment covers persons 25 years old and older; income covers persons 15 years old and older. 'Property income' includes interest, dividends, net rental income, income from trusts and estates, and net royalty income.

UNITS: Number of persons and persons by income in thousands of persons; median and mean income in current dollars.

Table 7.11 Median Weekly Earnings of Full-Time Wage and Salary Workers, by Sex and Age, 1980, 1985, 1988

	Black		White		All Races	
	male	female	male	female	male	female
1980						
All full-time wage and salary workers	$244	$185	$319	202	$312	$201
workers 16-24 years old	173	158	212	168	208	167
workers 25 years old and over	264	194	348	215	339	212
- workers 25-54 years old	267	197	349	217	340	214
- workers 55 years old and over	242	174	344	205	334	202
1985						
All full-time wage and salary workers	$304	$252	$417	$281	$406	$277
workers 16-24 years old	199	193	245	212	240	210
workers 25 years old and over	325	265	459	300	442	296
- workers 25-54 years old	326	268	457	303	441	298
- workers 55 years old and over	323	241	476	286	455	281
1988						
All full-time wage and salary workers	$347	$288	$465	318	$449	$315
workers 16-24 years old	224	218	266	237	261	235
workers 25 years old and over	378	301	497	340	487	335
- workers 25-54 years old	380	304	495	344	485	338
- workers 55 years old and over	362	266	514	318	501	312

SOURCE: U.S. Department of Labor, Bureau of Labor Statistics, Handbook of Labor Statistics, 1989, pp. 161-162, table 41 (data from the Current Population Survey). L 2.3/5:989

NOTES: 'All Races' includes other races not shown separately.

UNITS: Median weekly earning in dollars.

Table 7.12 Median Annual Earnings of Year-Round, Full-Time Wage and Salary Workers, by Sex, 1980 - 1987

	Black		White		All Races	
	male	female	male	female	male	female
1980	$13,737	$10,609	$19,570	$11,413	$18,910	$11,287
1981	14,988	11,166	21,087	12,476	20,593	12,345
1982	15,596	12,355	22,149	13,520	21,542	13,352
1983	16,193	12,896	22,917	14,288	22,296	14,111
1984	16,687	13,716	24,683	15,110	23,816	15,006
1985	17,456	14,495	25,592	15,901	24,939	15,728
1986	18,148	14,814	26,441	16,571	25,676	16,336
1987	19,147	15,952	27,073	17,209	26,312	17,047

SOURCE: U.S. Department of Labor, Bureau of Labor Statistics, Handbook of Labor Statistics, 1989, p. 231, table 53 (data from the Current Population Survey). L 2.3/5:989

NOTES: 'All Races' includes other races not shown separately. Data covers the earnings of wage and salary workers who usually worked 35 or more hours per week for 50 to 52 weeks during the year.

UNITS: Median annual earning in dollars.

Table 7.13 Per Capita Money Income in Current and Constant Dollars, 1975 - 1987

	Black	White	All Races
Current dollars			
1975	$ 2,972	$ 5,072	$ 4,818
1980	4,804	8,233	7,787
1981	5,129	8,979	8,476
1982	5,360	9,527	8,980
1983	5,755	10,125	9,548
1984	6,277	10,939	10,328
1985	6,840	11,671	11,013
1986	7,207	12,352	11,670
1987	7,499	13,031	12,287
Constant dollars			
1975	$ 6,276	$10,710	$10,174
1980	6,626	11,355	10,740
1981	6,409	11,220	10,592
1982	6,311	11,218	10,573
1983	6,565	11,550	10,892
1984	6,868	11,969	11,301
1985	7,226	12,330	11,635
1986	7,470	12,803	12,096
1987	7,499	13,031	12,287

SOURCE: U.S. Bureau of the Census, Statistical Abstract of the United States, 1989, p. 450, table 730 (data from the Current Population Survey). C 3.134.989

NOTES: 'All Races' includes other races not shown separately.

UNITS: Median money income per capita in current and constant dollars, as shown.

Table 7.14 Families Below the Poverty Level, 1975 - 1987

	Black	White	All Races
Number below the poverty level			
1975	1,513	3,838	5,450
1980	1,826	4,195	6,217
1981	1,972	4,670	6,851
1982	2,158	5,118	7,512
1983	2,161	5,254	7,681
1984	2,094	4,925	7,277
1985	1,983	4,983	7,223
1986	1,987	4,811	7,023
1987	2,149	4,592	7,059
Percent below the poverty level			
1975	27.1%	7.7%	9.7%
1980	28.9	8.0	10.3
1981	30.8	8.8	11.2
1982	33.0	9.6	12.2
1983	32.3	9.7	12.4
1984	30.9	9.1	11.6
1985	28.7	9.1	11.4
1986	28.0	8.6	10.9
1987	29.9	8.2	10.8

SOURCE: U.S. Bureau of the Census, Statistical Abstract of the United States, 1989, p. 455, table 739 (data from the Current Population Survey). C 3.134:989

NOTES: 'All Races' includes other races not shown separately.

UNITS: Number below the poverty level in thousands of families; percent as a percent of all families, by race, as shown.

Table 7.15 Selected Characteristics of Families Below the Poverty Level, 1980 - 1987

	number			poverty rate		
	Black	White	All Races	Black	White	All Races
1980						
All families below poverty	1,626	4,195	6,217	28.9%	8.0%	10.3%
Age of the householder						
15-24 years old	260	534	821	48.0	16.9	21.8
65 years old and over	221	603	837	28.3	7.3	9.1
Region of residence						
Northeast	309	831	1,153	26.6%	7.2%	9.0%
Midwest	405	948	1,377	31.7	6.7	8.8
South	1,018	1,601	2,669	30.9	9.4	13.0
West	95	816	1,017	16.2	8.2	9.0
Size of family						
2 persons	467	1,527	2,034	23.8%	7.1%	8.6%
3 persons	400	897	1,330	26.5	7.3	9.5
4 persons	372	81	1,234	29.3	7.5	9.9
5 persons	252	490	765	33.5	9.6	12.7
6 persons	151	248	414	36.2	12.6	16.8
7 persons	94	121	234	51.1	18.8	26.5
8 persons	46	54	111	38.0	22.0	27.4
9 persons or more	44	47	94	46.0	28.6	32.5
mean size	3.93	3.48	3.64			
Education of the householder						
less than 8 years of school	372	827	1,262	35.8%	21.5%	24.9%
8 years of school	141	417	565	36.5	10.8	13.1
1-3 years high school	489	747	1,267	38.0	11.7	16.2
4 years high school	417	1,144	1,593	22.7	6.4	8.0
1 or more years college	147	526	708	12.0	3.0	3.7
Work experience						
worked in 1980	701	2,277	3,073	16.3%	5.4%	6.5%
worked 50-52 weeks in 1980	261	922	1,217	8.6	2.8	3.3

continued on the next page

Table 7.15 continued

	number			poverty rate		
	Black	White	All Races	Black	White	All Races
1985						
All families below poverty	1,983	4,983	7,223	28.7%	9.21%	11.4%
Age of the householder						
15-24 years old	283	661	957	62.1	24.7	30.2
65 years old and over	188	506	708	22.0	5.6	7.0
Region of residence						
Northeast	330	931	1,281	26.3	8.0	9.7
Midwest	450	1,274	1,769	32.9	9.0	11.2
South	1,088	1,746	2,875	29.3	9.5	13.0
West	115	1,043	1,298	19.5	9.6	10.4
Size of family						
2 persons	539	1,735	2,325	24.8	7.6	9.1
3 persons	497	1,172	1,705	27.5	8.9	11.1
4 persons	411	1,050	1,513	29.0	9.1	11.3
5 persons	262	594	913	30.0	11.9	14.9
6 persons	120	240	387	35.6	15.2	19.0
7 persons or more	155	192	380	49.7	25.0	32.1
mean size	3.75	3.45	3.56	-	-	-
mean number of children per family with children	2.39	2.14	2.23	-	-	-
Education of the householder						
less than 8 years of school	262	771	1,068	33.8	24.1	26.2
8 years of school	119	456	592	32.7	13.9	15.9
1-3 years high school	489	904	1,429	39.4	15.0	19.4
4 years high school	584	1,498	2,163	25.0	7.9	9.9
1 or more years college	234	637	921	13.7	3.1	4.0
Work experience						
worked in 1985	792	2,721	3,630	16.9	6.4	7.5
worked 50-52 weeks in 1985	294	1,148	1,484	8.6	3.4	3.9

continued on the next page

Table 7.15 continued

	number			poverty rate		
	Black	White	All Races	Black	White	All Races
1987						
All families below poverty	2,149	4,592	7,059	29.9%	8.2%	10.8%
Age of the householder						
15-24 years old	285	558	863	56.7	23.8	29.5
65 years old and over	215	511	751	23.7	5.4	7.2
Region of residence						
Northeast	312	859	1,220	26.3	7.2	9.1
Midwest	467	1,090	1,620	33.6	7.7	10.2
South	1,237	1,636	2,925	31.1	8.8	12.8
West	133	1,007	1,293	21.3	8.8	9.9
Size of family						
2 persons	609	1,645	2,346	25.4	6.9	8.7
3 persons	519	1,040	1,622	28.4	7.9	10.5
4 persons	457	906	1,414	29.5	7.7	10.3
5 persons	280	538	864	37.4	11.1	14.8
6 persons	137	273	453	40.3	17.1	22.0
7 persons or more	148	191	360	46.6	23.5	29.5
mean size	3.70	3.44	3.54	-	-	-
mean number of children per family with children	2.36	2.19	2.25	-	-	-
Education of the householder						
less than 8 years of school	299	827	1,207	36.4	25.4	28.3
8 years of school	133	403	552	34.9	14.4	17.1
1-3 years high school	55	810	1,406	42.6	13.4	18.8
4 years high school	685	1,377	2,132	27.8	6.9	9.3
1 or more years college	191	617	899	11.2	2.9	3.7
Work experience						
worked in 1987	840	2,349	3,311	17.5	5.4	6.7
worked 50-52 weeks in 1987	286	1,012	1,334	8.2	2.9	3.4

continued on the next page

Table 7.15 continued

SOURCE: U.S. Bureau of the Census, Current Population Reports: Characteristics of the Population Below the Poverty Level, 1980, Series P-60, # 133, pp. 19-20, table 4; pp. 76-78, tables 17, 18, 19; p. 107, table 26; p. 128, table 31. C 3.186:P-60/133

U.S. Bureau of the Census, Current Population Reports: Poverty in the United States 1985, Series P-60, #158, p. 73, table 14; p. 97, table 21; pp. 119-121, table 26. C 3.186/22:985

U.S. Bureau of the Census, Current Population Reports: Money Income and Poverty Status in the United States: 1987, Series P-60, #161, pp. 12-14, table 2; p. 36, table 19. C 3.186/11:987

NOTES: 'All Races' includes other races not shown separately. Families as of March of the following year. 'Education of the householder' covers householders 25 years old and older. 'Work experience' restricted to families with civilian workers.

UNITS: Number below the poverty level in thousands of families; poverty rate as a percent of all families, by race, as shown.

Table 7.16 Persons Below the Poverty Level, 1975 - 1987

	Black	White	All Races
Number below the poverty level			
1975	7.5	17.8	25.9
1980	8.6	19.7	29.3
1981	9.2	21.6	31.8
1982	9.7	23.5	34.4
1983	9.9	24.0	33.3
1984	9.5	23.0	33.7
1985	8.9	22.9	33.1
1986	9.0	22.2	32.4
1987	9.7	21.4	32.5
Percent below the poverty level			
1975	31.3%	9.7%	12.3%
1980	32.5	10.2	13.0
1981	34.2	11.1	14.0
1982	35.6	12.0	15.0
1983	35.7	12.1	15.2
1984	33.8	11.5	14.4
1985	31.3	11.4	14.0
1986	31.1	11.0	13.6
1987	33.1	10.5	13.5

SOURCE: U.S. Bureau of the Census, Statistical Abstract of the United States, 1989, p. 452, table 734 (data from the *Current Population Survey*). C 3.134:989

NOTES: 'All Races' includes other races not shown separately.

UNITS: Number below the poverty level in millions of persons; percent as a percent of all persons, by race, as shown.

Table 7.17 Children Below the Poverty Level, 1975 - 1987

	Black	White	All Races
Number below the poverty level			
1975	3,884	6,748	10,882
1980	3,906	6,817	11,114
1981	4,170	7,429	12,068
1982	4,388	8,282	13,139
1983	4,273	8,534	13,427
1984	4,320	8,086	12,929
1985	4,057	7,838	12,483
1986	4,039	7,714	12,257
1987	4,297	7,550	12,435
Percent below the poverty level			
1975	41.4%	12.5%	16.8%
1980	42.1	13.4	17.9
1981	44.9	14.7	19.5
1982	47.3	16.5	21.3
1983	46.2	17.0	21.8
1984	46.2	16.1	21.0
1985	43.1	15.6	20.1
1986	42.7	15.3	19.8
1987	45.1	15.0	20.0

SOURCE: U.S. Bureau of the Census, Statistical Abstract of the United States, 1989, p. 454, table 738 (data from the Current Population Survey). C 3.134:989

NOTES: 'All Races' includes other races not shown separately. Data covers only related children under 18 years of age living in families.

UNITS: Number below the poverty level in thousands of children; percent as a percent of all children, by race, as shown.

Table 7.18 Persons Below the Poverty Level, and Poverty Rate Using Alternative Methods of Valuing Noncash Benefits, 1987

	Black	White	All Races
Number below the poverty level			
current poverty definition	9,683	21,409	32,546
market value definition			
valuing food and housing	8,349	19,336	29,004
valuing food, housing, and medical benefits, excluding institutional expenditures	5,475	14,086	20,440
recipient value definition			
valuing food and housing	8,713	19,757	29,821
valuing food, housing, and medical benefits, excluding institutional expenditures	7,768	17,664	26,575
Percent below the poverty level			
current poverty definition	33.1%	10.5%	13.5%
market value definition			
valuing food and housing	28.5	9.5	12.0
valuing food, housing, and medical benefits, excluding institutional expenditures	18.7	6.9	8.5
recipient value definition			
valuing food and housing	29.8	9.7	12.4
valuing food, housing, and medical benefits, excluding institutional expenditures	26.5	8.7	11.0

continued on the next page

Table 7.18 continued

SOURCE: U.S. Bureau of the Census, Statistical Abstract of the United States, 1989, p. 457, table 743. C 3.134:989

NOTES: 'All Races' includes other races not shown separately. Official poverty thresholds do not account for the value of noncash benefits received by persons. In an effort to account for the value of food stamps, school lunch programs, medical care programs, housing subsidies, the Bureau of the Census has formulated two approaches to valuing such benefits. The market value approach assigns a market value to in-kind transfers, equal to the private market value of the benefits received. The recipient value method assigns a value to the noncash benefit that would make the recipient feel just as well off as the noncash value itself. This value never exceeds (and in most cases is less than) the market value.

UNITS: Number below the poverty level in thousands of persons; percent as a percent of all persons, by race, as shown.

Table 7.19 Persons Receiving Benefits from Major Assistance Programs, by Length of Time of Receipt, 1986

	Black	White	All Races
Receipt of major assistance			
no months	51.5%	86.1%	81.7%
one month or more	48.5	13.9	18.3
1-6 months	7.8	3.6	4.1
7-24 months	12.2	4.2	5.1
25 months or more	28.5	6.1	9.0
32 months	24.0	4.7	7.2
mean number of months	11.2	2.6	3.7
Receipt of cash assistance			
no months	73.3%	93.8%	91.2%
one month or more	26.7	6.2	8.8
1-6 months	3.7	1/3	1.6
7-24 months	7.9	1.8	2.6
25 months or more	15.1	3.0	4.6
32 months	11.3	2.2	3.4
mean number of months	6.1	1.3	1.9
Receipt of food stamps			
no months	62.8%	90.1%	86.6%
one month or more	37.2	9.9	13.4
1-6 months	7.0	2.9	3.4
7-24 months	13.4	3.6	4.9
25 months or more	16.8	3.4	5.1
32 months	10.9	2.2	3.3
mean number of months	7.5	1.7	2.4
Months in which assistance accounted for 50% or more of income			
no months	70.4%	93.6%	90.7%
one month or more	29.6	6.4	9.3
1-6 months	6.4	1.9	2.5
7-24 months	10.1	2.3	3.2
25 months or more	13.1	2.2	3.6
32 months	8.2	1.4	2.4
mean number of months	5.8	1.1	1.7

continued on the next page

Table 7.19 continued

	Black	White	All Races
Proportion of income accounted for by assistance			
none	58.4%	88.8%	85.0%
one percent or more	41.6	11.2	15.0
1-9 percent	4.7	1.9	2.3
10-24 percent	8.6	2.9	3.6
25-49 percent	7.0	2.4	3.9
50-74 percent	7.4	1.2	1.9
75-99 percent	6.3	1.6	2.3
100 percent	7.5	1.3	2.1
mean percent	22.0	4.8	7.0

SOURCE: U.S. Bureau of the Census, Current Population Reports: Household Economic Studies - Characteristics of Persons Receiving Benefits from Major Assistance Programs, Series P-70, #14, p. 2, table A. C 3.186/P-70/14

NOTES: 'All Races' includes other races not shown separately. 'Major assistance programs' include AFDC (Aid to Families with Dependent Children), General Assistance, SSI (Supplemental Security Income), food stamps, Medicaid, and housing assistance. 'Major cash assistance programs' include AFDC (Aid to Families with Dependent Children), General Assistance, SSI (Supplemental Security Income). In tabulating proportion of income in which assistance accounted for more than 50%, the value of food stamps was included, but not the value of any other noncash benefit.

UNITS: Percent as a percent of all persons in households, 100.0%.

Table 7.20 Households Owning Assets, by Type of Asset, 1984

	Black	White	All Races
Assets by type of asset, 1984			
interest-earning assets at financial institutions			
total	43.8%	75.4%	71.8%
passbook savings accounts	41.6	65.7	62.9
money market deposits	2.6	17.4	15.7
certificates of deposit	4.2	21.2	19.1
interest-earning checking accounts	7.2	27.0	24.9
other interest-earning assets			
total	2.1%	9.4%	8.5%
money market funds	0.9	4.2	3.8
U.S. Government securities	0.1	1.6	1.4
municipal and corporate bonds	0.3	2.9	2.6
other interest-earning assets	1.0	3.0	2.8
regular checking account	32.0%	56.9%	53.9%
stocks and mutual fund shares	5.4	22.0	20.0
own business or profession	4.0	14.0	12.9
motor vehicle	65.0	88.5	85.8
own home	43.8	67.3	64.3
rental property	6.6	10.1	9.8
other real estate	3.3	10.9	10.0
mortgages	0.1	3.3	2.9
U.S. Savings Bonds	7.4	16.1	15.0
IRA or KEOGH account	5.1	21.4	19.5
other assets	0.7	3.9	3.5

SOURCE: U.S. Bureau of the Census, Current Population Reports: Household Economic Studies - Household Wealth and Asset Ownership, 1984, Series P-70, #7, pp. 8-12, tables 1, 2. C 3.186/P70/14

NOTES: 'All Races' includes other races not shown separately.

UNITS: Percent of households owning assets by type of asset, as a percent of all households, 100.0%.

Table 7.21 Households Owning Assets: Median and Mean Value of Type of Asset; Distribution of Household Net Worth, 1984

	Black	White	All Races
Median value by type of asset, 1984			
interest-earning assets at financial institutions	$ 739	$ 3,457	$ 3,066
other interest-earning assets	na	9,826	9,471
regular checking account	318	457	449
stocks and mutual fund shares	2,777	3,903	3,892
equity in own home	24,077	41,999	40,597
rental property equity	27,291	34,516	34,556
other real estate equity	10,423	15,488	14,791
equity in own business or profession	2,054	7,113	6,298
motor vehicle	2,691	4,293	4,104
U.S. Savings Bonds	200	305	300
IRA or KEOGH account	2,450	4,922	4,805
other assets	na	13,098	12,789
Median net worth	$ 3,397	$39,135	$32,667
Mean value by type of asset, 1984			
interest-earning assets at financial institutions	$ 3,135	$16,865	$15,815
other interest-earning assets	na	29,624	28,962
regular checking account	599	947	922
stocks and mutual fund shares	2,813	27,694	26,867
equity in own home	29,914	51,939	50,574
rental property equity	38,142	73,831	72,121
other real estate equity	14,423	35,102	34,434
equity in own business or profession	33,997	64,495	63,103
motor vehicle	3,446	5,707	5,516
U.S. Savings Bonds	550	2,624	2,492
IRA or KEOGH account	3,441	9,047	8,851
other assets	na	57,235	55,788
Mean net worth	$20,241	$86,332	$78,734

continued on the next page

Table 7.21 continued

	Black	White	All Races
Distribution of net worth, 1984			
Total	100.0%	100.0%	100.0%
zero or negative net worth	30.5	8.4	11.0
$1-$4,999	23.9	14.0	15.3
$5,000-$9,999	6.8	6.3	6.4
$10,000-$24,999	14.0	12.2	12.4
$25,000-$49,999	11.7	15.0	14.5
$50,000-$99,999	9.3	20.7	19.3
$100,000-$249,999	3.3	16.9	15.3
$250,000-$499,999	0.5	4.4	4.0
$500,000 or over	0.1	2.1	1.9

SOURCE: U.S. Bureau of the Census, Current Population Reports: Household Economic Studies - Household Wealth and Asset Ownership, 1984, Series P-70, #7, pp. 14-23, tables 3, 4, 5.
C 3.186/P-70/14

NOTES: 'All Races' includes other races not shown separately.

UNITS: Median and mean value of assets, by type of asset, in dollars.

Table 8.01 Social Security Benefits and Beneficiaries, 1980, 1985, 1987

	Black	White	All Races
1980			
Beneficiaries			
total	3,576,014	31,431,133	35,584,955
retired workers	1,533,904	17,780,617	19,562,085
disabled workers	432,449	2,376,823	2,858,680
wives	229,177	3,147,297	3,436,099
husbands	3,719	36,728	41,328
children	645,162	3,501,249	4,606,517
widowed mothers and fathers	115,235	428,822	562,316
widows (nondisabled)	288,931	3,935,175	4,262,607
widowers (nondisabled)	2,208	17,870	20,328
widows (disabled)	20,168	104,847	126,679
widowers (disabled)	139	747	901
parents	1,921	12,052	14,779
special age-72 beneficiary	2,986	88,098	91,808
wife of special age-72 beneficiary	15	808	828
Average monthly benefit			
total	$236.00	$308.60	$300.20
retired workers	281.60	346.90	341.40
disabled workers	325.30	379.70	370.70
wives	119.00	168.30	164.20
husbands	111.50	132.10	130.00
children	154.00	200.00	187.60
widowed mothers and fathers	196.60	261.70	246.20
widows (nondisabled)	244.80	316.90	311.00
widowers (nondisabled)	210.00	243.20	239.40
widows (disabled)	169.80	212.60	205.40
widowers (disabled)	131.50	148.10	145.70
parents	247.00	282.60	276.00
special age-72 beneficiary	104.90	104.90	104.90
wife of special age-72 beneficiary	52.60	52.60	52.60

continued on the next page

Table 8.01 continued

	Black	White	All Races
1985			
Beneficiaries			
total	3,515,354	32,847,468	37,058,317
retired workers	1,755,138	20,337,090	22,431,930
disabled workers	424,530	2,166,631	2,656,638
wives	201,439	3,071,114	3,337,464
husbands	4,208	31,318	37,135
children	685,635	2,486,253	3,319,490
widowed mothers and fathers	72,569	280,874	371,659
widows (nondisabled)	346,486	4,324,753	4,725,618
widowers (nondisabled)	3,712	25,18	30,182
widows (disabled)	18,870	85,058	105,816
widowers (disabled)	248	913	1,189
parents	1,290	7,436	9,541
special age-72 beneficiary	1,226	29,973	31,513
wife of special age-72 beneficiary	5	137	142
Average monthly benefit			
total	$345.50	$439.70	$429.10
retired workers	398.20	486.30	478.60
disabled workers	429.80	295.80	483.80
wives	176.20	241.90	236.80
husbands	146.70	170.10	166.70
children	na	na	na
widowed mothers and fathers	279.90	350.70	332.40
widows (nondisabled)	341.80	442.20	433.90
widowers (nondisabled)	286.10	322.80	317.80
widows (disabled)	268.30	328.20	316.60
widowers (disabled)	186.30	193.50	191.80
parents	344.50	387.30	378.20
special age-72 beneficiary	138.30	138.10	138.20
wife of special age-72 beneficiary	138.50	137.00	137.00

continued on the next page

Table 8.01 continued

	Black	White	All Races
1987			
Beneficiaries			
total	3,605,950	33,683,100	38,166,760
retired workers	1,822,840	21,159,270	23,418,290
disabled workers	456,390	2,227,630	2,787,950
wives	199,520	3,071,620	3,346,780
husbands	4,550	32,300	39,390
children	671,700	2,401,720	3,246,160
widowed mothers and fathers	61,520	248,800	329,710
widows (nondisabled)	363,880	4,405,440	4,832,080
widowers (nondisabled)	3,830	28,150	32,790
widows (disabled)	19,730	82,450	104,710
widowers (disabled)	240	1,120	1,410
parents	1,080	6,000	7,960
special age-72 beneficiary	670	18,600	19,530
Average monthly benefit			
total	$372.70	$473.00	$461.30
retired workers	428.00	521.30	512.90
disabled workers	454.60	521.90	508.50
wives	190.70	260.00	254.50
husbands	141.60	169.70	164.60
children	na	na	na
widowed mothers and fathers	298.00	372.60	353.10
widows (nondisabled)	370.80	478.00	468.90
widowers (nondisabled)	310.00	349.90	344.40
widows (disabled)	288.10	348.70	335.80
widowers (disabled)	188.70	205.70	199.20
parents	366.60	415.30	406.20
special age-72 beneficiary	146.10	145.30	145.30

continued on the next page

Table 8.01 continued

SOURCE: U.S. Department of Health & Human Services, Social Security Administration, Social Security Bulletin, Annual Statistical Supplement, 1982, pp. 112-123, table 54; 1987, pp. 145-155, table 70; 1988, pp. 153-163, table 5.A1 (1987). HE 3.3/3(year)

NOTES: 'All Races' includes other races not shown separately.

UNITS: Beneficiaries in number of beneficiaries, average monthly benefit in current dollars.

Table 8.02 Selected Characteristics of Farms and Farm Operators, 1987

	Black farms	All farms
Characteristics of farms		
Farms and land in farms		
farms (number)	22,954	2,087,759
land in farms (acres)	2,636,896	964,470,625
harvested croplands (acres)	794,377	282,223,880
Farms by size		
1-9 acres	3,182	181,257
10-49 acres	7,993	412,437
50-139 acres	7,363	na
140-219 acres	2,137	na
220-499 acres	1,647	na
500 acres or more	732	368,922
Owned and rented land in farms		
owned land in farms		
farms	20,648	1,238,547
acres	1,668,576	317,787,149
rented or leased land in farms		
farms	8,000	240,200
acres	968,320	126,868,953
Market value of agricultural products sold, in thousands of dollars)		
total	$332,444	$136,048,516
crops (including nursery and greenhouse crops)	182,371	58,931,085
livestock, poultry and their products	150,073	77,117,431
Farms by value of sales		
less than $2,500	10,662	490,296
$2,500-$9,999	7,866	537,890
$10,000-$19,999	1,943	na
$20,000-$24,000	469	na
$25,000 or more	2,014	733,407

continued on the next page

Table 8.02 continued

	Black farms	All farms
Farms by Standard Industrial Classification		
cash grains	3,150	458,396
field crops except cash grains	4,311	243,628
cotton	627	27,674
tobacco	2,460	87,776
sugarcane and sugarbeets; Irish potatoes; field crops except cash grains not elsewhere classified	1,224	123,553
vegetables and melons	703	28,801
fruits and tree nuts	298	88,323
horticultural specialties	110	31,469
general farms, primarily crop	666	57,888
livestock, except dairy, poultry and animal specialties	12,593	892,267
beef cattle, except feedlots	8,539	643,831
dairy farms	246	138,311
poultry and eggs	285	38,494
animal specialties	368	87,855
general farms, primarily livestock and animal specialties	224	22,327
Characteristics of the farm operator		
Residence		
on farm operated	13,255	1,487,937
not on farm operated	6,468	442,613
not reported	3,231	157,209
Principal occupation		
farming	10,071	1,138,179
other	12,883	949,580
Days of work off farm		
none	8,666	844,476
any	12,333	1,115,560

continued on the next page

Table 8.02 continued

	Black farms	All farms
Characteristics of the farm operator - continued		
Days of work off farm - continued		
1-99 days	2,426	200,031
100-199 days	2,348	178,323
200 days or more	7,559	737,206
Years on present farm		
2 years or less	1,195	113,554
3 or 4 years	1,221	135,473
5 to 9 years	2,456	303,875
10 years or more	9,671	1,163,336
average on present farm	19.6	18.8
Age		
under 25 years old	172	35,851
25-34 years old	1,261	242,688
35-44 years old	3,309	411,153
45-54 years old	4,285	454,910
55-59 years old	2,574	247,908
60-64 years old	3,000	247,908
65-69 years old	2,985	191,435
70 years old and over	5,366	255,906
average age	57.9	52.0
Sex		
male	20,901	1,956,118
female	2,053	131,641

SOURCE: U.S. Bureau of the Census, 1987 Census of Agriculture, Vol. 1 Geographic Area Series, Pt. 51, U.S. Summary and State Data, pp. 7-8, table 1; pp. 20-23, tables 16, 17, 18.
C 3.31/4:987/v. 1/ pt. 51

NOTES: 'All farms' includes farms owned/operated by persons of all races.

UNITS: Farms, farms by size, farms by organization, farms by value of sales, farms by Standard Industrial Classification, in number of farms; land in farms and harvested crop lands in acres; market value of agricultural products sold in thousands of dollars. Characteristics of farm operators in number of farm operators.

Table 8.03 Summary of Results of the 1986 Consumer Expenditure Survey

	Black consumer units	All consumer units
Number of consumer units	10,314	94,044
income before taxes	$16,964	$25,460
income after taxes		
Average number of:		
persons in consumer unit	2.8	2.6
earners in consumer unit	1.2	1.4
vehicles in consumer unit	1.2	2.0
children under 18 years old	1.0	0.7
persons over 65 years old	0.2	0.3
Average annual expenditures		
Total	$16,203	$23,866
food	1,251	3,448
food at home	1,723	1,993
- cereals and bakery products	233	275
cereals and cereal products	95	93
bakery products	138	183
- meats, poultry, fish, and eggs	656	562
beef	181	189
pork	167	116
other meats	82	79
poultry	117	85
fish and seafood	74	64
eggs	35	30
- dairy products	159	251
fresh milk and cream	91	122
other dairy products	67	128
- fruits and vegetables	275	320
fresh fruits	78	102
fresh vegetables	74	92
processed fruits	71	72
processed vegetables	52	54

continued on the next page

Table 8.03 continued

	Black consumer units	All consumer units
food at home - continued		
- other food at home	$ 393	$ 554
sugar and other sweets	58	74
fats and oils	45	51
miscellaneous foods	141	236
nonalcoholic beverages	149	193
- food prepared by consumer unit on out of town trips	7	31
food away from home	778	1,455
alcoholic beverages	128	271
housing	$ 5,269	$ 7,292
shelter	2,793	3,979
- owned dwellings	1,068	2,305
mortgage interest	668	1,431
property taxes	136	418
maintenance, repair, insurance, other	264	456
- rented dwellings	1,550	1,262
- other lodging	176	412
utilities, fuels and public services	1,540	1,645
- natural gas	299	248
- electricity	588	674
- fuel oil and other fuels	59	107
- telephone	478	471
- water and other public services	116	145
household operations	201	354
- personal services	136	168
- other household expenses	65	186
housekeeping supplies	206	316
- laundry and cleaning supplies	88	92
- other household products	68	126
- postage and stationary	49	98

continued on the next page

Table 8.03 continued

	Black consumer units	All consumer units
household furnishings and equipment	$ 530	$ 998
- household textiles	61	105
- furniture	196	304
- floor coverings	25*	55
- major appliances	114	156
- small appliances, misc. housewares	31	56
- misc. household equipment	103	322
apparel and services	$ 1,212	$ 1,346
- men and boys	222	343
men, 16 years old and over	149	278
boys, 2-15 years old	72	66
- women and girls	501	544
women, 16 years old and over	421	472
girls, 2-15 years old	80	72
- children under 2 years old	52	56
- footwear	234	167
- other apparel and services	203	236
transportation	$ 3,041	$ 4,842
- vehicle purchases	1,250	2,338
cars and trucks (new) net outlay	710	1,415
cars and trucks (used) net outlay	539	893
other vehicles	1*	29
- gasoline and motor oil	675	915
- other vehicle expenses	910	1,342
vehicle finance charges	204	269
maintenance and repairs	366	492
vehicle insurance	258	420
vehicle rental, license and other charges	83	161
- public transportation	206	248

continued on the next page

Table 8.03 continued

	Black consumer units	All consumer units
health care	$ 696	$ 1,135
- health insurance	257	371
- medical services	295	502
- drugs	111	192
- medical supplies	32	69
entertainment	$ 557	$ 1,149
- fees and admissions	113	308
- televisions, radios, sound equipment	292	371
- pets, toys, playground equipment	75	202
- other entertainment equipment, supplies and services	77	268
personal care products and services	$ 249	$ 303
reading	70	140
education	167	314
tobacco products and smoking supplies	196	230
miscellaneous	438	522
cash contributions	400	746
personal insurance and pensions	1,280	2,127
- life and other personal insurance	261	292
- pensions and Social Security	1,019	1,834
Sources on income and personal taxes		
Money income before taxes	$ 16,964	$ 25,460
wages and salaries	13,498	19,524
self employment income	370	1,618
Social Security, private and government retirement	1,697	2,555

continued on the next page

Table 8.03 continued

	Black consumer units	All consumer units
Money income before taxes - continued		
interest, dividends, rental income, other property income	122	973
unemployment, workers' compensation, veterans benefits	253	208
public assistance, supplemental security income, food stamps	864	273
regular contributions for support	101	223
other income	58	86
Personal taxes	$ 1,285	$ 2,288
federal income taxes	998	1,812
state income taxes	272	412
other taxes	16	64
Income after taxes	$ 15,678	$ 23,172
Addenda		
Net increase in total assets	$ 1,735	$ 3,241
Net increase in total liabilities	312	2,046
Estimated market value of owned home	21,793	49,642

SOURCE: U.S. Department of Labor, Bureau of Labor Statistics, Consumer Expenditure Survey: Integrated Survey Data, 1984-86, pp. 30-33, table 7. L 2.3:2333

NOTES: 'All consumer units' includes consumer units of all races. *Data are like to have large sampling errors.

UNITS: Number of consumer units in thousands; average numbers as shown; average annual expenditures by category, average income by source of income, and addenda, averages in current dollars.

Table 8.04 Selected Characteristics of Occupied Housing Units, by Tenure, 1985

	Black households	All households
Owner occupied housing units	4,310	56,145
Units in structure		
single family detached	3,427	46,703
single family attached	359	2.211
2-4 units	171	1,996
5-9 units	8	344
10-19 units	31	261
20-49 units	16	287
50 units or more	57	438
mobile home or trailer	240	3,906
Stories in structure		
one story	2,439	26,188
two stories	796	16,561
three stories	865	11,741
4-6 stories	156	1,295
7 or more stories	54	360
Year structure built		
1939 or earlier	1,139	12,029
1940-1949	586	5,001
1950-1959	648	9,419
1960-1969	734	10,035
1970-1979	915	14,128
1980 or later	287	5,534
median year	1957	1962
Percent of occupied units:		
lacking some or all plumbing facilities	1.2%	0.4%
with public water system or private company	88.2	81.1
with public sewer	78.7	68.7
with air conditioning	25.7	37.0

continued on the next page

Table 8.04 continued

	Black households	All households
Value of specified owner occupied units		
less than $20,000	622	2,506
$20,000-$29,999	432	2,492
$30,000-$39,999	602	4,282
$40,000-$49,999	511	5,279
$50,000-$59,999	338	4,686
$60,000-$69,999	318	5,048
$70,000-$79,999	227	4,014
$80,000-$89,999	309	5,977
$100,000-$119,999	115	3,046
$120,000-$149,999	103	2,881
$150,000-$199,999	58	2,319
$200,000-$299,999	24	1,621
$300,000 and over	8	723
median value	$43,500	$66,300
Monthly housing costs		
less than $300	1,938	22,502
$300 $399	502	6,483
$400-$499	397	5,333
$500-$599	347	4,260
$600-$699	211	3,171
$700-$799	152	2,546
$800-$999	195	3,127
$1,000 or more	158	4,223
median amount	$ 302	$ 348
Monthly housing costs as a percent of income		
less than 5%	91	1,877
5-9%	557	8,986
10-14%	629	9,729
15-19%	584	8,441
20-24%	476	6,472

continued on the next page

Table 8.04 continued

	Black households	All households
Month housing costs as a percent of income - continued		
25-29%	342	4,690
30-34%	301	3,184
35-39%	172	1,911
40% or more	701	5,906
median percent	21%	18%
Median monthly costs		
electricity	$ 63	$ 64
piped gas	66	56
fuel oil	64	66
Renter occupied housing units	5,593	32,280
Units in structure		
single family detached	1,249	8,373
single family attached	400	1,890
2-4 units	1,554	8,221
5-9 units	780	4,029
10-19 units	597	3,500
20-49 units	390	2,627
50 units or more	577	2,792
mobile home or trailer	45	848
Stories in structure		
one story	1,557	9,255
two stories	1,725	10,112
three stories	1,167	7,466
4-6 stories	677	3,530
7 or more stories	467	1,917
Year structure built		
1939 or earlier	1,733	9,022
1940-1949	656	2,919
1950-1959	621	3,376

continued on the next page

Table 8.04 continued

	Black households	All households
Year structure built - continued		
1960-1969	813	4,915
1970-1979	1,471	9,254
1980 or later	297	2,796
median year	1957	1962
Percent of occupied units:		
lacking some or all plumbing facilities	3.0%	1.3%
with public water system or private company	96.3	93.0
with public sewer	94.2	88.7
with air conditioning	20.2	26.9
Gross rent of specified renter occupied units		
less than $200	1,360	4,369
$200-$249	499	2,634
$250-$299	594	3,233
$300-$349	724	3,717
$350-$399	595	3,658
$400-$449	528	3,246
$450-$499	312	2,382
$500-$599	383	3,133
$600-$699	165	1,694
$700-$799	79	832
$800-$999	45	673
$1000 and over	38	482
no cash rent	226	1,753
median gross rent	$ 314	$ 365
Monthly housing costs		
less than $300	2,465	10,337
$300-$399	1,319	7,422
$400-$499	840	5,637
$500-$599	386	3,151

continued on the next page

Table 8.04 continued

	Black households	All households
Monthly housing costs - continued		
$600-$699	165	1,703
$700-$799	79	835
$800-$999	45	678
$1,000 or more	38	486
median amount	$ 314	$ 364
Month housing costs as a percent of income		
less than 5%	20	228
5-9%	93	991
10-14%	469	3,012
15-19%	615	4,300
20-24%	653	4,418
25-29%	667	3,767
30-34%	438	2,550
35-39%	310	1,862
40% or more	1,885	8,455
median percent	31%	27%
Median monthly costs		
electricity	$ 44	$ 43
piped gas	40	34
fuel oil	64	56

SOURCE: U.S. Bureau of the Census, Statistical Abstract of the United States, 1989, pp. 707-708, tables 1244, 1245, 1246. C 3.134:989

NOTES: 'All households' includes households occupied by persons of all races.

UNITS: Housing units in thousands of housing units; percent as a percent of total as shown; median value and median gross rent in dollars; median monthly costs in current dollars.

GLOSSARY

ACUTE CONDITION see **CONDITION (HEALTH)**.

AGE ADJUSTMENT Age adjustment, using the direct method, is the application of the age specific rates in a population of interest to a standardized age distribution in order to eliminate the differences in observed rates that result from age differences in population composition. This adjustment is usually done when comparing two or more populations at one point in time, or one population at two or more points in time.

AGGRAVATED ASSAULT see **CRIME**.

ARSON see **CRIME**.

AVERAGE see **MEAN; MEDIAN**.

BED (HOSPITAL; NURSING HOME) Any bed that is staffed for use by inpatients is counted as a bed in a facility.

BED-DISABILITY DAY see **DISABILITY DAY**.

BIRTH see **LIVE BIRTH**.

BURGLARY see **CRIME**.

CAUSE OF DEATH For the purpose of national mortality statistics, every death is attributed to one underlying condition, based on information reported on the death certificate and utilizing the international rules (International Classifications of Disease) for selecting the underlying cause of death from reported conditions. Selected causes of death are shown on tables.

CHRONIC CONDITION see **CONDITION (HEALTH)**.

CIVILIAN LABOR FORCE All persons (excluding members of the Armed Forces) who are either employed or unemployed. (The experienced civilian labor force is a subgroup of the civilian labor force, composed of all persons, employed and unemployed, that have worked before.)

Employed persons are those persons 16 years old and over who were either a) "at work"- those who did any work at all as paid employees, or in their own business or profession, or on their own farm, or worked 15 or more hours as unpaid workers on a family farm or in a family business; or b) "with a job but not at work"- those who did not work during the reference period but had jobs or businesses from which they were temporarily absent due to illness, bad weather, industrial dispute, vacation, or other personal reasons. Excluded from the employed are persons whose only activity consisted of work around the house or volunteer work for religious, charitable, and similar organizations.

Employed persons are classified as either full-time workers, those who worked 35 hours or more per week; or part-time workers, those who worked less that 35 hours per week.

Unemployed persons are those who were neither "at work" nor "with a job, but not at work" and who were a) looking for work, and b) available to accept a job. Also included as unemployed are persons who are waiting to be called back to a job from which they have been laid off. The unemployed are divided into four groups according to reason for unemployment:

--job losers (including those who have been laid off)
--job leavers who have left their job voluntarily
--reentrants, persons who have worked before and are reentering the labor force
--new entrants to the labor force looking for work

CIVILIAN NONINSTITUTIONAL POPULATION see **POPULATION**.

CIVILIAN POPULATION see **POPULATION**.

COLLEGE A postsecondary school which offers a general or liberal arts education, usually leading to an associate, bachelor's, master's, doctor's, or first professional degree. Junior colleges and community colleges are included. See also, Institution of Higher Education; University.

COMMUNITY HOSPITAL All non-federal short term hospitals, excluding hospital units of institutions, whose services are available to the public. Short term hospitals are those where the average length of stay is less than 30 days.

CONDITION (HEALTH) A health condition is a departure from a state of physical or mental well-being. Based on duration, there are two categories of conditions: acute and chronic.

An acute condition is one that has lasted less than three months, and has involved either a physician visit (medical attention) or restricted activity.

A chronic condition is any condition lasting three months or more, or is one classified as chronic regardless of the time of onset. See also, Health Limitation of Activity.

CONSOLIDATED METROPOLITAN STATISTICAL AREA (CMSA) A geographic area concept introduced in June, 1984, which, in combination with Metropolitan Statistical Area (MSA), and Primary Metropolitan Statistical Area (PMSA), replace the Standard Metropolitan Statistical Area (SMSA) concept. CMSAs are designated in accordance with criteria established by the federal Office of Management and Budget (OMB). In general CMSAs are MSAs with a population of one million or more, and which have component PMSAs. See also Metropolitan Statistical Area.

CONSUMER EXPENDITURE SURVEY A survey of current consumer expenditures reflecting the buying habits of American consumers. Begun in 1979 and conducted jointly by the U.S. Bureau of Labor Statistics and the U.S. Bureau of the Census, the survey consists of two parts: an interview panel survey in which the expenditures of consumer units are obtained in five interviews conducted every three months, and a diary or recordkeeping survey completed by the participating households for two consecutive one-week periods. See also Consumer Unit.

The Consumer Expenditure Survey, which collects data on expenditures, should not be confused with the Consumer Price Index, which measures the average change in prices of consumer goods and services.

CONSUMER UNIT An entity used as the basis of the Consumer Expenditure Survey. A consumer unit comprises either

--all the members of a particular household who are related by blood, marriage, adoption, or other legal arrangements; or

--a person living alone or sharing a household with others, or living as a roomer in a private home or lodging house or in a permanent living quarters in a hotel or motel, but who is financially independent; or

--two or more persons living together who pool their income to make joint expenditure decisions.

A consumer unit may or may not be a household.

CRIME A crime is an action which is prohibited by law. Their are two major statistical programs which measure crime in the United States. The first is the Uniform Crime Reporting (UCR) program, administered by the FBI. The Bureau receives monthly and annual reports from most police agencies around the country (covering approximately 97% of the population). These reports contain information on eight major types of crime (called collectively, serious crime), which are known to police. Serious crime consists of four violent crimes (murder and non-negligent manslaughter, which includes willful felonious homicides and is based on police investigations rather than determinations of a medical examiner; forcible rape, which includes attempted rape; robbery, which includes stealing or taking anything of value by force or violence, or by threat of force or violence, and includes attempted robbery; and aggravated assault which includes intent to kill), and four property crimes (burglary, which includes any unlawful entry to commit a felony or theft and includes attempted burglary and burglary followed by larceny; larceny, which includes theft of property or articles of value without use of force, violence, or fraud, and excludes embezzlement, con games, forgery, etc.; motor vehicle theft, which includes all cases where vehicles are driven away and abandoned, but excludes vehicles taken for temporary use and returned by the taker; and arson, which includes any willful or malicious burning or attempt to burn, with or without the intent to defraud, of a dwelling house, public building, motor vehicle, aircraft, or personal property of another.)

The second approach to the measurement of crime is through the National Crime Survey (NCS) administered by the Bureau of Justice Statistics. The survey is based on a representative sample of approximately 49,000 households, inhabited by about 102,000 persons age 12 and over. Although the categories of crime are similar to those used by the FBI in the UCR, the NCS is based on reports of victimization directly by victims, as opposed to crimes reported to police as in the UCR. As might be imagined, not all crimes are reported or known to police, therefore NCS estimates of crime tend to be significantly higher than UCR figures. The NCS also differs from the UCR in that only crimes whose victims can be interviewed are included (hence there are no homicide statistics), and only victims who are 12 years old or older are counted. The two central concepts in the NCS are victimization, which is the specific criminal act as it affects a single victim, and a criminal incident, which is a specific criminal act involving one or more victims. Thus in regard to personal crime, there are more victimizations, than incidents.

DEATH see **CAUSE OF DEATH; INFANT MORTALITY**.

DISABILITY The presence of a physical, mental, or other health condition which has lasted six or more months and which limits or prevents a particular type of activity. See also Work Disability.

DISABILITY DAY A day on which a person's usual activity is reduced because of illness or injury. There are four types of disability days (which are not mutually exclusive). They are

--a restricted-activity day, a day on which a person cuts down on his or her usual activities because of illness or an injury.

--a bed-disability day, a day on which a person stays in bed more than half of the daylight hours (or normal waking hours) because of a specific illness or injury. All hospital days are bed-disability days. Bed disability days may also be work-loss days or school loss days.

--a work-loss day, a day on which a person did not work at his or her job or business for at least half of his or her normal workday because of a specific illness or injury. Work loss days are determined only for employed persons.

--a school-loss day, a day on which a child did not attend school for at least half of his or her normal schoolday because of a specific illness or injury. School-loss days are determined only for children 6 to 16 years of age.

DISPOSABLE INCOME see **INCOME.**

EMPLOYED PERSONS see **CIVILIAN LABOR FORCE.**

EMPLOYMENT STATUS see **LABOR FORCE STATUS.**

ENROLLMENT The total number of students registered in a given school unit at a given time, generally in the fall of the year. See also Full-Time Enrollment; Part-Time Enrollment.

EVER MARRIED PERSONS see **MARITAL STATUS.**

EXPERIENCED CIVILIAN LABOR FORCE That portion of the Civilian Labor Force, both employed and unemployed, that have worked before. Excludes new entrants to the Civilian Labor Force. See also Civilian Labor Force.

EXPERIENCED WORKER see **EXPERIENCED CIVILIAN LABOR FORCE.**

FAMILY A type (subgroup) of household in which there are two or more persons living together (including the householder) who are related by birth, marriage, or adoption. All such related persons in one housing unit are considered as members of one family. (For example, if the son or daughter of the family householder and that son's or daughter's spouse and/or children are members of the household, they are all counted as part of the householder's family.) However, non-family members who are not related to the householder (such as a roomer or boarder and his or her spouse, or a resident employee and his or her spouse who are living in), are not counted as family members but as unrelated individuals living in a family household. Thus for Census purposes, a housing unit can contain only one household, and a household can contain only one family. See also Family Type; Household; Householder; Unrelated Individual.

FAMILY INCOME see **INCOME**.

FAMILY TYPE Families are classified by type according to the sex of the householder and the presence of a spouse and children. The three main types of households are: Married Couples, in which a husband and wife live together (with or without other persons in the household); Male Householder, No Wife Present, in which a male householder lives together with other members of his family but without a wife; and Female Householder, No Husband Present, in which a female householder lives together with other members of her family but without a husband. See also Family; Family Household; Household.

FARM As defined by the Bureau of the Census (and adopted by the Department of Agriculture), a farm is any place from which $1,000 or more of agricultural products were sold, or would have been sold during a given year. Control of the farm may be exercised through ownership or management, or through a lease, rental or cropping arrangement. In the case of landowners who have one or more tenants or renters, the land operated by each is counted as a separate farm. This definition has been in effect since 1974.

FARMLAND All land under the control of a farm operator, including land not actually under cultivation or not used for pasture or grazing. Rent free land is included as part of a farm only if the operator has sole use of it. Land used for pasture or grazing on a per head basis that is neither owned nor leased by the farm operator is not included except for grazing lands controlled by grazing associations leased on a per acre basis.

FARM INCOME Gross farm income comprises cash receipts from farm marketings of crops and livestock, federal government payments made directly to farmers for farm-related activities, rental value of farm homes, value of farm products consumed in farm homes, and other farm-related income such as machine hire and custom work.

FULL-TIME ENROLLMENT (HIGHER EDUCATION) The number of students enrolled in higher education courses with a total credit load equal to at least 75% of the normal full-time course load.

FULL-TIME WORKERS see **CIVILIAN LABOR FORCE.**

HEALTH LIMITATION OF ACTIVITY A characteristic of persons with chronic conditions. Each person identified as having a chronic condition is classified as to the extent to which his or her activities are limited by the condition as follows:

--persons unable to carry on a major activity (that is the principal activity of a person of his or her age-sex group: for persons 1-5 years of age, it refers to ordinary play with other children; for persons 6-16 years of age, it refers to school attendance; for persons 17 years of age and over, it usually refers to a job, housework, or school attendance.)
--persons limited in the amount or kind of major activity performed.
--persons not limited in major activity, but otherwise limited.
--persons not limited in activity.

See also Condition (Health).

HEALTH MAINTENANCE ORGANIZATION (HMO) A prepaid health plan delivering comprehensive care to members through designated providers, having a fixed monthly payment for health care services, and requiring members to be in the plan for a specified period of time (usually one year). HMOs are distinguished by the relationship of the providers to the plan. HMO model types are:

Group -- an HMO that delivers health services through a physician group controlled by the HMO, or an HMO that contracts with one or more independent group practices to provide health services.

Individual Practice Association (IPA) -- an HMO that contracts directly with physicians in independent practice, and/or contracts with one or more associations of physicians in independent practice, and/or contracts with one or more multispecialty group practices (but the plan is predominantly organized around solo-single specialty practices).

HIGHER EDUCATION see **INSTITUTION OF HIGHER EDUCATION.**

HISPANIC see **SPANISH ORIGIN.**

HOME OWNERSHIP see **TENURE.**

HOSPITAL see **COMMUNITY HOSPITAL.**

HOSPITAL DAY A hospital day is a night spent in a hospital by a person admitted as an inpatient.

HOUSEHOLD The person or persons occupying a housing unit. There are two main types of households: family households, which consist of two or more persons related by birth, marriage, or adoption living together (see Family; Family Type); and non-family households, which consist of a person living alone, or together with unrelated individuals (see Unrelated Individuals). See also Householder.

HOUSEHOLD INCOME see **INCOME.**

HOUSEHOLD TYPE see **HOUSEHOLD.**

HOUSEHOLDER The person in whose name a housing unit is rented or owned.

HOUSING UNIT A house, apartment, mobile home or trailer, group of rooms, or single room occupied as a separate living quarter, or, if vacant, intended for occupancy as a separate living quarter. Separate living quarters are those in which the occupants live and eat separately from any other persons in the building and which have direct access from the outside of the building or through a common hall.

Both occupied and vacant housing units are counted in many surveys, however recreational vehicles, boats, caves, tents, railroad cars, and the like are only included if they are occupied as someone's usual place of residence. Vacant mobile homes are included if they are intended for occupancy on the site where they stand. Vacant mobile homes on dealer's sales lots, at the factory, or in storage yards are excluded.

Most housing unit data is for year-round housing units which comprises all occupied housing units plus vacant housing units intended for year round use. Vacant units held for seasonal use or migratory labor are excluded.

See also Occupancy Status, Rooms, Specified Owner-Occupied Housing Units, Tenure, Value (Housing).

HOUSING TENURE see **TENURE**.

INCIDENT see **CRIME**.

INCOME The term income has different definitions depending on how it is modified and in what situation it is used. Like many government statistical terms, income can be viewed hierarchically.

Personal income is the current income received by persons from all sources, minus their personal contributions for social insurance. Persons include individuals (including owners of unincorporated firms), non-profit institutions serving individuals, private trust funds, and private non-insured welfare funds. Personal income includes transfers (payments not resulting from current production) from government and business such as Social Security benefits, public assistance, etc., but excludes transfers among persons. Also included are certain non-monetary types of income, chiefly estimated net rental value to owner-occupants of their homes, the value of services furnished without payment by financial intermediaries, and food and fuel produced and consumed on farms.

Disposable personal income is personal income less personal tax and non-tax payments. It is income available to persons for spending and saving. Personal tax and non-tax payments are tax payments (net of refunds) by persons (excluding contributions for social insurance) that are not chargeable to business expenses, and certain personal payments to general government that are treated like taxes. Personal taxes include income, estate and gift, personal property, and motor vehicle licenses. Non-tax payments include passport fees, fines and penalties, donations, tuition and fees paid to schools and hospitals mainly operated by the government.

Money income is a smaller less inclusive category than personal income. Money income is the sum of the amounts received from wages and salaries, self-employment income (including losses), Social Security, Supplemental Security Income, public assistance, interest, dividends, rents, royalties, estate or trust income, veterans payments, unemployment and workers' compensation payments, private and government retirement and disability pensions, alimony, child support, and any other source of money income which was regularly received. Capital gains or losses and lump-sum or one-time payments, such as life insurance settlements, are excluded.

Also excluded are non-cash benefits such as food stamps, health benefits, housing subsidies, rent-free housing, and the goods produced and consumed on farms. Money income is reported for households and various household types as well as for unrelated individuals. (In regard to family money income it should be noted that only the amount received by all family members 15 years old and over is counted, and excludes income received by household members not related to the householder.) It is reported in aggregate, median, mean, and per capita amounts. Money income is also used for determining the poverty status of families and unrelated individuals.

INFANT MORTALITY The deaths of live-born children who do not reach their first birthday. Infant mortality is usually expressed as a rate per 1,000 live births.

INPATIENT DAYS (HOSPITALS) The number of adult and pediatric days of care rendered during a given period. See also Hospital Day.

INSTITUTION OF HIGHER EDUCATION An institution which offers programs of study beyond the secondary school level terminating in an associate, baccalaureate, or higher degree. See also College; University.

JAIL A facility, usually operated by a local law enforcement agency, holding persons detained pending adjudication and/or persons committed after adjudication to a sentence of one year or less.

LABOR FORCE STATUS A term which refers to whether or not a person is in the labor force, and, if in the labor force, whether he or she is employed or unemployed, a full-time worker or a part-time worker, etc. Persons are in the labor force if they are in the civilian labor force or in the Armed Forces.

The civilian labor force consists of both employed and unemployed persons, full-time and part-time workers. Generally, persons outside the labor force consist of full-time homemakers, students who do not work, retired persons, and inmates of institutions. "Discouraged workers," those who do not have a job and have not been seeking one, are also considered to be not in the labor force. See also Civilian Labor Force.

LARCENY see **CRIME**.

LIMITATION OF ACTIVITY see **HEALTH LIMITATION OF ACTIVITY**.

LIVE BIRTH The live birth of an infant, defined as the complete expulsion or extraction from its mother of a product of conception, irrespective of the duration of the pregnancy, which, after such separation, breathes or shows any evidence of life such as heartbeat, umbilical cord pulsation, or definite movement of voluntary muscles, whether or not the umbilical cord has been cut or the placenta is attached. Each such birth is considered live born.

MARITAL STATUS All persons 15 years of age and older are classified by the Bureau of the Census according to marital status. The Bureau defines two broad categories of marital status:

Single - all those persons who have never been married (including persons whose marriage has been annulled), and

Ever married - which is composed of the now married, the widowed, and the divorced.

Now married persons are those who are legally married (as well as some persons who have common law marriages, along with some unmarried couples who live together and report their marital status as married), and whose marriage has not ended by widowhood or divorce. The now married are sometimes further subdivided: married, spouse present; separated; married, spouse absent; married, spouse absent, other.

--married, spouse present covers married couples living together.

--separated includes those persons legally separated or otherwise absent from their spouse because of marital discord (such as persons who have been deserted or who have parted because they no longer want to live together but who have not obtained a divorce). Separated includes persons with a limited divorce.

--married, spouse absent covers those households where the both the husband and the wife were not counted as members of the same household, (or where both husband and wife lived together in group quarters). This classification was used for the 1980 Census.

--married, spouse absent, other, includes those married persons whose spouse was not counted as a member of the same household, besides those who are separated. Included are persons whose spouse was employed and living away at from home, absent in the armed forces, or was an inmate of an institution. This classification was used for the 1980 Census.

Widowed - widows and widowers who have not remarried.
Divorced - persons who are legally divorced and have not remarried.

MARRIED COUPLES see **FAMILY TYPE**.

MARRIED PERSONS see **MARITAL STATUS**.

MEAN The arithmetic average of a set of values. It is derived by dividing the sum of a group of numerical items by the total number of items. Mean income (of a population), for example, is defined as the value obtained by dividing the total or aggregate income by the population. Thus, the mean income for families is obtained by dividing the aggregate of all income reported by persons in families by the total number of families. See also Median.

MEDIAN In general, a value that divides the total range of values into two equal parts. For example, to say that the median money income of families in the United States in 1985 was $27,735 indicates that half of all families had incomes larger than that value, and half had less. See also Mean.

MEDICAID A federally funded but state administered and operated program which provides medical benefits to certain low income persons in need of medical care. The program, authorized in 1965 by Title XIX of the Social Security Act, categorically covers participants in the Aid to Families with Dependent Children (AFDC) program, as well as some participants in the Supplemental Security Income (SSI) program, along with those other people deemed medically needy in each participating state. Each state determines the benefits covered, rates of payment to providers, and methods of administering the program.

MEDICARE A federally funded nationwide health insurance program providing health insurance protection to people 65 years of age and over, people eligible for social security disability payments for more than two years, and people with end-state renal disease, regardless of income. The program was enacted July 30, 1965, as title XVIII, Health Insurance for the Aged, of the Social Security Act, and became effective on July 1, 1966. It consists of two separate but coordinated programs: hospital insurance (Part A), and supplementary medical insurance (Part B).

METROPOLITAN AREA see **CONSOLIDATED METROPOLITAN STATISTICAL AREA; METROPOLITAN STATISTICAL AREA; PRIMARY METROPOLITAN STATISTICAL AREA; STANDARD CONSOLIDATED STATISTICAL AREA; STANDARD METROPOLITAN STATISTICAL AREA**

METROPOLITAN STATISTICAL AREA (MSA) A geographic concept introduced in June, 1984, to replace the Standard Metropolitan Statistical Area (SMSA). In general, an MSA is a geographic area consisting of a large population nucleus, together with adjacent communities that have a high degree of economic and social integration with that nucleus. MSAs are designated in accordance with a detailed 16 section criteria established by the federal Office of Management and Budget (OMB). In general, MSAs are a county based concept which must include a city that, with contiguous, densely settled territory, constitutes a Census Bureau defined urbanized area having at least 50,000 population. (However, if an MSA's largest city has less than 50,000 population, the MSA as a whole must have a total population of at least 100,000). Adjacent MSAs are consolidated into a single MSA if certain conditions relating to commuting to work, size, and geographic proximity are met. See also, Consolidated Metropolitan Statistical Area; New England County Metropolitan Area; Primary Metropolitan Statistical Area.

NEW ENGLAND COUNTY METROPOLITAN AREA (NECMA) A geographic concept developed for the New England states (Massachusetts, Connecticut, Rhode Island, Maine, New Hampshire, Vermont) to present data that is only available on a county-level basis . Unlike the rest of the country, Metropolitan Statistical Areas (MSAs) in the New England states are officially defined in terms of cities and towns instead of counties. As a result New England MSA data may not be directly comparable to MSA data in the rest of the country. NECMAs are county-based geographic areas (which follow the same general guidelines of MSAs in other parts of the country) and thus provide a basis of comparison with other states. NECMAs do not replace the MSAs in New England, but supplement them.

MOBILE HOME see **HOUSING UNIT.**

MONEY INCOME see **INCOME.**

MURDER see **CRIME.**

NATIONAL CRIME SURVEY A twice yearly survey of 49,000 households comprising over 102,000 inhabitants 12 years of age and older. Administered by the Bureau of Justice Statistics, the survey measures criminal victimization by surveying victims directly. It differs from the FBI Uniform Crime Report (UCR) which is based on crimes reported to police. See also Crime.

NURSING HOME A facility with three or more beds providing adults with nursing care and/or personal care (such as help with bathing, eating, using toilet facilities, or dressing) and/or supervision over such activities as money management, walking, and shopping.

OCCUPANCY STATUS (HOUSING) The classification of all housing units as either occupied or vacant.

Occupied housing units are those that have one or more persons living in them as their usual residence, and include units whose usual occupants are temporarily absent (e.g., on vacation).

Vacant housing units are those that have no one living in them as their usual residence. Also classified as vacant are housing units that are temporarily occupied solely by persons who have a usual residence elsewhere, newly constructed units completed to the point where all exterior windows and doors are installed and final usable floors are in place, and vacant mobile homes or trailers intended to be occupied on the site on which they stand.

OCCUPATION The kind of work a person does at a job or business. Occupation is reported for a given survey period, (most frequently the period covered by the survey, the reference period, is the week including March 12). If the person was not at work during the reference period, occupation usually refers to the person's most recent job or business. Persons working at more than one job are asked to identify the job at which he or she works the most hours, which is then counted as his or her occupation.

Occupations are classified according to the Standard Occupational Classification system (SOC), a system promulgated by the federal Office of Management and Budget.

OWNER OCCUPIED HOUSING UNIT see **TENURE**.

PART-TIME ENROLLMENT (HIGHER EDUCATION) The number of students enrolled in higher education courses with a total credit load of less than 75% of the normal full-time credit load.

PART-TIME WORKERS see **CIVILIAN LABOR FORCE.**

PERSONAL INCOME see **INCOME.**

POPULATION The number of inhabitants of an area. The total population of the United States is the sum of all persons living within the United States, plus all members of the Armed Forces living in foreign countries, Puerto Rico, Guam, and the U.S. Virgin Islands. Other Americans living abroad (e.g., civilian federal employees and dependents of members of the Armed Forces or other federal employees are not included).

The resident population of the United States, is the population living within the geographic United States. This includes members of the Armed Forces stationed in the United States and their families as well as foreigners working or studying here. It excludes foreign military, naval, and diplomatic personnel and their families located here and residing in embassies or similar quarters, as well as Americans living abroad. Resident population is often the denominator when calculating birth and death rates, incidence of disease, and other rates.

The civilian population is the resident population excluding members of the Armed Forces. However, families of members of the Armed Forces are included.

The civilian non-institutional population is the civilian population not residing in institutions. Institutions include, correctional institutions; detention homes and training schools for juvenile delinquents; homes for the aged and dependent (e.g., nursing homes and convalescent homes); homes for dependent and neglected children; homes and schools for the mentally and physically handicapped; homes for unwed mothers; psychiatric, tuberculosis, and chronic disease hospitals; and residential treatment centers.

POVERTY STATUS Although the term poverty connotes a complex set of economic, social, and psychological conditions, the standard statistical definition provides for only estimates of economic poverty. These are based on the receipt of money income before taxes and exclude the value of government payments and transfers such as food stamps or Medicare; private transfers, such as health insurance premiums paid by employers; gifts; the depletion of assets; and borrowed money. Thus the term poverty as used by government agencies, classifies persons and families in relation to being above or below a specified income level, or poverty threshold. Those below this threshold are said to be in poverty, or more accurately, as below the poverty level. Poverty thresholds vary by size of family, number of children, and age of householder and are updated annually. Poverty status is also determined for unrelated individuals living in households, but not for those living in group quarters nor for persons in the Armed Forces. The poverty threshold is revised each year according to formula based on the Consumer Price Index.

PRIMARY METROPOLITAN STATISTICAL AREA (PMSA) This geographic concept, introduced in June, 1984, combines with Metropolitan Statistical Area (MSA) and Consolidated Metropolitan Statistical Ares (CMSA), to\ replace the Standard Metropolitan Statistical Area (SMSA) concept. PMSAs are designated according to criteria established by the federal Office of Management and Budget. In general PMSAs are those counties with populations of at least 100,000 (60% must be urban), in which less than 50% of its resident workers commute to jobs outside the county. PMSAs are parts of Consolidated Metropolitan Statistical Areas (CMSAs).

PRISON A confinement facility having custodial authority over adults sentenced to confinement for a period of more than one year. Prisons are usually run by sate or federal authorities.

PRIVATE SCHOOL see **SCHOOL.**

PROPERTY CRIME see **CRIME.**

PUBLIC SCHOOL see **SCHOOL.**

RACE The Bureau of the Census in many of its surveys (most notably in the 1980 decennial census of population) asks all persons to identify themselves according to race. The concept of race as used by the Bureau reflects the self-identification of the respondents. It is not meant to denote any clear cut scientific or biological definition.

Although it is often reported with racial categories, Spanish origin, or hispanic origin, is not a racial category. Persons may be of any race and of Spanish origin. Those who describe themselves as hispanic (or Mexican, Cuban, Chicano, etc) in response to a question about race, are included by the Bureau in the racial classification, "other." See also Spanish Origin.

RAPE see **CRIME.**

REFERENCE PERSON Most frequently, the person who responds to a government survey. Most surveys done by the federal government are based on households and begin by asking the initial respondent the name of the person in whose name the housing unit is owned or rented (this person is designated as the householder). Usually the householder is the reference person. Other household members are defined in relation to the householder.

REGION The Bureau of the Census has divided the United States into four regions. This division is the primary geographic subdivision of the nation for statistical reporting purposes. As a result, almost all federal agencies, along with many private data collectors, have adopted the regional subdivision and use it for presenting statistical data. The four regions are the Northeast (Maine, New Hampshire, Vermont, Massachusetts, Rhode Island, Connecticut, New York, New Jersey, Pennsylvania); the Midwest (Ohio, Indiana, Illinois, Michigan, Wisconsin, Minnesota, Iowa, Missouri, North Dakota, South Dakota, Kansas, Nebraska); the South (Delaware, Maryland, District of Columbia, Virginia, West Virginia, North Carolina, South Carolina, Georgia, Florida, Kentucky, Tennessee, Alabama, Mississippi, Arkansas, Louisiana, Oklahoma, Texas); and the West (Montana, Idaho, Colorado, Wyoming, New Mexico, Arizona, Utah, Nevada, Washington, Oregon, California, Alaska, Hawaii). In this book, all regional data conform to this definition.

REGULAR SCHOOL see **SCHOOL**.

RENTER OCCUPIED HOUSING UNIT see **TENURE**.

RESIDENT POPULATION see **POPULATION**.

RESTRICTED-ACTIVITY DAY see **DISABILITY DAY**.

ROBBERY see **CRIME**.

ROOMS (HOUSING) The number of whole rooms intended for living purposes in both occupied and vacant housing units. These rooms include living rooms, dining rooms, kitchens, bedrooms, finished recreation rooms, enclosed porches suitable for year-round use, and lodger's rooms. Excluded are strip or pullman kitchens, bathrooms, open porches, balconies, foyers, halls, half-rooms, utility rooms, unfinished attics or basements, or other space used for storage. A partially divided room, such as a dinette next to a kitchen or living room, is a separate room only if there is a partition from floor to ceiling, but not if the partition consists solely of shelves or cabinets.

RURAL see **URBAN/RURAL POPULATION**.

SCHOOL Elementary and secondary schools are divisions of the school system consisting of students in one or more grade groups or other identifiable groups, organized as one unit with one or more teachers giving instruction of a defined type, and housed in a school plant of one or more buildings. More than one school may be housed in one school plant as is the case where elementary and secondary programs are housed in the same building.

Regular schools generally are those which advance a person toward a diploma or degree. They include public and private nursery schools, kindergartens, graded schools, colleges, universities, and professional schools.

Public schools are controlled and supported by local, state, or federal government agencies.

Private schools are controlled and supported mainly by religious organizations, private persons, or private organizations.

SCHOOL ENROLLMENT see **ENROLLMENT**.

SCHOOL-LOSS DAY see **DISABILITY DAY**.

SELF-EMPLOYMENT INCOME A type of money income which comprises net income (gross receipts minus operating expenses) received by persons from an unincorporated business, profession, and/or from the operation of a farm as a farm owner, tenant, or sharecropper. See also Money Income.

SEPARATED PERSONS see **MARITAL STATUS**.

SERIOUS CRIME see **CRIME**.

SPANISH ORIGIN An aspect of a person's ancestry. The Bureau of the Census in many of its survey asks persons if they are of Spanish origin. There are four main subcategories of Spanish origin: Mexican, Puerto Rican, Cuban, and other Spanish. Spanish origin is not a racial classification. Persons may be of any race and of Spanish origin. Spanish origin is used interchangeably with hispanic and hispanic origin.

SINGLE PERSON HOUSEHOLDS see **HOUSEHOLD**.

SINGLE PERSONS see **MARITAL STATUS**.

SPECIFIED OWNER-OCCUPIED HOUSING UNITS Specified owner-occupied units are single family houses on less than ten acres, which have no commercial enterprise or medical practice on the property. Excluded are owner-occupied condominium housing units, mobile homes, trailers, boats, tents, or vans occupied as a usual residence as well as owner-occupied non-condominium units in multi-family buildings. See also Housing Unit.

STANDARD CONSOLIDATED STATISTICAL AREA (SCSA) A large concentration of metropolitan population composed of two or more contiguous Standard Metropolitan Statistical Areas (SMSAs) which together meet certain criteria of population size, urban character, social and economic integration, and/or contiguity of urbanized areas. Each SCSA must have a population of one million or more.

The SCSA concept was replaced with the new metropolitan area classifications in June, 1984. See Consolidated Metropolitan Statistical Area; Metropolitan Statistical Area; Primary Metropolitan Statistical Area.

STANDARD METROPOLITAN STATISTICAL AREA (SMSA) A geographic area concept used until 1984. In general, an SMSA is a large population nucleus and nearby communities which have a high degree of economic and social integration within that nucleus. Each SMSA consists of one or more entire counties (or county equivalents) that meet certain criteria of population, commuting ties, and metropolitan character. In New England, towns and cities rather than counties are the basic units and count as county equivalents. An SMSA includes a city and, generally, the entire surrounding urbanized area and the remainder of the county or counties in which the urbanized area is located. An SMSA also includes those additional outlying counties which meet specified criteria relating to metropolitan character and level of commuting ties.

The SMSA concept was developed in 1949 and has been refined for each succeeding decennial census since 1950. In June, 1984, SMSAs were superseded by three new metropolitan area concepts: Metropolitan Statistical Areas (MSAs), Consolidated Metropolitan Statistical Areas (CMSAs), and Primary Metropolitan Statistical Areas (PMSAs).

TAXES Compulsory contributions exacted by a government for public purposes (except employee and employer assessments for retirement and social insurance purposes, which are classified as insurance trust revenue). All tax revenue is classified as general revenue and comprises amounts received (including interest and penalties, but excluding protested amounts and refunds) from all taxes imposed by a government.

TENURE A concept relating to housing units. All occupied housing units are classified as being either owner-occupied or renter occupied. A housing unit is owner-occupied if the owner or co-owner lives in the unit even if the unit is mortgaged or not fully paid for. All other housing units are considered to be renter occupied, regardless of whether or not cash rent is paid for them by a member of the household. See also Housing Unit.

UNEMPLOYED PERSONS see **CIVILIAN LABOR FORCE**.

UNEMPLOYMENT see **CIVILIAN LABOR FORCE**.

UNIFORM CRIME REPORTING (UCR) PROGRAM A program administered by the FBI which collects reports from most police agencies in the nation (covering approximately 95% of the population) on serious crimes known to police (violent crime and property crime), arrests, police officers and related items. The Bureau issues monthly and annual summary reports based on the program. See also Crime.

UNIVERSITY An institution of higher education consisting of a liberal arts college, a diverse graduate program, and usually two or more professional schools or faculties and empowered to confer degrees in various fields of study. See also Higher Education.

UNRELATED INDIVIDUAL An unrelated individual is generally a person living in a household, and is either: 1) a householder living alone or only with persons who are not related to him or her by blood, marriage, or adoption, or; 2) a roomer, boarder, partner, roommate, or resident employee unrelated to the householder. Certain persons living in group quarters (who are not inmates of institutions) are also counted as unrelated individuals.

URBAN/RURAL POPULATION Urban and rural are type of area concepts rather than specific areas outlined on maps. The urban population comprises all persons living in urbanized areas and in places of 2,500 or more inhabitants outside urbanized areas. The rural population consists of everyone else. Therefore, a rural classification need not imply a farm or sparsely settled areas, since a small city or town is rural when it is outside an urbanized area and has fewer than 2,500 inhabitants. The terms urban and rural are independent of metropolitan and non-metropolitan; both urban and rural areas occur inside and outside metropolitan areas. See also Urbanized Area.

URBANIZED AREA A population concentration of at least 50,000 inhabitants, generally consisting of a central city and the surrounding, closely settled, contiguous territory (suburbs). The urbanized area criteria define a boundary based on a population density of at least 1,000 persons per square mile, but also include some less densely settled areas, such as industrial parks and railroad yards, if they are within areas of dense urban development. The density level of 1,000 persons per square mile corresponds approximately to the contiguously built-up area around a city or cities. The urban fringe is that part of the urbanized area outside of a central city or cities.

Typically, an entire urbanized area is included within an Standard Metropolitan Statistical Area (SMSA) or Metropolitan Statistical Area (MSA). The SMSA (or MSA) is usually much larger in terms of area and includes territory where the population density is less than 1,000. Occasionally more than one urbanized area is located within an SMSA (MSA). In some cases a small part of an urbanized area may extend beyond an SMSA (MSA) boundary, or possibly into an adjacent SMSA (MSA). Urbanized areas sometimes cross state boundaries as well.

VACANCY STATUS see **OCCUPANCY STATUS**.

VALUE (HOUSING UNITS) In surveys done by the Bureau of the Census, the value of owner-occupied housing units is the respondent's estimate of the current dollar worth of the property; for vacant units, the value is the price asked for the property. A property is defined as the house and the land on which it stands. Respondents are asked by the Bureau to estimate the value of the house and land even if they own only the house, or own the house jointly. Statistics for value are only gathered by the Bureau for owner-occupied condominium units and for specified owner-occupied units (single family houses on less than ten acres, and with no business on the property).

VICTIMIZATION see **CRIME**.

VIOLENT CRIME see **CRIME**.

VOTING AGE POPULATION All persons over the age of 18 (the voting age for federal elections) in a given geographic area comprise the voting age population. The voting age population does include a small number of persons who, although of voting age, are not eligible to vote (e.g. resident aliens, inmates of institutions, etc.). The voting age population is estimated in even numbered years by the Bureau of the Census.

WAGES AND SALARIES Wages and salaries are a type (subgroup) of money income and include civilian wages and salaries, Armed Forces pay and allowances, piece-rate payments, commissions, tips, National Guard or Reserve pay (received for training periods), and cash bonuses before deductions for taxes, pensions, union dues, etc. See also Money Income

WIDOWED PERSONS see **MARITAL STATUS**.

WORK DISABILITY A health condition which limits the kind or amount of work a person can do, or prevents working at a job. A person is limited in the kind of work he or she can do if the person has a health condition which restricts his or her choice of jobs. A person is limited in amount of work if he or she is not able to work at a full-time (35 hours or more per week) job or business. See also Condition (Health).

WORK-LOSS DAY see **DISABILITY DAY**.

INDEX